Law Made Simple

Personal
Bankruptcy
Simplified

Law Made Simple

Personal Bankruptcy Simplified

by Daniel Sitarz
Attorney-at-Law

Nova Publishing Company
Small Business and Consumer Legal Books and Software
Carbondale, Illinois

© 2004 Daniel Sitarz

All rights reserved. This publication may not be reproduced in whole or in part by any means without prior written consent.

Editorial assistance by Janet Harris Sitarz, Linda Jorgensen Buhman, and Melanie Bray. Manufactured in the United States.

ISBN 1-892949-01-6   Book only   ($22.95)   ISBN 1-892949-02-4   Book/CD   ($28.95)

Cataloging-in-Publication Data
   Sitarz, Dan, 1948-
      Personal bankruptcy simplified/by Daniel Sitarz. -- 3rd ed.
      (Formerly titled: *Debt Free: The National Bankruptcy Kit*).
      256 p. cm. -- (Law Made Simple series).
      CD contains forms and includes Adobe® Acrobat® reader software. Includes index.
      ISBN: 1-892949-01-6 (book only)   1-892949-02-4 (book/CD)
      1. Bankruptcy—United States—Popular works. 2. Bankruptcy—United States—
   States—Popular works. 3. Bankruptcy—United States—Forms. I. Title. II. Series.
   KF1524.6 .S58 2004   346.7307/8--dc22   0408

Nova Publishing Company is dedicated to providing up-to-date and accurate legal information to the public. All Nova publications are periodically revised to contain the latest available legal information.

| 3rd Edition; 1st Printing | August, 2004 | 1st Edition; 2nd Printing | May, 1997 |
| 2nd Edition; 1st Printing | December, 1998 | 1st Edition; 1st Printing | October, 1995 |

This publication is designed to provide accurate and authoritative information in regard to the subject matter covered. It is sold with the understanding that the publisher and author are not engaged in rendering legal, accounting, or other professional services. If legal advice or other expert assistance is required, the services of a competent professional person should be sought.
   —*From a Declaration of Principles jointly adopted by a Committee of the American Bar Association and a Committee of Publishers*

DISCLAIMER

Because of possible unanticipated changes in governing statutes and case law relating to the application of any information contained in this book, the author, publisher, and any and all persons or entities involved in any way in the preparation, publication, sale, or distribution of this book disclaim all responsibility for the legal effects or consequences of any document prepared or action taken in reliance upon information contained in this book. No representations, either express or implied, are made or given regarding the legal consequences of the use of any information contained in this book. Purchasers and persons intending to use this book for the preparation of any legal documents are advised to check specifically on the current applicable laws in any jurisdiction in which they intend the documents to be effective.

Nova Publishing Company
Small Business and Consumer Legal Books and Software
1103 West College St.
Carbondale, IL 62901
Editorial: (800) 748-1175

Distributed by:
National Book Network
4501 Forbes Blvd., Suite 200
Lanham, MD 20706
Orders: (800) 462-6420

This book is printed on recycled paper

Nova Publishing Company is committed to preserving ancient forests and natural resources. Our company's policy is to print all of our books on recycled paper, with no less than 30% post-consumer waste. As a result, for the printing of this book, we have saved:

   24.2 trees   7,056 gallons of water
   4,133 kilowatts hours of electricity   6 pounds of pollution

Nova Publishing Company is a member of Green Press Initiative, a nonprofit program dedicated to supporting publishers in their efforts to reduce their use of fiber obtained from endangered forests. For more information, go to www.greenpressinitiative.org

Table of Contents

PREFACE 9

CHAPTER 1: Understanding Bankruptcy 11
    An Overview of Chapter 7 Bankruptcy 11
    Non-Dischargeable Debts 12
    Understanding Chapter 7 Bankruptcy 12
    Other Types of Bankruptcy 14
        Chapter 13 14
        Chapter 11 14
        Chapter 12 15
    When Chapter 7 Bankruptcy Isn't the Answer 15

CHAPTER 2: The Chapter 7 Bankruptcy Process 17
    Filling out Your Draft Bankruptcy Forms 17
    Filling out the Official Bankruptcy Forms 18
    Determining Your Exemptions 19
    Filing Your Bankruptcy Papers 19
    The Creditors' Meeting 20
    Your Final Discharge 21
    Instructions for Married Couples 21
    Checklist of Actions for Obtaining a Chapter 7 Bankruptcy 22
    Checklist of Schedules, Statements, and Fees for a Chapter 7 Bankruptcy ... 23

CHAPTER 3: Gathering Information for Your Bankruptcy 25
    Bankruptcy Questionnaire 26
        What Are Your Assets? 26
        What Are Your Debts? 35
        What Is Your Monthly Income? 38
        What Are Your Monthly Expenses? 39

CHAPTER 4: Filling out the Bankruptcy Forms 41
    Instructions for the Voluntary Petition (Official Form 1) 43
        Page 1 of Official Form 1 43
        Page 2 of Official Form 1 46
    Instructions for the Schedules for Official Form 6 48
        Schedule A: Real Property 48

Schedule B: Personal Property 51
Schedule C: Property Claimed as Exempt 56
Schedule D: Creditors Holding Secured Claims 59
Schedule E: Creditors Holding Unsecured Priority Claims 63
Schedule F: Creditors Holding Unsecured Nonpriority Claims 68
Schedule G: Executory Contracts and Unexpired Leases 72
Schedule H: Codebtors 74
Schedule I: Current Income of Individual Debtor(s) 76
Schedule J: Current Expenditures of Individual Debtor(s) 79
Instructions for the General Continuation Sheet 81
Instructions for the Summary of Schedules (Official Form 6) 83
Instructions for the Declaration Concerning Debtor's Schedules 85
Instructions for the Statement of Financial Affairs (Official Form 7) 87
Instructions for the Statement of Social Security Number[s] (Official
  Form 21) 102
Instructions for the Chapter 7 Individual Debtor's Statement of Intention
  (Official Form 8) 104
Instructions for the Application to Pay Filing Fee in Installments
  (Official Form 3) 107
Instructions for the Mailing List of Creditors' Names and Addresses 111

CHAPTER 5: Completing Your Bankruptcy 112
Filing Your Bankruptcy Papers 112
The Creditors' Meeting 115
Surrendering Your Property 116
Your Final Discharge 117
After Your Bankruptcy 117

APPENDIX A: Federal Bankruptcy Forms 119
Voluntary Petition (Official Form 1) 121
Schedule A: Real Property 125
Schedule B: Personal Property 127
Schedule C: Property Claimed as Exempt 133
Schedule D: Creditors Holding Secured Claims 135
Schedule E: Creditors Holding Unsecured Priority Claims 139
Schedule F: Creditors Holding Unsecured Nonpriority Claims 145
Schedule G: Executory Contracts and Unexpired Leases 149
Schedule H: Codebtors 151
Schedule I: Current Income of Individual Debtor(s) 153
Schedule J: Current Expenditures of Individual Debtor(s) 155
General Continuation Sheet 157
Summary of Schedules (Official Form 6) 159
Declaration Concerning Debtor's Schedules 161

Statement of Financial Affairs (Official Form 7) 163
Statement of Social Security Number[s] (Official Form 21) 185
Chapter 7 Individual Debtor's Statement of Intention (Official Form 8) 187
Application to Pay Filing Fee in Installments (Official Form 3) 189

APPENDIX B: State and Federal Bankruptcy Exemptions 191
State Bankruptcy Exemptions 195
Federal Bankruptcy Exemptions 238
Federal Non-Bankruptcy Exemptions 239

APPENDIX C: Federal Bankruptcy Courts 240

GLOSSARY of Bankruptcy Legal Terms 247

INDEX 251

Preface

This book is part of Nova Publishing Company's continuing Law Made Simple series. The various legal guides in this series are prepared by licensed attorneys who feel that public access to the American legal system is long overdue. The books in this series are designed to provide concrete information to consumers in order to assist them in understanding and using the law with a minimum of outside assistance.

However, in an area as complex as bankruptcy, it is not always prudent to attempt to handle every situation that arises without the aid of a competent professional. Although the information presented in this book will give readers a basic understanding of bankruptcy, it is not intended that this text entirely substitute for experienced professional assistance in all situations. Throughout this book there are references to those particular situations in which the aid of a professional is strongly recommended.

Regardless of whether or not an attorney or other professional is ultimately retained in certain situations, the information in this handbook will enable the reader to understand the framework of bankruptcy and effectively use this knowledge. To try and make that task as easy as possible, technical legal jargon has been eliminated whenever possible and plain English used instead. When it is necessary in this book to use a legal term that may be unfamiliar to most people, the word will be shown in *italics* and defined when first used. A glossary of bankruptcy legal terms most often encountered is included at the end of this book.

> **NOTE**: As this edition of *Personal Bankruptcy Simplified* went to press, it contained all of the revisions to U.S. bankruptcy law that were in effect. However, the U.S. Congress has been attempting to pass various changes to the U.S. Bankruptcy Act which would directly affect your rights as a debtor under the law. Be aware that bankruptcy laws may change rapidly. Nova Publishing will update this book as soon as any further bankruptcy laws change. You can also check the official bankruptcy court website for any changes: www.uscourts.gov/bkforms

CHAPTER 1
Understanding Bankruptcy

The ability to file for bankruptcy and obtain a fresh start is an important and long-standing part of American law. Your right to file for bankruptcy is guaranteed under federal law and the U.S. Constitution. There are various chapters in the Federal Bankruptcy Code under which you may file for bankruptcy. Each chapter has certain requirements and each offers certain relief from creditors and debt. This book describes the process for filing for bankruptcy under Chapter 7 of the Federal Bankruptcy Code, which is commonly known as a personal bankruptcy. (Information regarding the other types of bankruptcy is included at the end of this section.) The culmination of a successful Chapter 7 bankruptcy is the elimination of most of your debts and the prevention of any efforts by creditors to collect on those debts.

An Overview of Chapter 7 Bankruptcy

Chapter 7 bankruptcy is designed for debtors in financial difficulty who do not have the ability to pay their existing debts. By obtaining a personal bankruptcy, individuals are able to restart their economic lives without the burden of their prior debts. There are several effects of filing for a Chapter 7 bankruptcy. Immediately upon filing for bankruptcy, an *automatic stay* goes into effect. This is a court order that prohibits creditors from harassing you or taking any further action to collect your debts while your bankruptcy is in court. A bankruptcy court trustee then takes possession of all of your property, except the property that you may claim as exempt under state or federal law. *Exempt property* is property that the law allows you to keep, even after you are granted a bankruptcy. Much personal property and real estate is exempt from being seized in a bankruptcy. You may also be allowed to keep property that you have purchased which is subject to a *security interest* (secured property). The trustee then *liquidates* (sells) your non-exempt property and uses the proceeds to pay your creditors according to the priorities of the Bankruptcy Code. The final result of filing Chapter 7 bankruptcy is to obtain a *discharge* of your existing debts, that is, their total elimination. If, however, you are found to have committed certain kinds of improper conduct described in the Bankruptcy Code, your discharge may be denied by the court, and the purpose for which you filed the bankruptcy petition defeated. If your bankruptcy is granted, however, most of your debts will be wiped clean forever. If you receive a discharge of your debts through bankruptcy, you will not be allowed to file for bankruptcy again for a period of six years.

Non-Dischargeable Debts

Even if you receive a discharge in bankruptcy, there are some debts that are not discharged under the law. These are referred to as *non-dischargeable debts*. Therefore, even after a successful bankruptcy, you may still be responsible for the following non-dischargeable debts:

- Federal, state, and local income taxes that came due within the last three years
- Student loans that became due within the last seven years
- Court-ordered alimony and child support payments. Also, property settlements or other divorce-related debts if your spouse objects to their discharge
- Criminal restitution and court-ordered fines
- Debts for death or personal injury caused while driving while intoxicated from alcohol or drugs
- Debts you incurred to pay off non-dischargeable tax debts
- Debts that you failed to list on your bankruptcy filing papers
- Debts based on fraud or dishonesty. This includes debts of over $1,150.00 that you incurred for cash advances, loans, or credit purchases of luxuries within 60 days of filing for bankruptcy and debts incurred when you knew you couldn't pay them
- Certain condominium association fees and charges

Understanding Chapter 7 Bankruptcy

Chapter 7 bankruptcy is also referred to as a *liquidation bankruptcy*. Chapter 7 requires you, the debtor, to pay the bankruptcy court a $209.00 filing fee (which includes a $39.00 administrative fee and a $15.00 trustee surcharge) upon filing. The filing fee may be paid in installments if you are unable to pay it all upon filing. In order to file for a bankruptcy of this type, you fill out various official forms that detail your entire recent economic life. These forms will require you to inform the court of the following:

- **The location and value of all of your real estate**. All of your real estate will have to be surrendered to the court unless you claim it as exempt from bankruptcy under a federal or state exemption or you agree in some manner to keep current on the payments
- **The location and value of all of your personal property**. All of your personal property will have to be surrendered to the court unless you claim it as exempt from bankruptcy under a federal or state exemption, you agree to pay the creditor what it is worth (if it was pledged as collateral for a debt), or you agree in some manner to keep current on the payments

- **The type of real estate and/or personal property you claim is exempt from being surrendered to the bankruptcy court**. You will be allowed to keep all of the property that is exempt. In most states, you will generally be allowed to keep much of your property. Every state allows you to use their own state exemptions. In addition, some states also allow you to choose to use federal bankruptcy exemptions instead of the state exemptions. The details of bankruptcy exemptions are listed in Appendix B
- **The details of any debts for which you have pledged any type of property as collateral or on which a lien has been created**. These are referred to as *secured debts*. Your liability for these debts may be eliminated by a bankruptcy (unless it is a type of debt that is non-dischargeable). However, you may have to surrender the collateral to the creditor
- **The details of any debts that are specified by bankruptcy law as having priority in their repayment**. These debts will be repaid first from any money or property that you will surrender to the bankruptcy court. These are referred to as *unsecured priority debts*. If there is insufficient money to pay off these debts, they will also be wiped out by bankruptcy, unless the debts are non-dischargeable
- **The details of any debts for which you have not pledged any collateral and which are not priority debts**. These are referred to as *unsecured non-priority debts*. If there is any money left after paying all other creditors, these debts will be paid off proportionately. Then they too will be eliminated forever, unless they are considered non-dischargeable
- **The details of any outstanding contracts or leases**. These may also be voided unless the court feels that they can earn you income that can be used to pay off your creditors.
- **The identity of any cosigners for any of your debts**. If you are successful in obtaining a bankruptcy, your liability on a dischargeable debt will be eliminated. However, anyone who has cosigned or guaranteed a debt will still be held liable for payment on your debt
- **The amount and sources of your current income**. Your ability to pay off your debts will be scrutinized by the court
- **The amount and type of expenses that you currently pay**. Your spending on monthly expenses will also be carefully examined by the court
- **Any financial transactions within the last two years that may have an effect on your ability to pay your current creditors**. The bankruptcy court has the power to void transactions if you have transferred property to a family member to shelter it from surrender, or if you have paid off one debt to the detriment of other creditors. If you made any transactions with the intention of hiding assets or otherwise tricking creditors, your entire bankruptcy may be denied

Upon filing the forms containing this information, an *automatic stay* or court order is put into effect that prevents most creditors from trying to collect on their debts. Then a bankruptcy trustee, and perhaps your creditors, will meet with you to go over your documents. The trustee will then take possession of your non-exempt property. If necessary, the trustee will sell your non-exempt property and use the proceeds to pay off your creditors as much as possible. Finally, the bankruptcy judge *discharges* or wipes out all of your current dischargeable debts that have not been paid off.

Other Types of Bankruptcy

There are four chapters of the Federal Bankruptcy Code under which you may file a bankruptcy petition. This book describes the Chapter 7 bankruptcy in detail. Each of the other types of bankruptcy is described, in general, as follows:

Chapter 13: This type of bankruptcy is referred to as "Repayment of All or Part of the Debts of an Individual with Regular Income." Chapter 13 is designed for individuals with regular income who are temporarily unable to pay their debts, but would like to pay them in installments over a period of time. You are only eligible for Chapter 13 if your debts do not exceed certain dollar amounts set forth in the Bankruptcy Code. Under Chapter 13, you must file a plan with the court stating how you will repay your creditors all or part of the money that you owe them, using your future earnings. Usually, the period allowed by the court to repay your debts is three years, but no more than five years. Your plan must be approved by the court before it can take effect. Under Chapter 13, unlike Chapter 7, you may keep all of your property, both exempt and non-exempt, as long as you continue to make payments under the plan. After completion of payments under your repayment plan, your debts are discharged, except for certain taxes, student loans, alimony and child support payments, criminal restitution, debts for death or personal injury caused while driving while intoxicated from alcohol or drugs, and long-term secured obligations. Chapter 13 bankruptcies are also available to small sole-proprietorship businesses and will allow the business to remain open while paying off burdensome debts over a period of up to five years.

A Chapter 13 bankruptcy has advantages over other types of bankruptcies in certain instances. If you are behind in payments on your house, you may file a Chapter 13 plan to keep your house and take three to five years to make up your delinquent payments. A Chapter 13 bankruptcy may be the best alternative if you have a large amount of secured debts (debts for which you have pledged some type of collateral). If you have a mortgage on your home, the mortgage debt is a secured debt. Under a Chapter 7 bankruptcy, you may lose your home. Under a Chapter 13 bankruptcy, however, you will be allowed to keep it. If this is your situation and you would like to keep your house, you should consult a competent attorney.

Chapter 11: This type of bankruptcy is referred to as a "Reorganization." Chapter 11 is designed primarily for the reorganization of a business, but is also available to consumer debtors. Its provisions are quite complicated and any decision by an individual to file a Chapter 11 petition should be reviewed with an attorney.

Chapter 12: This bankruptcy is a specialized type of bankruptcy only available to a family farmer. Chapter 12 is designed to permit family farmers to repay their debts over a period of time and is, in many ways, similar to Chapter 13. The eligibility requirements are restrictive, however, limiting its use to those whose income arises primarily from a family-owned farm.

As you begin to determine your need for bankruptcy, you should be aware that there are various other alternatives to bankruptcy. You can often personally negotiate with your creditors to obtain relief from your debts, either in terms of making smaller payments, lengthening the time for paying the debt back, or actually lowering the amount of the debt. Most creditors will consider these options. You can also just sit tight and forego payments on your debts until your situation improves. You should also review your entire financial situation and determine how you got in over your head into debt in the first place. This may reveal strategies that you can use to lower your overall debt, for example, by giving up a second car or spending less on entertainment. There are also specific circumstances when a Chapter 7 bankruptcy is not advisable, as listed below.

When Chapter 7 Bankruptcy Isn't the Answer

There are certain situations when a Chapter 7 bankruptcy may not be the best alternative. In those situations, you may need to contact an attorney or other financial professional for advice. A Chapter 7 bankruptcy may not be the answer if:

- You own your own house or have a lot of equity built up on a major investment (such as an expensive car). Under Chapter 7, you may lose your house or car. Negotiation with your creditor or a Chapter 13 bankruptcy may be a better alternative. You should seek the assistance of an attorney
- You have obtained a Chapter 7 bankruptcy within the past six years. You will not be allowed to file for bankruptcy again until the six-year period has elapsed
- You filed a prior Chapter 7 bankruptcy petition within the previous 180 days and it was dismissed. Generally, you will not be allowed to file again until after 180 days
- You have a cosigner on a debt. A Chapter 7 bankruptcy for you will leave your cosigner or guarantor liable for the entire debt
- You're involved in a business partnership or business corporation. You should definitely consult with a lawyer before you file a Chapter 7 bankruptcy
- You have been dishonest with your creditors in any manner, including lying on loan applications, concealing assets, or attempting to transfer property to relatives

- You have run up large debts in the last few months with no obvious way to repay them. The bankruptcy court will not discharge these types of debts
- Most of your debts are of the non-dischargeable type (for example, student loans or income taxes). Chapter 7 will offer little relief
- You wish to *reaffirm* (pay off a debt, regardless of bankruptcy) a current debt. You may do so under Chapter 7. However, you should seek the assistance of an attorney
- You wish to redeem property from the bankruptcy trustee. You may do so under Chapter 7. However, you should seek the assistance of an attorney
- You wish to discharge a student loan debt. You may be able to do so under Chapter 7. However, you should seek the assistance of an attorney
- You wish to avoid a lien on your property. You may be able to do so under Chapter 7. However, you should seek the assistance of an attorney
- Your situation fits any of the descriptions above. If so, you should consult an attorney. If you have decided that Chapter 7 bankruptcy may be the correct decision for you, the following chapter in this book will explain the entire Chapter 7 bankruptcy process in detail

Remember, you have a legal constitutional right to file for bankruptcy. In fact, in the official bankruptcy court instructions, this statement is made:

> An individual, of course, has the right to file a bankruptcy case without employing an attorney. Before doing so, the debtor should read a "self-help" book on filing bankruptcy.

You are doing just what the bankruptcy court has advised. In addition, the court advises you to:

> Read all instructions thoroughly before beginning to fill out any forms. A worksheet, from an extra copy of the form, should be completed for each form. After you have completed and reviewed each worksheet, and are satisfied that the forms have been completed correctly, you should transfer the information from each worksheet to a clean blank form. The completed forms should be set aside for signing and filing.

CHAPTER 2
The Chapter 7 Bankruptcy Process

Once you have considered the alternatives and have decided that a Chapter 7 bankruptcy may be the answer to your financial problems, you will need an understanding of the entire bankruptcy process. A Chapter 7 bankruptcy can generally be obtained, from start to final discharge, in about four months. The process consists, generally, of completing numerous forms to file with the court that detail your financial situation, meeting with the bankruptcy trustee (and perhaps creditors), turning over your non-exempt property to the trustee, and finally eliminating your debts. Within this basic framework, there are various details that must be understood in order for you to emerge from your bankruptcy as financially intact as possible. Throughout the entire process of filing for bankruptcy, you must be entirely honest. All of your documents, statements, and dealings with the bankruptcy court will be under close scrutiny. The bankruptcy judges and trustees are extremely adept at detecting fraud or dishonesty. Your efforts to obtain a bankruptcy will be greatly diminished if you feel that you can trick the court or your creditors. Bankruptcy can provide a welcome relief from the burden of excessive debts. However, a bankruptcy court will not grant this relief to a person whom it feels has attempted to trick or defraud the court or creditors in any manner.

There are five basic steps in obtaining your bankruptcy using this book:

- Filling out draft copies of the bankruptcy forms
- Filling out the official bankruptcy forms
- Filing the completed forms with the bankruptcy court
- Attending a short meeting with the court-appointed bankruptcy trustee
- Obtaining the final discharge of all your debts from the bankruptcy court

Filling out Your Draft Bankruptcy Forms

The first step in obtaining your Chapter 7 bankruptcy will be to carefully fill in draft versions of the bankruptcy forms. On these forms, you will list all of the property that you own, both real estate and personal property. Every single piece of property that you own or possess must be listed, regardless of how trivial or special it may be to you. You will also list all of the various debts that you currently owe. Again, every debt that you owe must be listed. If you neglect to list a debt, that particular debt may not be wiped out by your bankruptcy. You must be scrupulously honest when filling out the official bankruptcy forms. If you attempt to hide your assets in any way to prevent them from being lost to bankruptcy, or if you lie on any of the forms or to the court, the bankruptcy judge will most likely deny your bankruptcy. You may also be subject to penalties for fraud and/or perjury, which can be up to $500,000.00 and/or five years in prison. On these forms, you will be asked to fill in considerable detail about both your property and your debts. Information regarding ownership, creditors' addresses, account numbers, and various other details will need to be listed. The gathering and recording of this information, however, will constitute the bulk of your efforts in obtaining a bankruptcy. You will need before you all of the paperwork you have that regards your finances. It will be necessary to consult your bills, payment records, paycheck stubs, mortgages, loan applications, checkbooks, tax returns, and all other financial information in order to complete these forms. If you are filing jointly, you will need to include totals for both spouses.

The Voluntary Petition (Official Form 1) is your official request for bankruptcy. The bankruptcy schedules (A through J) for the Summary of Schedules (Official Form 6) contain all of the details regarding your current assets, debts, income, and expenses. Schedules A and B contain the details of your real estate and personal property. Schedule C contains a listing of the property that you claim as exempt from bankruptcy, by virtue of either state or federal bankruptcy exemption laws. See "Determining Your Exemptions" on the next page for details. On Schedules D, E, and F, you will divide your debts into three general categories: 1. *secured debts* (those for which you have pledged some type of collateral or against which a lien exists); 2. *unsecured priority debts* (those that are, by law, to be paid off first if you have any money or assets to apply to pay your debts); or 3. *unsecured nonpriority debts* (essentially, all of your debts that are not secured or priority debts). For all of your debts, you must also determine if they fit into four other subcategories: 1. *contingent debt* (a known debt with an uncertain value, such as a claim against you stemming from an auto accident, but has yet to be resolved by a court); 2. *disputed debt* (a debt for which you dispute either the amount of the debt or the entire debt itself); 3. *liquidated debt* (a debt of yours for which a court judgment has been issued); or 4. *unliquidated debt* (a known undisputed debt that has not been the subject of a court action). Note that the majority of most people's debts will normally be unliquidated debts. On Schedule G, you will list any outstanding contracts or unexpired leases. Schedule H will list any codebtors: either cosigners on a debt or guarantors of a debt. All of your current income will be listed on Schedule I and your current expenditures on Schedule J. You will also complete a Statement of Financial Affairs (Official Form 7) on which you will answer various questions regarding your financial situation and most recent transactions.

Filling out the Official Bankruptcy Forms

The second step in the process will be to prepare the official court forms for filing for bankruptcy. These consist of a two-page Voluntary Petition, Schedules A through J, a few additional forms (a summary of all of your schedules [Official Form 6], an application to pay the filing fee in installments [Official Form 3], a statement of your intentions regarding your secured debts if you have any [Official Form 8]), and a mailing list of your creditors' names and addresses. You will use your completed draft copies to transfer all of the information regarding your assets and debts to the appropriate official bankruptcy schedules. When you have completed these official forms, your work in obtaining a bankruptcy will almost be over.

Determining Your Exemptions

The preparation of Schedule C: Property Claimed as Exempt of your bankruptcy papers is the most important form in terms of the property that you will get to keep at the end of your bankruptcy case. It is on this form that you will list all of your property that you claim is totally exempt from bankruptcy. Every state allows certain property to be excluded from being surrendered in bankruptcy. Many states also allow you to choose to use their list of exempt property or choose from the list of federal exemptions. In general, most states' exemption lists allow you to keep household goods, clothing, tools (up to certain limits), health aids (wheelchairs, crutches, etc.), public aid, unemployment, worker's compensation, pensions, and many insurance benefits. In addition, most states also allow you to exempt a certain value for a car and real estate. Most states also allow you to retain 75 percent of your wages. Some states are very liberal in their exemptions, allowing your residence to be retained regardless of value and other states are far more restrictive. In those states that allow a choice between federal or state exemptions, you will need to carefully determine which set of exemptions will be most beneficial to you in your particular circumstances. A detailed listing of state and federal exemptions is contained in Appendix B. As you fill out your Schedule C, you will need to consult your own state's listing and, possibly, the federal exemption list in that appendix.

Filing Your Bankruptcy Papers

The filing of the Voluntary Petition is the act that officially begins your bankruptcy. If there is no emergency, you should file all of your completed official bankruptcy forms at the same time. However, if there is an emergency (such as a creditor about to foreclose on your property or garnish your wages), you may file the Voluntary Petition and Mailing List of Creditors' Names and Addresses first and the remaining documents within 15 days. The filing of your Voluntary Petition is your official request to the court for bankruptcy relief. It also creates the *automatic stay*. The automatic stay is an official court order that automatically goes into effect upon the filing of your Voluntary Petition. Its effect is to prohibit your creditors from taking any action against you while your bankruptcy is pending. The stay has several effects:

- Lawsuits against you are suspended (with a few exceptions, such as paternity or child support suits)
- Creditors cannot repossess any of your property
- Banks cannot foreclose on your home while the stay is in effect
- Landlords cannot evict you
- Utility companies cannot disconnect your utilities. However, this relief only lasts 20 days, at which time a utility company can insist that you furnish a security deposit for future payment of your bills
- Even the Internal Revenue Service cannot collect on your past-due taxes
- Creditors are blocked by the automatic stay from taking any action to collect or recover any debt. They may not call you or contact your place of employment and they may not harass or annoy you in any way

There are a few exceptions to the blanket power of the automatic stay against creditors. Criminal prosecutions are not halted. The IRS can still audit you. Alimony and child support will likely be required to be paid, regardless of the stay. Creditors can also ask that the stay be lifted for certain debts or property. They may do this in particular to protect their collateral on one of your debts. In addition, a Chapter 7 automatic stay does not prevent a creditor from continuing collection procedures against a codebtor, unless the codebtor is your spouse and you have filed a joint bankruptcy petition. The automatic stay is a powerful tool to help you as you struggle to get back on your financial feet. If necessary to prevent immediate creditor action, you may decide to file your Voluntary Petition first in order to take advantage of this weapon against creditors. You, yourself, may then send a copy of your filed Voluntary Petition to creditors in order to alert them of the issuance of the automatic stay. In an emergency situation, waiting for the bankruptcy court to send notice of the automatic stay may take precious weeks.

The Creditors' Meeting

About a month after you file your Voluntary Petition, you will be required to attend a short creditors' meeting. Generally, no creditors will actually be present at this meeting, but they may attend if they seek to challenge some part of your claim to exemptions or dischargeability. Someone who will definitely attend the meeting, however, is the *bankruptcy trustee*. This is a court-appointed person who will take charge of your property and pay off your creditors with your assets to the best of his or her ability. All of your property and your right to receive property is together referred to as your *bankruptcy estate*. Upon filing for a personal bankruptcy, the bankruptcy court obtains total control over all of your property—your bankruptcy estate. Until your case is concluded, the court has full authority over your bankruptcy estate. While your bankruptcy case is pending, you must not sell, give away, or dispose of any property without notifying the bankruptcy trustee and obtaining permission. Your creditors' meeting will generally last less than one hour. At the meeting, your bankruptcy trustee will carefully review your documents with you. The trustee will look for any discrepancies, such as undervaluing property or claiming too many expenses. At this time, he or she will decide if there is any non-exempt property or cash that he or she feels can be used to pay off your creditors. If the trustee decides that there is certain property that is not exempt and that could be sold to pay off your creditors, he or she will ask that you surrender it to him or her. The same goes for any cash or bank accounts. Generally, the trustee will not take any used property with little cash value, even if it isn't exempt. After the meeting, the trustee will then use either the cash or proceeds from a sale of your non-exempt property to pay off your creditors according to a priority list set up by the Federal Bankruptcy Code.

Your Final Discharge

Once the bankruptcy trustee has reviewed your case, collected any non-exempt property, and used the proceeds to pay your creditors, you will be granted a final discharge by the bankruptcy court. This will be the official elimination of the rest of your dischargeable debts. From that moment on, you will cease to have those debts. Your creditors can take no legal action to collect on those discharged debts. All of the exempt property that you were allowed to keep is yours, free and clear from any claims by your previous creditors. You are ready to begin anew. Up until your final discharge, you may voluntarily ask the court to dismiss your bankruptcy. You may wish to do this if you feel that you have become able to pay off your debts or if you have reached an agreement with your creditors. If you wish to have your bankruptcy dismissed, you are advised to seek legal assistance.

Instructions for Married Couples

If you are currently married, you must decide how you will file for your bankruptcy. You have several choices. One of you may file individually, both of you may file individually, or you can file jointly. There are several factors that may influence your decision on which way to file for your bankruptcy. In general, there are benefits to jointly filing for bankruptcy. By doing so, all of the dischargeable debts, both joint and individual, belonging to both you and your spouse, will be wiped out. If you both file individually, you both will incur double filing and administrative fees. In addition, you will each have to complete a separate set of official bankruptcy forms. If you and your spouse have separated and have little or no jointly owned property or debts, you may wish to file alone. If your spouse individually owns valuable property that could be taken by the court in a joint bankruptcy, you may also wish to file for bankruptcy as an individual. In most cases, however, in which there is little property to be surrendered to the court, you will be safe in filing your bankruptcy petition jointly. Note that the forms have numerous places to indicate if you are filing jointly. If you have any questions regarding the choice on how to file, please consult a competent attorney. For those married couples who live in community property states (Arizona, California, Idaho, Louisiana, Nevada, New Mexico, Texas, Washington, and Wisconsin), some separate rules apply. *Note*: Alaska allows spouses to designate property as community property if done in writing. If you both file jointly, your situation is similar to married couples in all other states. However, if one of you chooses to file for bankruptcy individually, the community property of the non-filing spouse may be taken by the court to pay off the bills and debts of the spouse who filed for bankruptcy. In addition, however, the *community debts* of both spouses (generally, those debts incurred during the marriage) will be totally discharged (providing that they are of the dischargable type).

Checklist of Actions for Obtaining a Chapter 7 Bankruptcy

- ❏ Carefully read through this entire book

- ❏ Gather all of your financial records, bills, deeds, titles, checkbooks, checkstubs, and other paperwork together in one place

- ❏ Using your own financial documents, complete the bankruptcy questionnaire and the draft bankruptcy forms

- ❏ Contact the local bankruptcy court clerk for information on local court rules and mailing lists

- ❏ Using your completed draft bankruptcy forms, fill in the official bankruptcy form. You will need to either type the fill-ins or use good handwriting in ink. However, your mailing list must be typed

- ❏ Sign all official forms where indicated. If you are filing jointly, your spouse must also sign

- ❏ Make the required number of copies of the completed official bankruptcy forms

- ❏ File the original and required number of copies of your complete set of official forms. Retain an additional copy for yourself. Upon filing, you must either pay the required fees in full or fill out an application to pay the filing fee in installments.

❏ Attend a creditors' meeting and meet with the bankruptcy trustee

❏ Surrender any non-exempt property to the bankruptcy trustee, if required

❏ Obtain a final discharge of all dischargeable debts from the bankruptcy court

Checklist of Schedules, Statements, and Fees for a Chapter 7 Bankruptcy

❏ **Filing Fee**: $209.00 ($155.00 filing fee + $39.00 administrative fee + $15.00 trustee surcharge), payable in cash, money order, or certified bank check. You may choose to pay this fee in installments. If the fee is to paid in installments, the debtor must be an individual and must submit a signed application for court approval on an Application to Pay Filing Fee in Installments (Official Form 3). This form is supplied with this book and additional copies can be obtained from the clerk of your local bankruptcy court

❏ **Voluntary Petition (Official Form 1)**: Names and addresses of all creditors of the debtor MUST be submitted with the petition. This is not required, however, if debtor submits schedules of debts (Schedules D through F) for Official Form 6 with the petition. Form 1 is supplied with this book and you can obtain additional copies if necessary from the clerk of your local bankruptcy court

❏ **Schedules of Assets and Liabilities (Official Form 6)–Schedules A through F**: MUST be submitted with the petition or within 15 days. These forms are supplied with this book and you can obtain additional copies if necessary from the clerk of your local bankruptcy court

❏ **Schedule G: Executory Contracts and Unexpired Leases** *and* **Schedule H: Codebtors**: MUST be submitted with the petition or within 15 days. These forms are supplied with this book and copies are available from the clerk of your local bankruptcy court

The Chapter 7 Bankruptcy Process

- ❏ **Schedule I: Current Income of Individual Debtor(s)** *and* **Schedule J: Current Expenditures of Individual Debtor(s)**: MUST be submitted with the petition or within 15 days. These forms are supplied with this book and you can obtain additional copies if necessary from the clerk of your local bankruptcy court

- ❏ **Statement of Financial Affairs (Official Form 7)**: MUST be submitted with the petition or within 15 days. This form is supplied with this book and you may obtain additional copies if necessary from the clerk of your local bankruptcy court

- ❏ **Chapter 7 Individual Debtor's Statement of Intention (Official Form 8)**: Required only if the debtor is an individual and Schedule D: Creditors Holding Secured Claims contains consumer debts that are secured by property of the debtor. If so, this form MUST be submitted within 30 days of filing of the petition or by the date set for the creditors' meeting, whichever is earlier. This form is supplied with this book and copies can be obtained from the clerk of your local bankruptcy court

- ❏ **Statement of Social Security Number(s) [Official Form 21]**: MUST be filed with the Voluntary Petition (Official Form 1). Form 21 is supplied with this book and you can obtain additional copies if necessary from the clerk of your local bankruptcy court

- ❏ **Statement Disclosing Compensation Paid or to Be Paid a Bankruptcy Petition Preparer**: Only required if you are using a bankruptcy petition preparer. This form is not supplied with this book and may be obtained from the clerk of your local bankruptcy court

- ❏ **Statement Disclosing Compensation Paid or to Be Paid to an Attorney for the Debtor**: Only required if you are using an attorney. This form is not supplied with this book and may be obtained from the clerk of your local bankruptcy court

- ❏ **Mailing List of Creditors' Names and Addresses**: MUST be filed with the Voluntary Petition. This form varies with local bankruptcy courts. Check with the court for local rules. This form is not supplied with this book and can be obtained from the clerk of your local bankruptcy court

CHAPTER 3
Gathering Information for Your Bankruptcy

Before you begin to actually prepare your bankruptcy papers, you must have a clear record of what your assets, debts, income, and expenses are. This information regarding your current financial situation will help you understand your overall position and will eventually be used on the various bankruptcy forms which you prepare for the court. It is helpful to gather all of the information regarding your personal financial situation together in one place. The following Bankruptcy Questionnaire will assist you in that task and should provide you with all of the necessary information to make the actual preparation of your bankruptcy papers a relatively easy task. In addition, the actual process of filling out these questions will force you to think about your current financial situation. You must complete this questionnaire and the related bankruptcy papers with absolute honesty. Any attempts, however minor, to hide your property or trick creditors in any manner may result in the denial of your bankruptcy by the court.

To prepare this questionnaire, you will need before you all of the paperwork that you have regarding your finances. It will be necessary to consult your bills, payment records, paycheck stubs, mortgages, loan applications, checkbooks, tax returns, and all other financial information in order to complete this questionnaire. If you are filing jointly, include totals for both spouses. When you have finished completing the questionnaire, have it before you as you fill in your official bankruptcy forms found in Appendix A. By referring to this completed questionnaire, you should be able to quickly and easily fill in all of the necessary legal documents for your bankruptcy.

Bankruptcy Questionnaire

What Are Your Assets?

Real Estate

Personal Residence
Description _____
Location _____
Market Value: $ _____
How held and percent held? (Joint tenants, tenancy-in-common, etc?)
_____ / _____ %
Value of your share .... $ _____
Amount of mortgage or other debt .... $ _____

Vacation Home
Description _____
Location _____
Market Value: $ _____
How held and percent held? (Joint tenants, tenancy-in-common, etc?)
_____ / _____ %
Value of your share .... $ _____
Amount of mortgage or other debt .... $ _____

Vacant Land
Description _____
Location _____
Market Value: $ _____
How held and percent held? (Joint tenants, tenancy-in-common, etc?)
_____ / _____ %
Value of your share .... $ _____
Amount of mortgage or other debt .... $ _____

Other Property
Description _____
Location _____
Market Value: $ _____
How held and percent held? (Joint tenants, tenancy-in-common, etc?)
_____ / _____ %
Value of your share .... $ _____
Amount of mortgage or other debt .... $ _____

Other Property
Description _____
Location _____
Market Value: $ _____
How held and percent held? (Joint tenants, tenancy-in-common, etc?)
_____ / _____ %
Value of your share .... $ _____
Amount of mortgage or other debt .... $ _____

Total Real Estate .... $ _____

Personal Property

Cash and Bank Accounts

Cash .... $ _____

Checking account .... $ _____
Bank _____
Address _____
Account # _____
Name(s) on account _____

Savings account .... $ _____
Bank _____
Address _____
Account # _____
Name(s) on account _____

Certificate of deposit .... $ _____
Held by _____
Address _____
Expiration date _____
Name(s) on account _____

Other account .... $ _____
Bank _____
Address _____
Account # _____
Name(s) on account _____

Total Cash and Bank Accounts .... $ _____

Security Deposits (Held by Utilities, Landlords, etc.)

Security deposit .... $ _____
Held by _____
Address _____
Reason for deposit _____
Name(s) on account _____

Security deposit .... $ _____
Held by _____
Address _____
Reason for deposit _____
Name(s) on account _____

Total Security Deposits .... $ _____

Miscellaneous Household and Personal Property

Household furnishings .... $ _____
Description _____
Location _____

Audio or video equipment .... $ _____
Description _____
Location _____

Computer equipment .... $ _____
Description _____
Location _____

Books, pictures, or artwork .... $ _____
Description _____
Location _____

Stamp, coin, or other collections .... $ _____
Description _____
Location _____

Clothing .... $ _____
Description _____
Location _____

Jewelry and furs .... $ _____
Description _____
Location _____

Firearms and sporting equipment .... $ _____
Description _____
Location _____

Camera and hobby equipment .... $ _____
Description _____
Location _____

Any other miscellaneous household and personal property .... $ _____
Description _____
Location _____

Total Miscellaneous Household and Personal Property .... $ _____

Insurance and Annuity Contracts

Life insurance (face value) .... Policy Amount $ _____
Policy # _____
Company _____
Address _____
Cash surrender value .... $ _____

Annuity contract (face value) .... Policy Amount $ _____
Policy # _____
Company _____
Address _____
Cash surrender value .... $ _____

Total Insurance and Annuity Contracts .... $ _____

IRA, Keogh, and/or Pension/Profit-Sharing Plans

Company or administrator _____
Address _____
Plan type _____
Net value .... $ _____

Company or administrator _____
Address _____
Plan type _____
Net value .... $ _____

Total IRA, Keogh, and/or Pension/Profit-Sharing Plans .... $ _____

Stocks and Mutual Funds

Company _____
CUSIP or Certificate # _____
Number and type of shares _____
Value .... $ _____

Company _____
CUSIP or Certificate # _____
Number and type of shares _____
Value .... $ _____

Total Stocks and Mutual Funds .... $ _____

Business Interests

Sole Proprietorship
Name _____
Location _____
Type of business _____
Your net value .... $ _____

Interest in Partnership
Name _____
Location _____
Type of business _____
Gross value $ _____
Percentage share held _____
Your net value .... $ _____

Corporation Interest
Name _____
Location _____
Type of business _____
Gross value $ _____
Percentage shares held _____
Your net value .... $ _____

Joint Venture Interest
Name _____
Location _____
Type of business _____
Gross value $ _____
Percentage share held _____
Your net value .... $ _____

Total Business Interests .... $ _____

Bonds and Mutual Bond Funds

Company _____
CUSIP or Certificate # _____
Number and type of shares _____
Value .... $ _____

Company _____
CUSIP or Certificate # _____
Number and type of shares _____
Value .... $ _____

Total Bonds and Mutual Bond Funds .... $ _____

Accounts Receivable

Accounts owed to you .... $ _____
Due from _____
Address _____

Accounts owed to you .... $ _____
Due from _____
Address _____

Total Accounts Receivable .... $ _____

Alimony, Support, or Property Settlements Owed to You

Alimony .... $ _____
Due from _____
Address _____

Property settlement .... $ _____
Due from _____
Address _____

Total Alimony, Support, or Property Settlements Owed to You .... $ _____

Other Debts Owed to You

Other debt owed to you .... $ _____
Due from _____
Address _____

Other debt owed to you .... $ _____
Due from _____
Address _____

Total Other Debts Owed to You .... $ _____

Tax Refunds Due to You

Federal income tax .... $ _____
Address of IRS office _____

State income tax .... $ _____
Name of state _____
Address of tax authority _____

Other tax .... $ _____
Name of tax authority _____
Address of tax authority _____

Total Tax Refunds Due to You .... $ _____

Miscellaneous Property Interests

Future interest and/or life estates .... $ _____
Description _____
Location _____

Interests in estates of decedents, etc. .... $ _____
Description _____
Location _____

Interests in another person's life insurance policy .... $ _____
Description _____
Location _____

Other contingent or unliquidated claims .... $ _____
Description _____
Location _____

Royalties, patents, copyrights, etc. .... $ _____
Description _____
Location _____

Licenses, franchises, etc .... $ _____
Description _____
Location _____

Auto, truck, or other vehicles .... $ _____
Description _____
Location _____

Boat, marine motor, etc. .... $ _____
Description _____
Location _____

Airplane and accessories .... $ _____
Description _____
Location _____

Office equipment, supplies, and furnishings .... $ _____
Description _____
Location _____

Machinery, business equipment, etc. .... $ _____
Description _____
Location _____

Business inventory .... $ _____
Description _____
Location _____

Animals .... $ _____
Description _____
Location _____

Crops (growing or harvested) .... $ _____
Description _____
Location _____

Farm equipment .... $ _____
Description _____
Location _____

Farm supplies and seed .... $ _____
Description _____
Location _____

33

Tools .... $ _____
Description _____
Location _____

Season tickets .... $ _____
Description _____
Location _____

Any other personal property not listed .... $ _____
Description _____
Location _____

Any other personal property not listed .... $ _____
Description _____
Location _____

Any other personal property not listed .... $ _____
Description _____
Location _____

Any other personal property not listed .... $ _____
Description _____
Location _____

Total Miscellaneous Property Interests .... $ _____

Summary of Assets

(Insert totals from previous pages)

Real Estate Total .... $ _____
Cash and Bank Accounts Total .... $ _____
Security Deposits Total .... $ _____
Miscellaneous Household and Personal Property Total .... $ _____
Insurance and Annuity Contracts Total .... $ _____
Ira, Keogh, and/or Pension/Profit-Sharing Plans Total .... $ _____
Stocks and Mutual Funds Total .... $ _____
Business Interests Total .... $ _____
Bonds and Mutual Bond Funds Total .... $ _____
Accounts Receivable Total .... $ _____
Alimony, Support, or Property Settlements Owed to You Total .... $ _____
Other Debts Owed to You Total .... $ _____
Tax Refunds Due to You Total .... $ _____
Miscellaneous Property Interests Total .... $ _____

Total Assets .... $ _____

What Are Your Debts?

Mortgages You Owe (Home or Business)

Payable to _____ Mortgage # _____
Address _____
Property location _____
Reason for debt _____
Place debt originated _____ Date incurred _____
Do you dispute debt? _____ Did you sign contract? _____
Any legal action on this debt? _____ Name of co-signer (if any)? _____
Length of term _____ Interest rate _____
Total amount now due.. $ _____

Payable to _____ Mortgage # _____
Address _____
Property location _____
Reason for debt _____
Has there been any legal action regarding this debt? _____
Place debt originated _____ Date incurred _____
Do you dispute debt? _____ Did you sign contract? _____
Any legal action on this debt? _____ Name of co-signer (if any)? _____
Length of term _____ Interest rate _____
Total amount now due.. $ _____

Total Mortgages You Owe .... $ _____

Loans You Owe (Finance Company, Bank, Auto, or Personal)

Payable to _____ Loan # _____
Address _____
Collateral _____ Reason for debt _____
Place debt originated _____ Date incurred _____
Do you dispute debt? _____ Did you sign loan contract? __
Any legal action on this debt? _____ Name of co-signer (if any)? _____
Length of term _____ Interest rate _____
Total amount now due.. $ _____

Payable to _____ Loan # _____
Address _____
Collateral _____ Reason for debt _____
Place debt originated _____ Date incurred _____
Do you dispute debt? _____ Did you sign loan contract? __
Any legal action on this debt? _____ Name of co-signer (if any)? _____
Length of term _____ Interest rate _____
Total amount now due.. $ _____

Total Loans You Owe .... $ _____

Accounts Payable You Owe (Medical, Dental, Stores, etc.)

Payable to _____ Account # _____
Address _____
Reason for debt _____
Place debt originated _____ Date incurred _____
Do you dispute debt? _____ Did you sign contract? _____
Is account past due? _____ Interest rate _____
Total amount now due.. $ _____

Payable to _____ Account # _____
Address _____
Reason for debt _____
Place debt originated _____ Date incurred _____
Do you dispute debt? _____ Did you sign contract? _____
Is account past due? _____ Interest rate _____
Total amount now due.. $ _____

Payable to _____ Account # _____
Address _____
Reason for debt _____
Place debt originated _____ Date incurred _____
Do you dispute debt? _____ Did you sign contract? _____
Is account past due? _____ Interest rate _____
Total amount now due.. $ _____

Total Accounts Payable You Owe .... $ _____

Rent You Owe

Payable to _____
Address _____
Address of rental property _____ Date incurred _____
Do you dispute debt? _____ Did you sign lease? _____
Is rent past due? _____ Late charge _____
Total amount now due.. $ _____

Payable to _____
Address _____
Address of rental property _____ Date incurred _____
Do you dispute debt? _____ Did you sign lease? _____
Is rent past due? _____ Late charge _____
Total amount now due.. $ _____

Total Rent You Owe .... $ _____

Taxes Due

Federal income (name of tax authority _____) ...... $ _____
State income (name of tax authority _____) .... $ _____
Personal property (name of tax authority _____) .... $ _____
Real estate (name of tax authority _____) .... $ _____
Other (name of tax authority _____) .... $ _____

Total Taxes Due .... $ _____

Credit Card Debts

Credit card company _____ Credit card account # _____
Address _____
Reason for debt _____
Place debt originated _____ Date incurred _____
Do you dispute debt? _____ Did you sign contract? _____
Amount due.. $ _____

Credit card company _____ Credit card account # _____
Address _____
Reason for debt _____
Place debt originated _____ Date incurred _____
Do you dispute debt? _____ Did you sign contract? _____
Amount due.. $ _____

Credit card company _____ Credit card account # _____
Address _____
Reason for debt _____
Place debt originated _____ Date incurred _____
Do you dispute debt? _____ Did you sign contract? _____
Amount due.. $ _____

Total Credit Card Debts .... $ _____

Miscellaneous Debts

To whom due _____
Address _____
Collateral _____ Reason for debt _____
Place debt originated _____ Date incurred _____
Do you dispute debt? _____ Did you sign contract? _____
Any legal action on this debt? _____ Name of co-signer (if any)? _____
Term _____ Interest rate _____
Amount due.. $ _____

To whom due _____
Address _____
Collateral _____ Reason for debt _____
Place debt originated _____ Date incurred _____
Do you dispute debt? _____ Did you sign contract? _____
Any legal action on this debt? _____ Name of co-signer (if any)? _____
Term _____ Interest rate _____
Amount due .... $ _____

Total Miscellaneous Debts .... $ _____

Summary of Debts

(Insert totals from previous pages)

Mortgages You Owe Total .... $ _____
Loans You Owe Total .... $ _____
Accounts Payable You Owe Total .... $ _____
Rent You Owe Total .... $ _____
Taxes Due Total .... $ _____
Credit Card Debts Total .... $ _____
Miscellaneous Debts Total .... $ _____

Total Debts .... $ _____

What Is Your Monthly Income?

Occupation _____
How long employed? _____
Name of employer _____
Address of employer _____

	You	*Spouse*

Monthly Wage Income
Gross wages, salary, and commissions
(*pro-rate if not paid monthly*): .... $ _____ $ _____
    Estimated monthly overtime: .... $ _____ $ _____
    Total Monthly Wages .... $ _____ $ _____

Less payroll deductions:
    Taxes .... $ _____ $ _____
    Social Security .... $ _____ $ _____
    Insurance .... $ _____ $ _____
    Union dues .... $ _____ $ _____

Other (Specify: _____) .... $ _____ $ _____
Other (Specify: _____) .... $ _____ $ _____
Subtotal Of Payroll Deductions .... $ _____ $ _____

Total Net Monthly Wage Income (take-home pay:
total monthly wages minus payroll deductions) .... $ _____ $ _____

Do you anticipate any change of more than 10% in any of the above categories within the next year? Explain: _____

Monthly Non-Wage Income   *You*   *Spouse*
Income from business, profession, or farm: .... $ _____ $ _____
Income from real property: .... $ _____ $ _____
Interest and dividends: .... $ _____ $ _____
Alimony or child support payments: .... $ _____ $ _____
Social Security or other government assistance: .... $ _____ $ _____
Pension or retirement income: .... $ _____ $ _____
Other monthly income: .... $ _____ $ _____

Total Monthly Non-Wage Income .... $ _____ $ _____

Do you anticipate any change of more than 10% in any of the above categories within the next year? Explain: _____

Summary of Monthly Income

(Insert totals from previous pages)

                                                     You   *Spouse*
Total Net Monthly Wage Income .... $ _____ $ _____
Total Monthly Non-Wage Income .... $ _____ $ _____

Total Monthly Income .... $ _____ $ _____

What Are Your Monthly Expenses?

Rent or home mortgage payment (include lot rent for mobile home): .... $ _____
Real estate taxes .... $ _____
Property insurance .... $ _____
Utilities:
    Electricity and heating fuel .... $ _____
    Water and sewer .... $ _____
    Telephone .... $ _____
    Other .... $ _____
    Subtotal of Utilities .... $ _____

Home maintenance (repairs and upkeep): .... $ _____
Food: .... $ _____
Clothing: .... $ _____
Laundry and dry cleaning: .... $ _____
Medical and dental expenses: .... $ _____
Transportation (not including car payments): .... $ _____
Recreation, clubs and entertainment, newspapers, magazines, etc.: .... $ _____
Charitable contributions: .... $ _____
Insurance (not deducted from wages or included in mortgage payments):
    Homeowner's or renter's .... $ _____
    Life .... $ _____
    Health .... $ _____
    Auto .... $ _____
    Other .... $ _____
    Subtotal of Insurance .... $ _____
Taxes (not deducted from wages or included in mortgage payments): .... $ _____
Installment payments:
    Auto .... $ _____
    Other .... $ _____
    Other .... $ _____
    Subtotal of Installment Payments .... $ _____
Alimony, maintenance, and support paid to others: .... $ _____
Support of dependents not living at your home: .... $ _____
Regular expenses from operation of business, profession, or farm: .... $ _____
Other: .... $ _____
Other: .... $ _____
Other: .... $ _____

Total Monthly Expenses .... $ _____

Do you anticipate any change of more than 10% in any of the above categories within the next year? Explain: _____

Financial Summary

(Insert totals from previous pages)

Total Assets .... $ _____

Total Debts .... $ _____

                                                                             You   *Spouse*

Total Monthly Income .... $ _____ $ _____

Total Monthly Expenses .... $ _____

CHAPTER 4
Filling out the Bankruptcy Forms

On the following pages you will find instructions for filling in each of the required forms for a Chapter 7 bankruptcy. The instructions for each form will explain who will need to use the form and, specifically, how to fill in the form. After each set of instructions, you will also find a sample filled-in form, showing information from a fictional bankruptcy proceeding. Before you begin, you should carefully read through this entire chapter to gain an understanding of the entire procedure of bankruptcy form completion and to determine which forms you will personally need to use.

Please note that there are also instructions for a Continuation Sheet. This particular form is to be used, if necessary, to add additional information to bankruptcy schedules or forms. Bankruptcy Schedules B, D, E, and F already have pre-printed continuation sheets that you should use for additional information for those forms. As you prepare each of the necessary forms, you should have before you all of your financial information that you filled in on your Bankruptcy Questionnaire. Referring to a client's financial information is, in fact, the same method that a bankruptcy attorney would use to fill in these forms. The difference is that the attorney would be charging you over $100.00 per hour to fill in these forms.

You should then make photocopies of the necessary forms from the blank originals included in Appendix A of this book. The photocopies must be on single-sided white 8½" x 11" paper. You should make two copies of each blank form that you need: the first copy will be for your first draft, which you may fill in with pencil. The other copy of the blank forms will be used for your final copy, which should be completed by typing or with very neat handwriting in black ink. *Note*: If you are using the version of this book that includes Forms-on-CD, please refer to the instructions for completing the forms that are on the readme document that is included on the CD.

Be absolutely honest in filling out these forms. Do not, in any way, attempt to hide property from the court. You must list every single piece of property that you own and every source of income that you have. If the court discovers any evidence of deceit, your case will most likely be dismissed and you will not be allowed to attempt to refile for bankruptcy for at least six months. You may also be subject to fines or imprisonment. Be extremely thorough. The schedules are the forms on which you will enter the information regarding what you own (your *assets*); what you owe (your *debts*) and to whom you owe them; what you make (your *income*); and what you spend (your *expenditures*). As you list your debts, assets, income, and expenditures, be certain that you have listed every possible item. It is very easy to overlook many common items or debts. Read the instructions and forms very carefully for clues on what you should include. The only debts that the bankruptcy court will eliminate are those that you list. If a debt is not listed by you on the appropriate schedule, you may go through bankruptcy and still owe that debt. Equally important is the careful listing of the exact address of each person you owe. Creditors must be given notice that you are filing for bankruptcy or your debt to them will not be discharged. Recall that you need to include all transactions for a full year prior to your filing for bankruptcy. Also note that you have the right to amend your Voluntary Petition at any time, if you find that you made a mistake.

On the completed final copy, you will sign and date each form if necessary before filing it with the bankruptcy court. *Note*: If you need additional copies of these forms, you can obtain them from your local bankruptcy court or on the internet. Please note that certain bankruptcy courts may require specific localized forms in addition to the main bankruptcy forms supplied in this book. Additional copies of official bankruptcy forms can be obtained from the clerk of the U.S. Bankruptcy Court for your area. Please check the listing in Appendix C for the address of your area court. In addition, official bankruptcy forms may be downloaded from the internet at: www.uscourts.gov/bkforms/

In general, you will use every form provided. Please refer to the instructions for each individual form. When filling in your copy of these forms, please be careful that your information is listed in the proper columns and on the correct form. Some of these forms are complicated and several forms are very similar. Do not make any stray marks on the forms. Type your information if possible. You may use legible handwriting in black ink to complete the forms (except the mailing list which must be typed).

NOTE: If you purchased a version of this book without an accompanying CD-ROM that contains fill-in copies of the official bankruptcy forms, you can order the CD-ROM for $12.95, plus shipping and handling. For credit card purchases, please call 1-800-462-6420 and specify "Personal Bankruptcy Simplified Forms-on-CD only" (ISBN# 0-892949-03-2).

Instructions for the Voluntary Petition (Official Form 1)

(Page 1 of Official Form 1)

This form is your official request for bankruptcy. By filing this form, you are voluntarily agreeing to give control over everything you own to the court. In turn, you will be allowed to keep all of your property that is exempt from bankruptcy and all of your debts that are dischargeable in bankruptcy will be wiped out.

Court Name: Fill in the full name of the judicial district in which you will be filing your papers (such as "Southern District of Illinois"). This should be where you reside and maintain your primary home.

Name of Debtor: Fill in your full name (last name first) that you regularly use to sign checks, etc.

Name of Joint Debtor: Fill in your spouse's name, if you are married and filing a joint petition with your spouse. Use the name he or she regularly uses (last name first).

All Other Names used by the Debtor in the last 6 years: Fill in any other names that you have used (nicknames, shortened, maiden, or initials-only names, etc.). If you have recently operated a business, fill in any business name that you used.

All Other Names used by the Joint Debtor in the last 6 years: Fill in any other names that your spouse has used (nicknames, shortened, maiden, or initials-only names, etc.). If he or she has recently operated a business, fill in any business name that was used.

Last four digits of Soc. Sec. No./Complete EIN or other Tax I.D. No.: Fill in your (debtor) and your spouse's (joint debtor) last four Social Security number digits and/or any full Federal Employer Tax ID numbers, if applicable.

Street Address of Debtor and Joint Debtor: Fill in the actual street address of your home or homes. This cannot be a post office box or other address where you merely receive mail.

County of Residence or of the Principal place of Business: List the county of your mainplace of residence. "Place of business" does not apply.

Mailing Address of Debtor and Joint Debtor: Here is where you list your actual mailing address if it is different from your street address (can be a post office box).

Location of Principal Assets of Business Debtor: This is only for those debtors who have operated a business. Normally, this address will be that of your business, but if

Filling out the Bankruptcy Forms   43

not, specify where the majority of your business possessions are located. If you have not operated a business, enter *N/A* for "not applicable."

Venue: This indicates your residency. Put an *X* in the top box.

Type of Debtor: Place an *X* in front of "Individual(s)."

Chapter or Section of Bankruptcy Code Under Which the Petition is Filed: Place an *X* before "Chapter 7."

Nature of Debts: Most will place an X in front of "Non-Business/Consumer." However, if you have operated a business in the last few years and many of your debts are business-related, place an *X* in front of "Business."

Chapter 11 Small Business: Ignore this box.

Filing Fee: Check the first box if you will attach the entire filing fee of $209.00. Check the second box if you will be requesting to pay the fee in installments. If so, you will need to fill out an Application to Pay Filing Fee in Installments (Official Form 3), explained later. In a few states, low-income debtors may request a waiver of the entire filing fee. Check with the bankruptcy court clerk if you wish to pursue this option and don't check any box.

Statistical/Administrative Information: When you have a clear idea of the necessary amounts, check the appropriate boxes. The answers here may be your best estimates.

(Official Form 1) (12/03)

FORM B1	United States Bankruptcy Court __Northern__ District of __Illinois__	Voluntary Petition

Name of Debtor (if individual, enter Last, First, Middle): Smith, Mary Ellen	Name of Joint Debtor (Spouse) (Last, First, Middle): Smith, John Alan
All Other Names used by the Debtor in the last 6 years (include married, maiden, and trade names): Ellen Smith Ellen Harris (maiden)	All Other Names used by the Joint Debtor in the last 6 years (include married, maiden, and trade names): J.A. Smith
Last four digits of Soc. Sec. No./Complete EIN or other Tax I.D. No. (if more than one, state all): **5555**	Last four digits of Soc. Sec. No./Complete EIN or other Tax I.D. No. (if more than one, state all): **8888**
Street Address of Debtor (No. & Street, City, State & Zip Code): 16 Main Street Centerville, IL 61111	Street Address of Joint Debtor (No. & Street, City, State & Zip Code): 16 Main Street Centerville, IL 61111
County of Residence or of the Principal Place of Business: Superior County	County of Residence or of the Principal Place of Business: Superior County
Mailing Address of Debtor (if different from street address): P.O. Box 120 Centerville, IL 61111	Mailing Address of Joint Debtor (if different from street address): P.O. Box 120 Centerville, IL 61111
Location of Principal Assets of Business Debtor (if different from street address above): n/a	

Information Regarding the Debtor (Check the Applicable Boxes)

Venue (Check any applicable box)
- [✓] Debtor has been domiciled or has had a residence, principal place of business, or principal assets in this District for 180 days immediately preceding the date of this petition or for a longer part of such 180 days than in any other District.
- [ ] There is a bankruptcy case concerning debtor's affiliate, general partner, or partnership pending in this District.

Type of Debtor (Check all boxes that apply)
- [✓] Individual(s)
- [ ] Corporation
- [ ] Partnership
- [ ] Other _____
- [ ] Railroad
- [ ] Stockbroker
- [ ] Commodity Broker
- [ ] Clearing Bank

Chapter or Section of Bankruptcy Code Under Which the Petition is Filed (Check one box)
- [✓] Chapter 7
- [ ] Chapter 9
- [ ] Chapter 11
- [ ] Chapter 12
- [ ] Chapter 13
- [ ] Sec. 304 - Case ancillary to foreign proceeding

Nature of Debts (Check one box)
- [✓] Consumer/Non-Business
- [ ] Business

Filing Fee (Check one box)
- [✓] Full Filing Fee attached
- [ ] Filing Fee to be paid in installments (Applicable to individuals only) Must attach signed application for the court's consideration certifying that the debtor is unable to pay fee except in installments. Rule 1006(b). See Official Form No. 3.

Chapter 11 Small Business (Check all boxes that apply)
- [ ] Debtor is a small business as defined in 11 U.S.C. § 101
- [ ] Debtor is and elects to be considered a small business under 11 U.S.C. § 1121(e) (Optional)

Statistical/Administrative Information (Estimates only)   THIS SPACE IS FOR COURT USE ONLY
- [ ] Debtor estimates that funds will be available for distribution to unsecured creditors.
- [ ] Debtor estimates that, after any exempt property is excluded and administrative expenses paid, there will be no funds available for distribution to unsecured creditors.

Estimated Number of Creditors
1-15	16-49	50-99	100-199	200-999	1000-over
[✓]	[ ]	[ ]	[ ]	[ ]	[ ]

Estimated Assets
$0 to $50,000	$50,001 to $100,000	$100,001 to $500,000	$500,001 to $1 million	$1,000,001 to $10 million	$10,000,001 to $50 million	$50,000,001 to $100 million	More than $100 million
[ ]	[✓]	[ ]	[ ]	[ ]	[ ]	[ ]	[ ]

Estimated Debts
$0 to $50,000	$50,001 to $100,000	$100,001 to $500,000	$500,001 to $1 million	$1,000,001 to $10 million	$10,000,001 to $50 million	$50,000,001 to $100 million	More than $100 million
[ ]	[✓]	[ ]	[ ]	[ ]	[ ]	[ ]	[ ]

(Page 2 of Official Form 1)

Name of Debtor(s): Enter your full name. If you are filing jointly, also enter your spouse's full name.

Prior Bankruptcy Case Filed Within Last 6 Years: Enter *N/A* if you, or your spouse if you are both filing jointly, have not filed for bankruptcy in the last six years. If you have filed for bankruptcy within the last six years, you may not be allowed to refile. In that case, you should consult an attorney.

Pending Bankruptcy Case Filed by any Spouse, Partner or Affiliate of this Debtor: Enter *N/A* if there are no other bankruptcy cases currently pending which involve your spouse, a partnership, or other business of which you are an owner. If there is a bankruptcy pending, consult an attorney.

Signature(s) of Debtor(s) (Individual/Joint): Sign the top line in the box and enter the appropriate date. If you are filing jointly, your spouse should sign the "Signature of Joint Debtor" line. Enter your phone number. By signing and filing this form, you will be officially asking the court to discharge your debts.

Signature of Attorney: Enter *N/A* in the box for the attorney signature.

Signature of Debtor (Corporate or Partnership): Enter *N/A* on the signature line.

Exhibit A: Leave blank. Exhibit A is not included in this kit. If the description applies to you or your spouse, you should consult an attorney.

Exhibit B: Enter *N/A* on the signature line.

Exhibit C: Check "No," unless your property includes very dangerous property. If your answer is "Yes," you should consult an attorney. Exhibit C is not included in this kit.

Signature of Non-Attorney Petition Preparer: Enter *N/A* on the signature line, unless you are using the services of a paid bankruptcy-form preparer.

(Official Form 1) (12/03) FORM B1, Page 2

| **Voluntary Petition**
(This page must be completed and filed in every case) | Name of Debtor(s):
Mary Ellen and John Alan Smith |

Prior Bankruptcy Case Filed Within Last 6 Years (If more than one, attach additional sheet)

| Location Where Filed: | Case Number: | Date Filed: |

Pending Bankruptcy Case Filed by any Spouse, Partner or Affiliate of this Debtor (If more than one, attach additional sheet)

| Name of Debtor: | Case Number: | Date Filed: |
| District: | Relationship: | Judge: |

Signatures

Signature(s) of Debtor(s) (Individual/Joint)

I declare under penalty of perjury that the information provided in this petition is true and correct.
[If petitioner is an individual whose debts are primarily consumer debts and has chosen to file under chapter 7] I am aware that I may proceed under chapter 7, 11, 12 or 13 of title 11, United States Code, understand the relief available under each such chapter, and choose to proceed under chapter 7.
I request relief in accordance with the chapter of title 11, United States Code, specified in this petition.

X *Mary Ellen Smith (handwritten signature)*
Signature of Debtor

X *John Alan Smith (handwritten signature)*
Signature of Joint Debtor

(444) 555-6666
Telephone Number (If not represented by attorney)

March 13, 2004
Date

Signature of Attorney

X n/a
Signature of Attorney for Debtor(s)

_____
Printed Name of Attorney for Debtor(s)

_____
Firm Name

_____
Address

_____
Telephone Number

_____
Date

Signature of Debtor (Corporation/Partnership)

I declare under penalty of perjury that the information provided in this petition is true and correct, and that I have been authorized to file this petition on behalf of the debtor.

The debtor requests relief in accordance with the chapter of title 11, United States Code, specified in this petition.

X n/a
Signature of Authorized Individual

_____
Printed Name of Authorized Individual

_____
Title of Authorized Individual

_____
Date

Exhibit A
(To be completed if debtor is required to file periodic reports (e.g., forms 10K and 10Q) with the Securities and Exchange Commission pursuant to Section 13 or 15(d) of the Securities Exchange Act of 1934 and is requesting relief under chapter 11)

☐ Exhibit A is attached and made a part of this petition.

Exhibit B
(To be completed if debtor is an individual whose debts are primarily consumer debts)
I, the attorney for the petitioner named in the foregoing petition, declare that I have informed the petitioner that [he or she] may proceed under chapter 7, 11, 12, or 13 of title 11, United States Code, and have explained the relief available under each such chapter.

X n/a
Signature of Attorney for Debtor(s)   Date

Exhibit C
Does the debtor own or have possession of any property that poses or is alleged to pose a threat of imminent and identifiable harm to public health or safety?

☑ Yes, and Exhibit C is attached and made a part of this petition.
☐ No

Signature of Non-Attorney Petition Preparer

I certify that I am a bankruptcy petition preparer as defined in 11 U.S.C. § 110, that I prepared this document for compensation, and that I have provided the debtor with a copy of this document.

_____
Printed Name of Bankruptcy Petition Preparer

_____
Social Security Number (Required by 11 U.S.C. § 110)

_____
Address

Names and Social Security numbers of all other individuals who prepared or assisted in preparing this document:

If more than one person prepared this document, attach additional sheets conforming to the appropriate official form for each person.

X n/a
Signature of Bankruptcy Petition Preparer

_____
Date

A bankruptcy petition preparer's failure to comply with the provisions of title 11 and the Federal Rules of Bankruptcy Procedure may result in fines or imprisonment or both 11 U.S.C. §110; 18 U.S.C. §156.

Instructions for the Schedules for Official Form 6

Schedule A: Real Property

All of the real estate that you own or have an interest in will be listed on Schedule A. All of your personal property will be listed on Schedule B. However, don't include leases; these will go on Schedule G. Note that if you own a home, you may lose it in a Chapter 7 bankruptcy. You may be better off using a Chapter 13 bankruptcy and should consult an attorney for advice in this situation. If more space is needed, use a Continuation Sheet, as explained later.

In Re: Enter your full name. If you're filing jointly, include your spouse's name.

Case No.: Leave this blank if filed with your petition. The court clerk will assign you a case number.

Description and Location of Property: Enter a brief description of the property and its street address. You should enter all homes, land, condos, business property, and buildings in which you have any ownership interest. Your description can simply be "home" or "lot" or some other simple description and the address or location. If you do not own any real estate, enter the "None" box and put *$0* in the space for "Total" and enter *$0* on your Summary of Schedules (explained later) and proceed to Schedule B.

Nature of Debtor's Interest in Property: Check the ownership language on your deed or mortgage, but in most cases property is held as "fee simple." Enter the term "fee simple" (which refers to a full ownership), unless you are certain that your property is held in some other form, such as a "tenant in common" or other form of joint ownership. If you are purchasing real estate under a contract, describe the contract by date and name.

Husband, Wife, Joint, or Community: If single, enter *N/A*. If married, enter *H* (for husband), *W* (wife), *J* (joint), or *C* (community property), depending if the property is owned individually by the husband or wife, is owned jointly by both (as joint tenants or tenants-by-the-entireties), or is owned as community property. Check the ownership language on the deed or other document of ownership. In community property states (Arizona, California, Idaho, Louisiana, Nevada, New Mexico, Texas, Washington, and Wisconsin), property that was acquired during a marriage is generally considered community property. In all other states, the ownership of property depends on the names on the title document or deed.

Current Market Value of Debtor's Interest in Property, without Deducting Any Secured Claim or Exemption: You should enter the full value at which the property could be sold today. Do not deduct any money that you may owe on the property, like a mortgage. You may need to obtain a market value estimate from a real estate broker.

However, you may determine the value yourself by checking the value of other similar property for sale in your locale. If you own the property jointly with someone who is not filing for bankruptcy with you, you should indicate your percentage of ownership and only note the market value of your share of the property (for example, your 33.33 percent ownership of a home owned jointly with your parents with a full market value of $60,000.00 would constitute a market value of $20,000.00 for your interest in the property).

Amount of Secured Claim: A *secured claim* is any mortgage, deed of trust, loan, lien, or other claim against the property that is in writing and for which the property acts as collateral. Enter the amount that is left to be paid on the mortgage or other obligation. You can get the current amount from the financial institution to which the money is owed. If there are no secured claims, enter the "None" box.

Total: Total the amounts in the "Current Market Value…" column (and from any continuation sheets if used), and enter here and also on the Summary of Schedules form, as explained later.

Form B6A
(6/90)

In re Mary Ellen and John Alan Smith   ,   Case No. (supplied by clerk)
             Debtor   (If known)

SCHEDULE A - REAL PROPERTY

Except as directed below, list all real property in which the debtor has any legal, equitable, or future interest, including all property owned as a co-tenant, community property, or in which the debtor has a life estate. Include any property in which the debtor holds rights and powers exercisable for the debtor's own benefit. If the debtor is married, state whether husband, wife, or both own the property by placing an "H," "W," "J," or "C" in the column labeled "Husband, Wife, Joint, or Community." If the debtor holds no interest in real property, write "None" under "Description and Location of Property."

Do not include interests in executory contracts and unexpired leases on this schedule. List them in Schedule G - Executory Contracts and Unexpired Leases.

If an entity claims to have a lien or hold a secured interest in any property, state the amount of the secured claim. See Schedule D. If no entity claims to hold a secured interest in the property, write "None" in the column labeled "Amount of Secured Claim."

If the debtor is an individual or if a joint petition is filed, state the amount of any exemption claimed in the property only in Schedule C - Property Claimed as Exempt.

DESCRIPTION AND LOCATION OF PROPERTY	NATURE OF DEBTOR'S INTEREST IN PROPERTY	HUSBAND, WIFE, JOINT, OR COMMUNITY	CURRENT MARKET VALUE OF DEBTOR'S INTEREST IN PROPERTY, WITHOUT DEDUCTING ANY SECURED CLAIM OR EXEMPTION	AMOUNT OF SECURED CLAIM
Personal home located at 16 Main Street, Centerville, IL 61111	Fee Simple	J	$48,000.00	$37,000.00
		Total ▶	$48,000.00	

(Report also on Summary of Schedules.)

Schedule B: Personal Property

On this form, you will list every other property that you own or have any claim of ownership in. Personal property includes all other property except real estate. This form includes extensive lists for many specific types of property. If your specific property is not listed, line 33 should be used for "other" property.

In re: Enter your full name. If you're filing jointly, include your spouse's name.

Case No.: Leave this blank if filed with your petition. The court clerk will assign you a case number.

None: If you do not own any of the type of property for that number, enter an *X*.

Description and Location of Property: Enter a brief description of the property and the street address of its location. You should separately enter each piece of individual property worth more than $25.00 in which you have any ownership interest at all. List wages that are owed to you under line 17 (liquidated debts). Your property should be listed under the appropriate number for that specific type of property (for example, enter an auto under line 23). Include a clear description of the property. For cash and bank accounts, list the source of the money (for example, from wages). At the top of this box, you may note that all of your property is located at a single address unless noted otherwise.

Husband, Wife, Joint, or Community: If you are single, enter *N/A*. If you are married, enter *H*, *W*, *J*, or *C*, depending if the property is owned individually by the husband or wife, is owned jointly by both (as joint tenants or tenants-by-the-entireties), or is owned as community property in a community property state. Check the ownership language on the title or other document of ownership. In community property states (Arizona, California, Idaho, Louisiana, Nevada, New Mexico, Texas, Washington, and Wisconsin), property that was acquired during a marriage is considered community property. In all other states, the ownership of property depends on the names on the title document and if there is no title, then it is generally jointly owned if it was acquired while you were married. In most states, property that was individually owned prior to a marriage is still considered individually owned during the marriage. *Note*: Spouses in Alaska can designate in writing that certain property is to be considered "community property."

Current Market Value of Debtor's Interest in Property, without Deducting Any Secured Claim or Exemption: You should enter the full value at which the property could be sold today. Do not deduct any money that you may owe on the property, like a loan. For life insurance, enter the cash surrender value only, not the amount of the policy. For other property, you may need to obtain market-value estimates from a used-car Blue Book at the library or by checking the value of other similar property for sale in your area. For very valuable property, you may need to consult an appraiser. If you own the property jointly with someone who is not filing for bankruptcy with you, you should indicate your percentage of ownership and only note the market value of your share of the property. If more space is needed, use a Continuation Sheet, as explained later.

Instructions for specific property:
1. Cash on hand should be the amount in your actual possession on the date of filing.
2. Includes all financial accounts you have.
3. Includes all credit accounts for your housing.
4–8. Include a brief description of the type of property. Include a lump sum total dollar amount for each category number.
9–13. Describe each item in detail. (For line 11, if your retirement plan is ERISA-qualified, do not enter an amount for its dollar value.)
14. Include any personal or cashier's checks, money orders, or promissory notes.
15–17. Include any money owed to you.
18–20. Include any property that will become yours in the future.
21–22 Include trademarks, trade secrets, and any royalties.
23–32. List each item in detail and include a continuation sheet if necessary.
33. List any property that does not fit into specific categories.

Total: On the last page, total the amounts in the "Current Market Value…" column on each page (and any continuation sheets) and enter here. Also enter this amount on the Summary of Schedules form. Enter the total number (if any) of continuations sheets that are attached.

Form B6B
(10/89)

In re **Mary Ellen and John Alan Smith**,   Case No. **(supplied by clerk)**
             Debtor   **(If known)**

SCHEDULE B - PERSONAL PROPERTY

Except as directed below, list all personal property of the debtor of whatever kind. If the debtor has no property in one or more of the categories, place an "x" in the appropriate position in the column labeled "None." If additional space is needed in any category, attach a separate sheet properly identified with the case name, case number, and the number of the category. If the debtor is married, state whether husband, wife, or both own the property by placing an "H," "W," "J," or "C" in the column labeled "Husband, Wife, Joint, or Community." If the debtor is an individual or a joint petition is filed, state the amount of any exemptions claimed only in Schedule C - Property Claimed as Exempt.

Do not list interests in executory contracts and unexpired leases on this schedule. List them in Schedule G - Executory Contracts and Unexpired Leases.

If the property is being held for the debtor by someone else, state that person's name and address under "Description and Location of Property."

TYPE OF PROPERTY	NONE	DESCRIPTION AND LOCATION OF PROPERTY	HUSBAND, WIFE, JOINT, OR COMMUNITY	CURRENT MARKET VALUE OF DEBTOR'S INTEREST IN PROPERTY, WITHOUT DEDUCTING ANY SECURED CLAIM OR EXEMPTION
1. Cash on hand.	☐	cash with debtors	J	$90.00
2. Checking, savings or other financial accounts, certificates of deposit, or shares in banks, savings and loan, thrift, building and loan, and homestead associations, or credit unions, brokerage houses, or cooperatives.	☐	Checking account at First Bank of Centerville, 120 Broadway, Centerville, IL 61111	J	$137.00
3. Security deposits with public utilities, telephone companies, landlords, and others.	☐	Centerville Electric Company, 14 Center Street, Centerville, IL 61111	J	$100.00
4. Household goods and furnishings, including audio, video, and computer equipment.	☐	washer, dryer, refrigerator, TV, stereo, and various household furnishings: all at family home	J	$2,500.00
5. Books; pictures and other art objects; antiques; stamp, coin, record, tape, compact disc, and other collections or collectibles.	☐	personal books, family photos, and 3 paintings	J	$150.00
6. Wearing apparel.	☐	personal clothing of debtors	J	$400.00
7. Furs and jewelry.	☐	wedding rings	J	$1,000.00
8. Firearms and sports, photographic, and other hobby equipment.	☐	Nikon camera	J	$140.00
9. Interests in insurance policies. Name insurance company of each policy and itemize surrender or refund value of each.	☐	Prudential Insurance Co., Policy 12345, Cash surrender value	W	$1,200.00
10. Annuities. Itemize and name each issuer.	✔			

53

Form B6B-Cont.
(10/89)

In re **Mary Ellen and John Alan Smith**, Case No. __(supplied by clerk)__
      Debtor   **(If known)**

SCHEDULE B - PERSONAL PROPERTY
(Continuation Sheet)

TYPE OF PROPERTY	NONE	DESCRIPTION AND LOCATION OF PROPERTY	HUSBAND, WIFE, JOINT, OR COMMUNITY	CURRENT MARKET VALUE OF DEBTOR'S INTEREST IN PROPERTY, WITHOUT DEDUCTING ANY SECURED CLAIM OR EXEMPTION
11. Interests in IRA, ERISA, Keogh, or other pension or profit sharing plans. Itemize.	☐	IRA accounts held at First Bank of Centerville, 120 Broadway, Centerville, IL 61111	H/W	$150.00
12. Stock and interests in incorporated and unincorporated businesses. Itemize.	✔			
13. Interests in partnerships or joint ventures. Itemize.	✔			
14. Government and corporate bonds and other negotiable and non-negotiable instruments.	✔			
15. Accounts receivable.	✔			
16. Alimony, maintenance, support, and property settlements to which the debtor is or may be entitled. Give particulars.	✔			
17. Other liquidated debts owing debtor including tax refunds. Give particulars.	✔			
18. Equitable or future interests, life estates, and rights or powers exercisable for the benefit of the debtor other than those listed in Schedule of Real Property.	✔			
19. Contingent and noncontingent interests in estate of a decedent, death benefit plan, life insurance policy, or trust.	✔			
20. Other contingent and unliquidated claims of every nature, including tax refunds, counterclaims of the debtor, and rights to setoff claims. Give estimated value of each.	✔			
21. Patents, copyrights, and other intellectual property. Give particulars.	✔			
22. Licenses, franchises, and other general intangibles. Give particulars.	✔			

54

Form B6B-cont.
(10/89)

In re **Mary Ellen and John Alan Smith**   ,   Case No. **(supplied by clerk)**
                Debtor   **(If known)**

SCHEDULE B - PERSONAL PROPERTY
(Continuation Sheet)

TYPE OF PROPERTY	N O N E	DESCRIPTION AND LOCATION OF PROPERTY	HUSBAND, WIFE, JOINT, OR COMMUNITY	CURRENT MARKET VALUE OF DEBTOR'S INTEREST IN PROPERTY, WITHOUT DEDUCTING ANY SECURED CLAIM OR EXEMPTION
23. Automobiles, trucks, trailers, and other vehicles and accessories.	☐	1994 Honda Accord, 1998 Chevy pick-up	H/W	$13,000.00
24. Boats, motors, and accessories.	✔			
25. Aircraft and accessories.	✔			
26. Office equipment, furnishings, and supplies.	✔			
27. Machinery, fixtures, equipment, and supplies used in business.	✔			
28. Inventory.	✔			
29. Animals.	✔	1 dog (pet)		$300.00
30. Crops - growing or harvested. Give particulars.	✔			
31. Farming equipment and implements.	✔			
32. Farm supplies, chemicals, and feed.	✔			
33. Other personal property of any kind not already listed. Itemize.	☐	tools used in trade as mechanic, and a piano		$1,800.00

___3___ continuation sheets attached   Total▶ $ 20,967.00

(Include amounts from any continuation sheets attached. Report total also on Summary of Schedules.)

Schedule C: Property Claimed as Exempt

You will use this form to claim the property that is exempt from being taken in your bankruptcy. Please consult Appendix B for details on the specific exemptions available in your state. In some states (Arkansas, Connecticut, District of Columbia, Hawaii, Massachusetts, Michigan, Minnesota, New Jersey, New Mexico, Pennsylvania, Rhode Island, South Carolina, Texas, Vermont, Washington, and Wisconsin) you have a choice between federal bankruptcy exemptions or state bankruptcy exemptions. In those states, fill in a separate copy of Schedule C for each set of exemptions (federal and state) and then decide which is the better choice. In all other states, you will use the state bankruptcy exemptions and federal *non-bankruptcy* exemptions. See Appendix B for details. *Note*: You must have resided in your state for at least 91 of the 180 days immediately preceding the date when you file your petition in order to use that state's exemptions.

In re: Enter your full name. If you're filing jointly, include your spouse's name.

Case No.: Leave this blank if filed with your petition. The court clerk will assign you a case number.

Debtor elects the exemptions to which debtor is entitled under: Select the top box if you choose to use the federal bankruptcy exemptions and the second box if you choose state and federal non-bankruptcy exemptions.

Description of Property: Carefully go through the exemption list that you have chosen and your Schedules A and B and decide which property can be claimed as exempt. For each item of property that you decide is exempt, use the same description of that property that you used on Schedules A or B. List each grouping of property under subheadings such as "Real Estate," "Household Goods," "Tools," etc. For pensions, all ERISA pensions are exempt under either federal or state bankruptcy exemptions. Check with your employer to see if yours is an ERISA pension. If not, your state may specifically exempt your particular pension. If in doubt, you will need to consult a lawyer to be certain that you do not lose your pension.

Specify Law Providing Each Exemption: Using your state's listing in Appendix B, list the exact name and chapter of your state's law that provides the exemption. You may state at the top of the form that "All references are to…" and then list the name of your state's statute (for example: Idaho Code). Then just list the chapter numbers for each exemption.

Value of Claimed Exemption: Based on the statute exemption limits, list the amount that you claim as exempt for each piece of property. If you are married and filing jointly, you may double the amount of most exemptions, unless noted in Appendix B that your state does not allow such doubling. Some states have separate exemptions that may apply to a single piece of property. If so, list both exemption amounts up to the market value of the property. If the exemption amount is more than the value of the property, you may use the rest of the exemption on another piece of similar property until the exemption limit is reached. If the exemption amount is less than the market value of the property, the property may be sold by the court, the exemption amount given to you as cash, and the rest of the proceeds used to pay off your creditors.

Current Market Value of Property without Deducting Exemption: Enter the full market value of each piece of property exactly as you have previously listed it on Schedule A or B. Don't make any deduction for your exemption amount. Use a Continuation Sheet if necessary.

Form B6C
(6/90)

In re Mary Ellen and John Alan Smith   ,   Case No. (supplied by clerk)
                     Debtor   (If known)

SCHEDULE C - PROPERTY CLAIMED AS EXEMPT

Debtor elects the exemptions to which debtor is entitled under:
(Check one box)

- [x] 11 U.S.C. § 522(b)(1): Exemptions provided in 11 U.S.C. § 522(d). **Note: These exemptions are available only in certain states.**
- [ ] 11 U.S.C. § 522(b)(2): Exemptions available under applicable nonbankruptcy federal laws, state or local law where the debtor's domicile has been located for the 180 days immediately preceding the filing of the petition, or for a longer portion of the 180-day period than in any other place, and the debtor's interest as a tenant by the entirety or joint tenant to the extent the interest is exempt from process under applicable nonbankruptcy law.

DESCRIPTION OF PROPERTY	SPECIFY LAW PROVIDING EACH EXEMPTION	VALUE OF CLAIMED EXEMPTION	CURRENT MARKET VALUE OF PROPERTY WITHOUT DEDUCTING EXEMPTION
personal residence	735-5/12-901	$15,000.00	$48,000.00
cash with debtors	735-5/12-1001(b)	$90.00	$90.00
checking account at First Bank of Centerville	735-5/12-1001(b)	$137.00	$137.00
security deposit with Centerville Electric Company	735-5/12-1001(b)	$100.00	$100.00
household goods, furnishings, washer, dryer, TV, stereo, refrigerator	735-5/12-1001(b)	$2,500.00	$2,500.00
pet dog	735-5/12-1001(b)	$300.00	$300.00

Schedule D: Creditors Holding Secured Claims

A *secured debt* is a debt for which you pledged some type of collateral (like a mortgage, consumer loan, car loan, etc.) or a debt based on a lien against your property (such as a judgment, tax, or mechanic's lien has been filed against property that you own). Even if a debt is only partially secured by collateral, you should list it here. If a creditor has more than one claim, such as debts arising from separate transactions, list each claim separately. You may have these debts canceled, but you will be required to either give up the collateral or buy it back from the court for its market value. Use the official Continuation Sheet if necessary. Please note that if you have a consumer debt secured by collateral, you must also file Chapter 7 Individual Debtor's Statement of Intention (Official Form 8) [see later instructions]. If you wish to keep such property, you should see an attorney.

In re: Enter your full name. If you're filing jointly, include your spouse's name.

Case No.: Leave this blank if filed with your petition. The court clerk will assign you a case number.

Check this box if debtor has no creditors holding secured claims to report on this Schedule D: If so, check box and go to Schedule E.

Creditor's Name, Mailing Address Including Zip Code, and Account Number: Fill in the complete name and address of each creditor (in alphabetical order). Include only the last four digits of an account number if there is one.

Codebtor: If someone else cosigned the debt documents, is a non-filing spouse or joint owner, or otherwise can be held liable for the debt, place an *X* in this box. In community property states, non-filing spouses are generally liable for debts undertaken during a marriage. In common-law states, non-filing spouses are generally liable for debts for necessities (food, clothing, shelter, etc.).

Husband, Wife, Joint, or Community: If you are single, enter *N/A*. If you are married, enter *H*, *W*, *J*, or *C*, depending if the particular debt is owed individually by the husband or wife, is owed jointly by both (as joint tenants or tenants-by-the-entireties), or is owed as a community debt in a community property state. Check the language on the debt document. In common-law states, the liability for the debt generally depends on the names on the debt document. In most states, debts that were individually undertaken prior to a marriage are considered individual debts during the marriage.

Date Claim Was Incurred, Nature of Lien, and Description and Market Value of Property Subject to Lien: List all pertinent information about each secured debt. List the date that you signed the debt documents or that the lien was recorded. The *nature* *of lien* is either a lien or a tax, judgment, child support, or mechanic's lien. For debts, each debt is either a *purchase money debt* (the property purchased is the collateral), *non-purchase money debt* (the property purchased was not the collateral), or *possessory non-purchase money debt* (you obtained a loan on property that the creditor has possession of, such as a pawn-shop loan). To describe the property and market value of the collateral for any debt or lien, use the description and value from Schedule A or B.

Contingent, Unliquidated, or Disputed: "Contingent" means the debt is based on an event that has not yet occurred. "Unliquidated" means an outstanding loan whose amount has not yet been determined, such as the amount of damages in a car accident that has not yet been established by court action. "Disputed" means that you dispute either the amount or even the existence of the debt. You may check more than one box.

Amount of Claim without Deducting Value of Collateral: List the amount required to pay off the entire debt or lien.

Unsecured portion, If Any: If the value of the collateral is less than the amount of the debt, enter the difference here. If the collateral is worth more than the debt, enter *$0*.

Subtotal and Total: Subtotal the amounts in the "Amount of Claim Without Deducting Collateral" column on each page and enter the total on the last page and also on the Summary of Schedules form. Also enter the amount of continuation sheets used, if any.

Form B6D
(12/03)

In re __Mary Ellen and John Alan Smith__,   Case No. __(supplied by clerk)__
        Debtor   (If known)

SCHEDULE D - CREDITORS HOLDING SECURED CLAIMS

State the name, mailing address, including zip code and last four digits of any account number of all entities holding claims secured by property of the debtor as of the date of filing of the petition. The complete account number of any account the debtor has with the creditor is useful to the trustee and the creditor and may be provided if the debtor chooses to do so. List creditors holding all types of secured interests such as judgment liens, garnishments, statutory liens, mortgages, deeds of trust, and other security interests. List creditors in alphabetical order to the extent practicable. If all secured creditors will not fit on this page, use the continuation sheet provided.

If any entity other than a spouse in a joint case may be jointly liable on a claim, place an "X" in the column labeled "Codebtor," include the entity on the appropriate schedule of creditors, and complete Schedule H - Codebtors. If a joint petition is filed, state whether husband, wife, both of them, or the marital community may be liable on each claim by placing an "H," "W," "J," or "C" in the column labeled "Husband, Wife, Joint, or Community."

If the claim is contingent, place an "X" in the column labeled "Contingent." If the claim is unliquidated, place an "X" in the column labeled "Unliquidated." If the claim is disputed, place an "X" in the column labeled "Disputed." (You may need to place an "X" in more than one of these three columns.)

Report the total of all claims listed on this schedule in the box labeled "Total" on the last sheet of the completed schedule. Report this total also on the Summary of Schedules.

☐ Check this box if debtor has no creditors holding secured claims to report on this Schedule D.

CREDITOR'S NAME, MAILING ADDRESS INCLUDING ZIP CODE, AND ACCOUNT NUMBER (See instructions above.)	CODEBTOR	HUSBAND, WIFE, JOINT, OR COMMUNITY	DATE CLAIM WAS INCURRED, NATURE OF LIEN, AND DESCRIPTION AND MARKET VALUE OF PROPERTY SUBJECT TO LIEN	CONTINGENT	UNLIQUIDATED	DISPUTED	AMOUNT OF CLAIM WITHOUT DEDUCTING VALUE OF COLLATERAL	UNSECURED PORTION, IF ANY
ACCOUNT NO. 987654321 Centerville Savings and Loan 169 Front Street Centerville, IL 61111	✔	J	Mortgage on personal home at 16 Main Street Centerville, IL 61111 dated 1/13/93 VALUE $ 48,000.00	☐	✔	☐	$37,000.00	$0.00
ACCOUNT NO. 	☐		 VALUE $	☐	☐	☐		
ACCOUNT NO. 	☐		 VALUE $	☐	☐	☐		
ACCOUNT NO. 	☐		 VALUE $	☐	☐	☐		

__0__ continuation sheets attached

Subtotal ➡ $ 37,000.00
(Total of this page)

Total ➡ $ 37,000.00
(Use only on last page)

(Report total also on Summary of Schedules)

Form B6D - Cont.
(12/03)

In re _____,   Case No. _____
               Debtor   (If known)

SCHEDULE D - CREDITORS HOLDING SECURED CLAIMS
(Continuation Sheet)

CREDITOR'S NAME, MAILING ADDRESS INCLUDING ZIP CODE AND ACCOUNT NUMBER (See instructions.)	CODEBTOR	HUSBAND, WIFE, JOINT, OR COMMUNITY	DATE CLAIM WAS INCURRED, NATURE OF LIEN, AND DESCRIPTION AND MARKET VALUE OF PROPERTY SUBJECT TO LIEN	CONTINGENT	UNLIQUIDATED	DISPUTED	AMOUNT OF CLAIM WITHOUT DEDUCTING VALUE OF COLLATERAL	UNSECURED PORTION, IF ANY
ACCOUNT NO.			VALUE $					
ACCOUNT NO.			VALUE $					
ACCOUNT NO.			VALUE $					
ACCOUNT NO.			VALUE $					
ACCOUNT NO.			VALUE $					

Sheet no. ___ of ___ continuation sheets attached to Schedule of Creditors Holding Secured Claims

Subtotal $ ➤
(Total of this page)

Total $ ➤
(Use only on last page)

(Report total also on Summary of Schedules)

Schedule E: Creditors Holding Unsecured Priority Claims

Unsecured priority claims are certain debts that are given priority in being paid off in a bankruptcy, but that have no collateral pledged. They include taxes that you might owe, wages you may owe to employees, alimony, child support, and certain other claims. Even if a debt is only partially subject to priority, you should only list it here. If a creditor has more than one claim, such as debts arising from separate transactions, list each claim separately. Use the official Schedule E Continuation Sheet if necessary.

In re: Enter your full name. If you're filing jointly, include your spouse's name.

Case No.: Leave this blank if filed with your petition. The court clerk will assign you a case number.

Check this box if debtor has no creditors holding unsecured priority claims to report on this Schedule E: If so, check the box and go on to Schedule F.

Type of Priority Claims: Read through each definition of the various priority claims carefully and check them against the debts that you have. The most likely unsecured priority claim will be for back taxes owed. Place an *X* before any of your debts that are considered priority claims.

Schedule E: Creditors Holding Unsecured Priority Claims Continuation Sheet Instructions

In re: Enter your full name. If you're filing jointly, include your spouse's name.

Case No.: Leave this blank if filed with your petition. The court clerk will assign you a case number.

Type of Priority: Enter the type of priority claim that was checked off on Schedule E.

Creditor's Name, Mailing Address Including Zip Code, and Account Number: Fill in the complete name and address of each creditor (in alphabetical order). Include the last four digits of account number if there is one.

Codebtor: If someone else has cosigned the debt documents, is a non-filing spouse or joint owner, or otherwise can be held liable for the debt, place an *X* in this box. In community-property states, debts undertaken during a marriage are generally considered community debts, and non-filing spouses are liable. In common-law states, non-filing spouses are generally only liable for debts for necessities (food, clothing, shelter, etc.).

Husband, Wife, Joint, or Community: If you are single, enter *N/A*. If you are married, enter *H*, *W*, *J*, or *C*, depending if the particular debt is owed individually by the husband or wife, is owed jointly by both (as joint tenants or tenants-by-the-entireties), or is owed as a community debt in a community property state. Check the language on the debt document. In common-law states, the liability for the debt generally depends on the names on the debt document. In most states, debts that were individually undertaken prior to a marriage are considered individual debts during the marriage.

Date Claim Was Incurred and Consideration For Claim: List the date that the debt was incurred and a description of the debt or claim, including what you received in exchange for the debt, such as "goods purchased, "hours worked," or "cash deposited."

Contingent, Unliquidated, or Disputed: "Contingent" means the debt is based on an event that has not yet occurred. "Unliquidated" means an outstanding loan whose amount has not yet been determined, such as the amount of damages in a car accident that has not yet been established by court action. "Disputed" means that you dispute either the amount or even the existence of the debt. You may check more than one box.

Amount of Claim: List the total amount of the claimed debt, including any amount over the actual priority amount limit listed under "Types of Priority Claims" on the first page of Schedule E. Note that these amounts may change on April 1, 2007. Check with the court clerk for current amount limits.

Amount Entitled to Priority: List the lesser of the total amount of claims or the maximum priority amount from the list under "Types of Priority Claims."

Subtotal and Total: Subtotal the amounts in the "Amount of Claim" column on each page and enter the total on the last page and also on the Summary of Schedules form. Also enter the number of the sheet attached to the Schedule of Creditors Holding Priority Claims and the total number of sheets attached (if any).

Form B6E
(04/04)

In re Mary Ellen and John Allen Smith   ,   Case No. (supplied by clerk)
                        Debtor   (if known)

SCHEDULE E - CREDITORS HOLDING UNSECURED PRIORITY CLAIMS

A complete list of claims entitled to priority, listed separately by type of priority, is to be set forth on the sheets provided. Only holders of unsecured claims entitled to priority should be listed in this schedule. In the boxes provided on the attached sheets, state the name, mailing address, including zip code, and last four digits of the account number, if any, of all entities holding priority claims against the debtor or the property of the debtor, as of the date of the filing of the petition. The complete account number of any account the debtor has with the creditor is useful to the trustee and the creditor and may be provided if the debtor chooses to do so.

If any entity other than a spouse in a joint case may be jointly liable on a claim, place an "X" in the column labeled "Codebtor," include the entity on the appropriate schedule of creditors, and complete Schedule H-Codebtors. If a joint petition is filed, state whether husband, wife, both of them or the marital community may be liable on each claim by placing an "H,""W,""J," or "C" in the column labeled "Husband, Wife, Joint, or Community."

If the claim is contingent, place an "X" in the column labeled "Contingent." If the claim is unliquidated, place an "X" in the column labeled "Unliquidated." If the claim is disputed, place an "X" in the column labeled "Disputed." (You may need to place an "X" in more than one of these three columns.)

Report the total of claims listed on each sheet in the box labeled "Subtotal" on each sheet. Report the total of all claims listed on this Schedule E in the box labeled "Total" on the last sheet of the completed schedule. Repeat this total also on the Summary of Schedules.

☐ Check this box if debtor has no creditors holding unsecured priority claims to report on this Schedule E.

TYPES OF PRIORITY CLAIMS (Check the appropriate box(es) below if claims in that category are listed on the attached sheets)

☐ **Extensions of credit in an involuntary case**

Claims arising in the ordinary course of the debtor's business or financial affairs after the commencement of the case but before the earlier of the appointment of a trustee or the order for relief. 11 U.S.C. § 507(a)(2).

☐ **Wages, salaries, and commissions**

Wages, salaries, and commissions, including vacation, severance, and sick leave pay owing to employees and commissions owing to qualifying independent sales representatives up to $4,925* per person earned within 90 days immediately preceding the filing of the original petition, or the cessation of business, whichever occurred first, to the extent provided in 11 U.S.C. § 507(a)(3).

☐ **Contributions to employee benefit plans**

Money owed to employee benefit plans for services rendered within 180 days immediately preceding the filing of the original petition, or the cessation of business, whichever occurred first, to the extent provided in 11 U.S.C. § 507(a)(4).

☐ **Certain farmers and fishermen**

Claims of certain farmers and fishermen, up to $4,925* per farmer or fisherman, against the debtor, as provided in 11 U.S.C. § 507(a)(5).

☐ **Deposits by individuals**

Claims of individuals up to $2,225* for deposits for the purchase, lease, or rental of property or services for personal, family, or household use, that were not delivered or provided. 11 U.S.C. § 507(a)(6).

Form B6E
(04/04)

In re Mary Ellen and John Allen Smith   ,   Case No. (supplied by clerk)
                    Debtor   (if known)

☐ **Alimony, Maintenance, or Support**

Claims of a spouse, former spouse, or child of the debtor for alimony, maintenance, or support, to the extent provided in 11 U.S.C. § 507(a)(7).

☑ **Taxes and Certain Other Debts Owed to Governmental Units**

Taxes, customs duties, and penalties owing to federal, state, and local governmental units as set forth in 11 U.S.C. § 507(a)(8).

☐ **Commitments to Maintain the Capital of an Insured Depository Institution**

Claims based on commitments to the FDIC, RTC, Director of the Office of Thrift Supervision, Comptroller of the Currency, or Board of Governors of the Federal Reserve System, or their predecessors or successors, to maintain the capital of an insured depository institution. 11 U.S.C. § 507 (a)(9).

* Amounts are subject to adjustment on April 1, 2007, and every three years thereafter with respect to cases commenced on or after the date of adjustment.

_1_ continuation sheets attached

Form B6E - Cont.
(04/04)

In re **Mary Ellen and John Allen Smith**, Case No. **(supplied by clerk)**
　　　　　Debtor　　　　　　　　　　　　　　　　　　　　　(If known)

SCHEDULE E - CREDITORS HOLDING UNSECURED PRIORITY CLAIMS
(Continuation Sheet)

　　　　　　　　　　　　　　　　　　　　　　　　　　　　taxes
　　　　　　　　　　　　　　　　　　　　　　　　　TYPE OF PRIORITY

CREDITOR'S NAME, MAILING ADDRESS INCLUDING ZIP CODE, AND ACCOUNT NUMBER (See instructions.)	CODEBTOR	HUSBAND, WIFE, JOINT, OR COMMUNITY	DATE CLAIM WAS INCURRED AND CONSIDERATION FOR CLAIM	CONTINGENT	UNLIQUIDATED	DISPUTED	AMOUNT OF CLAIM	AMOUNT ENTITLED TO PRIORITY
ACCOUNT NO. 555-12-5656 Internal Revenue Service Kansas City, MO 64999	☐	J	federal income taxes due on joint return filed April 15, 2003, for 2002 taxes.	☑	☐	☐	$850.00	$850.00
ACCOUNT NO.	☐			☐	☐	☐		
ACCOUNT NO.	☐			☐	☐	☐		
ACCOUNT NO.	☐			☐	☐	☐		
ACCOUNT NO.	☐			☐	☐	☐		

Sheet no. **3** of **3** sheets attached to Schedule of Creditors Holding Priority Claims

　　　　　　　　　　　　　　　　　　　　Subtotal▶　$　850.00
　　　　　　　　　　　　　　　　　　(Total of this page)
　　　　　　　　　　　　　　　　　　　　　Total▶　$　850.00
(Use only on last page of the completed Schedule E.)
(Report total also on Summary of Schedules)

Schedule F: Creditors Holding Unsecured Nonpriority Claims

Unsecured nonpriority claims are any other debts that you owe, other than leases or contractual obligations (that is, any debts that are not secured debts or unsecured priority debts). This includes, generally, all of your bills, including credit cards, medical bills, utility bills, personal loans with no collateral, and bills owed to stores. These debts will usually be cancelled by your bankruptcy. Every debt must be listed, even those that you dispute are actually valid debts, those you wish to pay off, and those that are non-dischargeable (such as a student loan or court-ordered fine). If a creditor has more than one claim, such as debts arising from separate transactions, list each claim separately. You must list your debts accurately for them to be discharged.

In re: Enter your full name. If you're filing jointly, include your spouse's name.

Case No.: Leave this blank if filed with your petition. The court clerk will assign you a case number.

Check this box if debtor has no creditors holding unsecured claims to report on this Schedule F: If so, check the box and go on to Schedule G.

Creditor's Name, Mailing Address Including Zip Code, and Account Number: Fill in the complete name and address of each creditor (in alphabetical order). Include only the last four digits of an account number if there is one. Include all collection agencies and attorneys who have contacted you regarding a debt, all cosigners on a debt you owe, all debtors with whom you have cosigned for a debt, and anyone who has sued you for a monetary amount. If you list multiple addresses for a single debt (such as if you list a credit card company and a collection agency for the same debt), do not repeat the description or amount of the debt, but note "same as above."

Codebtor: If someone else has cosigned the debt documents, is a non-filing spouse or joint owner, or otherwise can be held liable for the debt, place an *X* in this box. In community-property states, debts undertaken during a marriage are generally considered community debts, and non-filing spouses are liable. In common-law states, non-filing spouses are generally liable for debts for necessities.

Husband, Wife, Joint, or Community: If you are single, enter *N/A*. If you are married, enter *H*, *W*, *J*, or *C*, depending if the particular debt is owed individually by the husband or wife, is owed jointly by both (as joint tenants or tenants-by-the-entireties), or is owed as a community debt in a community-property state. Check the language on the debt document. In common-law states, the liability for the debt generally depends on the names on the debt document. In most states, debts that were individually undertaken prior to a marriage are considered individual debts during the marriage.

Date Claim Was Incurred and Consideration for Claim. If Claim Subject to Setoff, So State: List the date that the debt was incurred and a brief but clear description of the debt or claim. A *setoff* means that the creditor owes you money and will apply it to a debt. If there is a setoff, state the amount and reason for the setoff.

Contingent, Unliquidated, or Disputed: "Contingent" means the debt is based on an event that has not yet occurred. "Unliquidated" means an outstanding loan whose amount has not yet been determined, such as the amount of damages in a car accident that has not yet been established by court action. "Disputed" means that you dispute either the amount or even the existence of the debt. You may check more than one box.

Amount of Claim: List the total amount of the claimed debt. If there are multiple creditors for the same amount (as when a collection agency has taken over a debt) only list the total amount for one creditor (preferably the original creditor). If the amount is approximate, add "approx." after the amount.

Subtotal and Total: Subtotal the amounts in the "Amount of Claim" column of each page (and any continuation sheets) and enter the total on the last page of the form and also on the Summary of Schedules form. Add the number of the sheet attached to the Schedule of Creditors Holding Priority Claims and the total number of sheets attached (if any).

Form B6F (12/03)

In re **Mary Ellen and John Alan Smith**, Case No. **(supplied by clerk)**
Debtor (If known)

SCHEDULE F- CREDITORS HOLDING UNSECURED NONPRIORITY CLAIMS

State the name, mailing address, including zip code, and last four digits of any account number, of all entities holding unsecured claims without priority against the debtor or the property of the debtor, as of the date of filing of the petition. The complete account number of any account the debtor has with the creditor is useful to the trustee and the creditor and may be provided if the debtor chooses to do so. Do not include claims listed in Schedules D and E. If all creditors will not fit on this page, use the continuation sheet provided.

If any entity other than a spouse in a joint case may be jointly liable on a claim, place an "X" in the column labeled "Codebtor," include the entity on the appropriate schedule of creditors, and complete Schedule H - Codebtors. If a joint petition is filed, state whether husband, wife, both of them, or the marital community maybe liable on each claim by placing an "H," "W," "J," or "C" in the column labeled "Husband, Wife, Joint, or Community."

If the claim is contingent, place an "X" in the column labeled "Contingent." If the claim is unliquidated, place an "X" in the column labeled "Unliquidated." If the claim is disputed, place an "X" in the column labeled "Disputed." (You may need to place an "X" in more than one of these three columns.)

Report total of all claims listed on this schedule in the box labeled "Total" on the last sheet of the completed schedule. Report this total also on the Summary of Schedules.

☐ Check this box if debtor has no creditors holding unsecured claims to report on this Schedule F.

CREDITOR'S NAME, MAILING ADDRESS INCLUDING ZIP CODE, AND ACCOUNT NUMBER (See instructions above.)	CODEBTOR	HUSBAND, WIFE, JOINT, OR COMMUNITY	DATE CLAIM WAS INCURRED AND CONSIDERATION FOR CLAIM. IF CLAIM IS SUBJECT TO SETOFF, SO STATE.	CONTINGENT	UNLIQUIDATED	DISPUTED	AMOUNT OF CLAIM
ACCOUNT NO. 1234567 American Bank 1234 First Ave. Chicago, IL 60606	☐	J	Visa credit card charges, 1999-2004	☐	☑	☐	$3,500.00
ACCOUNT NO. 87654321 Barker Bank 654321 66th Street Springfield, IL 62700	☐	J	MasterCard credit card charges, 1999-2002	☐	☑	☐	$5,800.00
ACCOUNT NO. none Carter Car Repair 345 Oak Street Centerville, IL 61111	☐	J	Car repairs, September 2001	☐	☐	☑	$600.00
ACCOUNT NO. 123-456 Centerville Bank 9876 Main Street Centerville, IL 61111	☐	W	Student loan, October 1994	☐	☑	☐	$5,000.00

___1___ continuation sheets attached   Subtotal ▶ $ 14,900.00

Total ▶ $ (last page only)

(Report also on Summary of Schedules)

Form B6F - Cont.
(12/03)

In re Mary Ellen and John Alan Smith,   Case No. (supplied by clerk)
         Debtor   (If known)

SCHEDULE F - CREDITORS HOLDING UNSECURED NONPRIORITY CLAIMS
(Continuation Sheet)

CREDITOR'S NAME, MAILING ADDRESS INCLUDING ZIP CODE, AND ACCOUNT NUMBER (See instructions.)	CODEBTOR	HUSBAND, WIFE, JOINT, OR COMMUNITY	DATE CLAIM WAS INCURRED AND CONSIDERATION FOR CLAIM. IF CLAIM IS SUBJECT TO SETOFF, SO STATE.	CONTINGENT	UNLIQUIDATED	DISPUTED	AMOUNT OF CLAIM
ACCOUNT NO. 567890 Centerville Hospital 3 Hospital Lane Centerville, IL 61111	☐	H	Hospital bills, June 1997	☐	✔	☐	$12,000.00
ACCOUNT NO. 34567 Dwight Furniture 7878 Second Street Centerville, IL 61111	☐	J	Furniture, November 1999	☐	✔	☐	$1,000.00
ACCOUNT NO. none Dr. William Fredricks 35 Doctors Court Centerville, IL 61111	☐	H	Doctor's bills, 1999-2003	☐	✔	☐	$4,300.00
ACCOUNT NO 246810 Mobil Oil Company Box 1234 Houston, TX 77777	☐	J	Gas company credit card, 1998-2004	☐	✔	☐	$1,235.00
ACCOUNT NO. A-234 Personal Finance Company 6666 LaSalle Street Chicago, IL 60606	☐	J	Personal loan, December 1997	☐	✔	☐	$3,590.00

Sheet no. 2 of 2 sheets attached to Schedule of Creditors Holding Unsecured Nonpriority Claims

                                                     Subtotal ➤ $ 22,125.00
                                             (Total of this page)
                                                            Total ➤ $ 37,025.00
(Use only on last page of the completed Schedule F.)
(Report total also on Summary of Schedules)

Schedule G: Executory Contracts and Unexpired Leases

Executory contracts are contracts that are still in force and contain obligations that you or another party must still fulfill. *Unexpired leases* are leases that are still in force, either for residential or business property. These include any type of contract or lease that you have signed and is still in force, including insurance contracts and business contracts. Examples might be timeshare interests, orders for furniture, or layaway arrangements at clothing stores. If you are past due on payments on a lease or contract, that should be listed as a debt on Schedules D, E, or F. Schedule G is a master list of all leases and contracts that are outstanding, whether or not you are delinquent in payments. This includes leases where someone leases property from you.

In re: Enter your full name. If you're filing jointly, include your spouse's name.

Case No.: Leave this blank if filed with your petition. The court clerk will assign you a case number.

Check this box if debtor has no executory contracts or unexpired leases: If so, check the box and continue to Schedule H.

Name and Mailing Address, Including Zip Code, of Other Parties to Lease or Contract: List the name and address of every person who is a party to any current lease or contract. This will include anyone who signed the lease or contract and every company that is involved with the lease or contract. State whether you are the *lessor* (landlord) or *lessee* (tenant) of any lease.

Description of Contract or Lease and Nature of Debtor's Interest: State whether lease is for non-residential real property. State the date the lease or contract was signed and give a brief general description of the type of lease or contract that is included. In addition, briefly describe what the lease or contract requires of each party. If the contract is with any government agency or authority, list the contract number.

Form B6G
(10/89)

In re Mary Ellen and John Alan Smith ,　　　　　　　　　　Case No. (supplied by clerk)
　　　　　　　　Debtor　　　　　　　　　　　　　　　　　　　　　　　　　　(if known)

SCHEDULE G - EXECUTORY CONTRACTS AND UNEXPIRED LEASES

Describe all executory contracts of any nature and all unexpired leases of real or personal property. Include any timeshare interests. State nature of debtor's interest in contract, i.e., "Purchaser," "Agent," etc. State whether debtor is the lessor or lessee of a lease. Provide the names and complete mailing addresses of all other parties to each lease or contract described.

NOTE: A party listed on this schedule will not receive notice of the filing of this case unless the party is also scheduled in the appropriate schedule of creditors.

☐ Check this box if debtor has no executory contracts or unexpired leases.

NAME AND MAILING ADDRESS, INCLUDING ZIP CODE, OF OTHER PARTIES TO LEASE OR CONTRACT.	DESCRIPTION OF CONTRACT OR LEASE AND NATURE OF DEBTOR'S INTEREST. STATE WHETHER LEASE IS FOR NONRESIDENTIAL REAL PROPERTY. STATE CONTRACT NUMBER OF ANY GOVERNMENT CONTRACT.
Centerville Business Products 234 Business Lane Centerville, IL 61111	Co-signer with brother, William David Smith, on contract dated September 15, 1999 to buy computer

Schedule H: Codebtors

This schedule is a master list of all of the codebtors (other than a spouse who is jointly filing with you) that you have listed on Schedules D, E, and F. Codebtors may be cosignors, guarantors, and non-filing spouses who may be liable on a consumer debt. Review those forms and enter all of the codebtors again on this form.

In re: Enter your full name. If you're filing jointly, include your spouse's name.

Case No.: Leave this blank if filed with your petition. The court clerk will assign you a case number.

Check this box if debtor has no codebtors: If so, check the box and continue to Schedule I.

Name and Address of Codebtor: Enter the name and address of each codebtor listed on Schedules D, E, or F.

Name and Address of Creditor: Enter the name and address of each creditor for each of the codebtors listed in the first column. This should be identical to the information for creditors that you listed on Schedules D, E, or F where there were codebtors indicated.

Form B6H
(6/90)

In re Mary Ellen and John Alan Smith   ,   Case No. (supplied by clerk)
                    Debtor   **(if known)**

SCHEDULE H - CODEBTORS

Provide the information requested concerning any person or entity, other than a spouse in a joint case, that is also liable on any debts listed by debtor in the schedules of creditors. Include all guarantors and co-signers. In community property states, a married debtor not filing a joint case should report the name and address of the nondebtor spouse on this schedule. Include all names used by the nondebtor spouse during the six years immediately preceding the commencement of this case.

☐ Check this box if debtor has no codebtors.

NAME AND ADDRESS OF CODEBTOR	NAME AND ADDRESS OF CREDITOR
William David Smith 567 Elm Street Centerville, IL 61111	Centerville Business Products 234 Business Lane Centerville, IL 61111

Schedule I: Current Income of Individual Debtor(s)

This form contains information on all of your current income, whether from wages, salary, self-employment, farming, real estate, investments, alimony, Social Security, pensions, or any other source. You will calculate your income on a monthly basis. Include a copy of your latest tax return with Schedule I when you file it with the court.

In re: Enter your full name. If you're filing jointly, include your spouse's name.

Case No.: Leave this blank if filed with your petition. The court clerk will assign you a case number.

Debtor's Marital Status: Indicate whether you are single, married, divorced, or widowed.

Dependents of Debtor and Spouse: Enter the names, ages, and relationships of dependent children and others for whom you provide over half of the support.

Employment of Debtor and Spouse: Enter your occupation, name of employer, length of employment, and address of employer. Enter whether you are retired, disabled, or unemployed, if applicable.

Income: For you and your spouse (if filing jointly) enter your total *gross* (before taxes) monthly income from a regular job. Enter your average monthly overtime, if applicable. If your income varies monthly or seasonally, divide the last full year's income by 12. Subtotal these amounts.

Less Payroll Deductions: List the average monthly amount of all taxes, Social Security/Medicare, insurance, pensions, union dues, or other deductions that are taken out of your paycheck. Subtotal these amounts.

Total Net Monthly Take Home Pay: Deduct the "Subtotal of Payroll Deductions" from the "Subtotal" of monthly wages and enter here.

Regular income from operation of business or profession or farm: Enter the average monthly amount of income from a farm, business, or self-employment. Divide the last year's total income (taken from your latest tax return) by 12. Attach detailed statement on a continuation sheet.

Income from real property: List the average monthly income that you make from rental of real estate, either commercial or residential.

Interest and dividends: Enter the average monthly income from stocks, bank accounts, or other income-producing investments.

Alimony, maintenance or support payments payable: Enter the monthly average amount that you receive for yourself or the support of any dependent child.

Social security or other government assistance: List the monthly amount of any social security, unemployment, worker's compensation, disability, aid to families with dependent children, food stamps, veteran's benefits, or other government assistance. Specify the type of assistance.

Pension or retirement income: Enter the average monthly amount of any retirement benefits, including IRAs, KEOGHs, or annuities. Specify the type.

Other monthly income: Include the average monthly amount of any other type of income that you receive on a regular basis. Specify the source of the income.

Total Monthly Income: Add your "Total Net Monthly Take Home Pay" amount and all of the other income amounts and enter here.

Total Combined Monthly Income: Add together both "Total Monthly Income" amounts for you and your spouse and enter on this line and on the Summary of Schedules.

Describe any increase or decrease of more than 10%: If you know or anticipate any reason why your income will change by at least 10 percent in the next 12 months after you file your petition, explain here.

Form B6I
(12/03)

In re <u>Mary Ellen and John Alan Smith</u>, Case No. <u>(supplied by clerk)</u>
          Debtor   (if known)

SCHEDULE I - CURRENT INCOME OF INDIVIDUAL DEBTOR(S)

The column labeled "Spouse" must be completed in all cases filed by joint debtors and by a married debtor in a chapter 12 or 13 case whether or not a joint petition is filed, unless the spouses are separated and a joint petition is not filed.

Debtor's Marital Status: Married	DEPENDENTS OF DEBTOR AND SPOUSE	
	RELATIONSHIP none	AGE

Employment:	DEBTOR	SPOUSE
Occupation	Teacher	Mechanic
Name of Employer	Centerville Elementary School	Centerville Auto Repair Service
How long employed	3 years	2 years
Address of Employer	987 West Main Street	765 Elm Street
	Centerville, IL 61111	Centerville, IL 61111

	DEBTOR	SPOUSE
Income: (Estimate of average monthly income)		
Current monthly gross wages, salary, and commissions (pro rate if not paid monthly.)	$ 1,000.00	$ 2,000.00
Estimated monthly overtime	$ 0.00	$ 0.00
SUBTOTAL	$ 1,000.00	$ 2,000.00
LESS PAYROLL DEDUCTIONS		
a. Payroll taxes and social security	$ 127.00	$ 234.00
b. Insurance	$	$
c. Union dues	$ 23.00	$
d. Other (Specify: _____)	$	$
SUBTOTAL OF PAYROLL DEDUCTIONS	$ 150.00	$ 234.00
TOTAL NET MONTHLY TAKE HOME PAY	$ 850.00	$ 1,766.00
Regular income from operation of business or profession or farm (attach detailed statement)	$	$
Income from real property	$	$
Interest and dividends	$	$
Alimony, maintenance or support payments payable to the debtor for the debtor's use or that of dependents listed above.	$	$
Social security or other government assistance (Specify) _____	$	$
Pension or retirement income	$	$
Other monthly income (Specify) _____ _____	$	$
TOTAL MONTHLY INCOME	$ 850.00	$ 1,766.00

TOTAL COMBINED MONTHLY INCOME $ <u> 2,616.00 </u>   (Report also on Summary of Schedules)

Describe any increase or decrease of more than 10% in any of the above categories anticipated to occur within the year following the filing of this document:

none

Schedule J: Current Expenditures of Individual Debtor(s)

On this schedule, you will estimate your average monthly expenses. The amounts you list will be for your entire family's expenses, whether you are filing jointly, or are married and filing alone. If you are filing jointly, but you and your spouse do not live together, see below under "Check this Box." For all amounts, determine the average monthly expense amount. For expenditures that are made on a weekly, quarterly, or annual basis, calculate the monthly amount and enter.

In re: Enter your full name. If you're filing jointly, include your spouse's name.

Case No.: Leave this blank if filed with your petition. The court clerk will assign you a case number.

Check this box if a joint petition is filed and debtor's spouse maintains a separate household: Do so if you and your spouse are separated but are filing a joint petition. You will then need to complete separate Schedule Js for you and your spouse. Clearly label your spouse's Schedule J as "Spouse."

Expenditures: For each of the listed expense items, list your average monthly amount. If the amount is paid other than monthly (i.e., weekly, annually, etc.), calculate the monthly average amount. Include any types of expenses not listed under "Other."

Total Monthly Expenses: Total all expenses and list this amount also on your Summary of Schedules.

For Chapter 12 and Chapter 13 Debtors Only: Enter *N/A* on the amount line.

Form B6J
(6/90)

In re **Mary Ellen and John Alan Smith**   ,   Case No. **(supplied by clerk)**
           Debtor   (if known)

SCHEDULE J - CURRENT EXPENDITURES OF INDIVIDUAL DEBTOR(S)

Complete this schedule by estimating the average monthly expenses of the debtor and the debtor's family. Pro rate any payments made bi-weekly, quarterly, semi-annually, or annually to show monthly rate.

☐ Check this box if a joint petition is filed and debtor's spouse maintains a separate household. Complete a separate schedule of expenditures labeled "Spouse."

Rent or home mortgage payment (include lot rented for mobile home)	$ 650.00
Are real estate taxes included? Yes ✔ No ____	
Is property insurance included? Yes ✔ No ____	
Utilities Electricity and heating fuel	$ 175.00
Water and sewer	$ 78.00
Telephone	$ 109.00
Other cable TV	$ 45.00
Home maintenance (repairs and upkeep)	$ 375.00
Food	$ 200.00
Clothing	$ 50.00
Laundry and dry cleaning	$ 35.00
Medical and dental expenses	$ 160.00
Transportation (not including car payments)	$ 100.00
Recreation, clubs and entertainment, newspapers, magazines, etc.	$ 1,200.00
Charitable contributions	$ 0.00
Insurance (not deducted from wages or included in home mortgage payments)	
Homeowner's or renter's	$ 0.00
Life	$ 35.00
Health	$ 60.00
Auto	$ 117.00
Other ____	$ ____
Taxes (not deducted from wages or included in home mortgage payments) (Specify) ____	$ ____
Installment payments: (In chapter 12 and 13 cases, do not list payments to be included in the plan)	
Auto	$ 240.00
Other personal loan	$ 345.00
Other ____	$ ____
Alimony, maintenance, and support paid to others	$ ____
Payments for support of additional dependents not living at your home	$ ____
Regular expenses from operation of business, profession, or farm (attach detailed statement)	$ ____
Other ____	$ ____
TOTAL MONTHLY EXPENSES (Report also on Summary of Schedules)	**$ 3,974.00**

[FOR CHAPTER 12 AND 13 DEBTORS ONLY]
Provide the information requested below, including whether plan payments are to be made bi-weekly, monthly, annually, or at some other regular interval.

A. Total projected monthly income $ ____
B. Total projected monthly expenses $ ____
C. Excess income (A minus B) $ ____
D. Total amount to be paid into plan each _____
                                                                    (interval)

Instructions for General Continuation Sheet

You will use this unofficial form if you need to include any additional information on any of your schedules. If you use this form, it will be considered a continuation sheet and should be counted as a sheet when you need to list the total number of sheets for each schedule and on your Summary of Schedules (later in this chapter).

In re: Enter your full name. If you're filing jointly, include your spouse's name.

Case No.: Leave this blank. The court clerk will assign you a case number.

Continuation Sheet to Schedule: Here list the letter of the schedule which the sheet will supplement (for example, *Schedule A*).

On the rest of the sheet include any information which you may need to add in order to complete or explain anything on the official schedule. *Note*: Use only the official continuation sheets for Schedules D, E, and F.

In re: _____   Case No. _____
         Debtor

CONTINUATION SHEET TO SCHEDULE ____

Instructions for the Summary of Schedules (Official Form 6)

Here you will enter information from all schedules to act as a summary for the court.

Court Name: Fill in the full name of the judicial district in which you will be filing (as listed on your Voluntary Petition).

In re: Enter your full name. If you're filing jointly, include your spouse's name.

Case No.: Leave this line blank if filed with your petition. The court clerk will assign you a case number.

Attached (Yes/No): Indicate with a "yes" or "no" which schedules are attached. You should attach all schedules listed on the summary, even if one or some of the schedules do not apply to your situation.

No. of Sheets: For each schedule, count the number of pages. Include any continuation pages that you have used.

Amounts Scheduled: Enter asset totals from Schedules A and B; liability totals from Schedules D, E, and F; and income and expenditure totals from Schedules I and J. No amounts are listed for Schedules G and H.

Totals: Total the columns for the "Total Number of Sheets of all Schedules," "Total Assets," and "Total Liabilities."

FORM B6-Cont.
(6/90)

UNITED STATES BANKRUPTCY COURT
Northern District of Illinois

In re Mary Ellen and John Alan Smith, Case No. (supplied by clerk)
    Debtor   (If known)

SUMMARY OF SCHEDULES

Indicate as to each schedule whether that schedule is attached and state the number of pages in each. Report the totals from Schedules A, B, D, E, F, I, and J in the boxes provided. Add the amounts from Schedules A and B to determine the total amount of the debtor's assets. Add the amounts from Schedules D, E, and F to determine the total amount of the debtor's liabilities.

AMOUNTS SCHEDULED

NAME OF SCHEDULE	ATTACHED (YES/NO)	NO. OF SHEETS	ASSETS	LIABILITIES	OTHER
A - Real Property	yes	1	$ 48,000.00		
B - Personal Property	yes	3	$ 20,967.00		
C - Property Claimed as Exempt	yes	1			
D - Creditors Holding Secured Claims	yes	1		$ 37,000.00	
E - Creditors Holding Unsecured Priority Claims	yes	3		$ 850.00	
F - Creditors Holding Unsecured Nonpriority Claims	yes	2		$ 37,025.00	
G - Executory Contracts and Unexpired Leases	yes	1			
H - Codebtors	yes	1			
I - Current Income of Individual Debtor(s)	yes	1			$ 2,616.00
J - Current Expenditures of Individual Debtor(s)	yes	1			$ 3,974.00

Total Number of Sheets of ALL Schedules ➤ 15

Total Assets ➤ $ 68,967.00

Total Liabilities ➤ $ 74,875.00

84

Instructions for the Declaration Concerning Debtor's Schedules

This form is where you state that everything that you entered on all of the schedules is true and correct to the best of your knowledge. Everything that you enter on your bankruptcy forms must be absolutely true and you must be able to prove it with documents, receipts, bills, or other paper records. Keep in mind that the penalty for making a false statement on a bankruptcy form is a fine of up to $500,000.00 and imprisonment for up to five years, or both, and, of course, denial of your request to discharge your debts in bankruptcy.

In re: Enter your full name. If you're filing jointly, include your spouse's name.

Case No.: Leave this blank if filed with your petition. The court clerk will assign you a case number.

Declaration Under Penalty of Perjury by Individual Debtor: List the total number of sheets from your Summary of Schedules plus add one (for the Summary of Schedules itself). Date and sign (if joint, both spouses must sign).

Certification and Signature of Non-Attorney Bankruptcy Petition Preparer: Enter *N/A* on the signature line, unless you are using a bankruptcy petition preparer.

Declaration Under Penalty of Perjury on Behalf of a Corporation or Partnership: Enter *N/A* on the signature line.

Official Form 6-Cont.
(12/03)

In re **Mary Ellen and John Alan Smith**,
           Debtor

Case No. **(supplied by clerk)**
                  (If known)

DECLARATION CONCERNING DEBTOR'S SCHEDULES

DECLARATION UNDER PENALTY OF PERJURY BY INDIVIDUAL DEBTOR

I declare under penalty of perjury that I have read the foregoing summary and schedules, consisting of __**15**__ sheets, and that they are true and correct to the best of my knowledge, information, and belief.
(Total shown on summary page plus 1.)

Date _**March 13, 2004 (handwritten date)**_   Signature: _**Mary Ellen Smith (handwritten signature)**_
                                                                                Debtor

Date _**March 13, 2004 (handwritten date)**_   Signature: _**John Alan Smith (handwritten signature)**_
                                                                                (Joint Debtor, if any)

[If joint case, both spouses must sign.]

CERTIFICATION AND SIGNATURE OF NON-ATTORNEY BANKRUPTCY PETITION PREPARER (See 11 U.S.C. § 110)

I certify that I am a bankruptcy petition preparer as defined in 11 U.S.C. § 110, that I prepared this document for compensation, and that I have provided the debtor with a copy of this document.

_____   _____
Printed or Typed Name of Bankruptcy Petition Preparer   Social Security No.
                                                                                      (Required by 11 U.S.C. § 110(c).)

_____
Address

Names and Social Security numbers of all other individuals who prepared or assisted in preparing this document:

If more than one person prepared this document, attach additional signed sheets conforming to the appropriate Official Form for each person.

x _**n/a**_____   _____
Signature of Bankruptcy Petition Preparer   Date

A bankruptcy petition preparer's failure to comply with the provisions of title 11 and the Federal Rules of Bankruptcy Procedure may result in fines or imprisonment or both. 11 U.S.C. § 110; 18 U.S.C. § 156.

DECLARATION UNDER PENALTY OF PERJURY ON BEHALF OF A CORPORATION OR PARTNERSHIP

I, the _____ [the president or other officer or an authorized agent of the corporation or a member or an authorized agent of the partnership] of the _____ [corporation or partnership] named as debtor in this case, declare under penalty of perjury that I have read the foregoing summary and schedules, consisting of _____ sheets, and that they are true and correct to the best of my knowledge, information, and belief.   *(Total shown on summary page plus 1.)*

Date _____   Signature: _**n/a**_____

                                                                  _____
                                                                  [Print or type name of individual signing on behalf of debtor.]

[An individual signing on behalf of a partnership or corporation must indicate position or relationship to debtor.]

Penalty for making a false statement or concealing property: Fine of up to $500,000 or imprisonment for up to 5 years or both. 18 U.S.C. §§ 152 and 3571.

Instructions for the Statement of Financial Affairs (Official Form 7)

This form is used to describe your financial transactions over the last two years. You must truthfully answer all questions on this form. *Note*: For some questions, the answers require information going back six full years. The answers on this form will be checked very carefully by the court. In certain cases, the bankruptcy court may void certain transactions and take control of money or property that you transferred to others before you filed for bankruptcy. If you are filing jointly, list the information for each of you separately. If your answer for any question is "None," check the box to the left of the question. You can amend this statement at any time before your case is closed, but you must notify the bankruptcy trustee and any creditors of any changes.

Court Name: Fill in the full name of the judicial district in which you will be filing (as listed on your Voluntary Petition).

In re: Enter your full name. If you're filing jointly, include your spouse's name.

Case No.: Leave this blank if filed with your petition. The court clerk will assign you a case number.

1. Income from employment or operation of business: Two amounts are required. First, list all income from your job or business for this calendar year. Then, also list the total amount of income from your job or business during the two years prior to this calendar year. Use your tax returns to complete this section. Indicate the source used, such as your 2004 federal tax return.

2. Income other than from employment or operation of business: List all other income you have received from any source in the two years prior to filing for bankruptcy (tax refunds, alimony, bank account interest, for example). Use your tax returns to complete this section. Indicate the source used, such as your 2004 federal tax return.

3. Payments to creditors: Under "a.," list any payments totaling over $600.00 that you have made on any debts within the 90 days prior to filing for bankruptcy. Under "b.," list any payments for any amount made within one year prior to filing that were made to *insiders* (relatives, business partners, or other closely related parties).

4. Suits and administrative proceedings, executions, garnishments and attachments: Under "a.," list any lawsuits that you or your spouse were parties to within one year prior to filing for bankruptcy. Under "b.," list any property that has been garnished, attached, or seized within one year prior to filing.

5. Repossessions, foreclosures and returns: Enter any property that was repossessed, foreclosed, or voluntarily returned to a seller within one year prior to filing.

6. Assignments and receiverships: Under "a.," list any assignment of property made within 120 days prior to filing. Under "b.," list any property held by a receiver or other court official within one year prior to filing.

7. Gifts: List every gift (cash or property) that you or your spouse made within one year prior to filing if the gifts total over $200.00 worth to a family member or over $100.00 worth to any single charity.

8. Losses: List all fire, theft, gambling, or other losses within one year prior to filing or since filing.

9. Payments related to debt counseling or bankruptcy: List any payments or property transferred to any party for any bankruptcy or debt counseling or assistance within one year prior to filing.

10. Other transfers: List any other property that was transferred within one year prior to filing, except ordinary business or financial transactions.

11. Closed financial accounts: List information regarding any financial or bank accounts that were closed or transferred within one year prior to filing for bankruptcy.

12. Safe deposit boxes: List all safe deposit boxes in which you or your spouse held any valuables within one year prior to filing.

13. Setoffs: List any setoffs made against a debt by a creditor or bank within 90 days prior to filing. *Setoffs* are money that a creditor owes you which the creditor has applied against a debt that you owe the creditor.

14. Property held for another person: List any property that you or your spouse are currently holding for someone else.

15. Prior address of debtor: List any addresses where you or your spouse have lived within the last two years.

16. Spouses and Former Spouses: Complete only if you have resided with a spouse in a community-property state at any time during the past six years (Arizona, California, Idaho, Louisiana, Nevada, New Mexico, Puerto Rico, Texas, Washington, or Wisconsin). Otherwise check the "None" box. If "yes," list the name of any spouse or former spouse with whom you lived in any of these states within the last six years.

17. Environmental Information: Under "a.," list the name and address for any location or property, whether or not presently owned, for which you have received any notice from any governmental agency that there may be liability or a violation under any federal, state, or local environmental law or regulation. List the site name and address, the name and address of the government unit, the date of the notice, and the environmental law that applies. Under "b.," for any site for which you provided a release of hazardous material to any government unit, list the site name and address, the name and address of the government unit, the date of the notice, and the environmental law that applies. Under "c.," if you have been a party to any lawsuit or administrative proceeding, including any settlements or order relating to any environmental law, you must list the name and address of the governmental unit involved, the docket number of the case, and the status of the case.

18. Nature, location and name of business: Under "a.," list name, taxpayer I.D. number (FEIN or Social Security number), address, nature of the business, and the beginning and ending dates of every business that you or your spouse owned five percent or more of within the six years prior to filing for bankruptcy. Under "b.," enter name and address of any property listed as a business under "a" that consists of a single piece of real estate.

Note: Questions 19 through 25 should only be answered if you or your spouse have been in business (or owned five percent or more of a business) within the past six years; either as a corporation, partnership, sole proprietorship, or otherwise self-employed. These questions must be answered even if you are no longer in business at the time you file for bankruptcy. If you or a spouse have not been in business in the last six years, check the "None" box, skip these questions, and go directly to the signature page.

19. Books, records and financial statements: Under "a.," list the names and addresses of any bookkeepers and accountants who handled any of your business records within the six years prior to filing for bankruptcy. Under "b.," list any person or firm who has audited or prepared financial records for your business within the two years prior to filing. Under "c.," list any person or firm who had possession of any books or records of your business on the date of filing for bankruptcy. Under "d.," list any financial institution or creditor to whom the business gave a financial statement within the two years prior to filing for bankruptcy.

20. Inventories: Under "a.," list the dates and amounts for each of the last two business inventories. Also list the name of the person who supervised each inventory. Under "b.," enter the name and address of the person who has possession of the records of those inventories.

21. Current Partners, Officers, Directors and Shareholders: Under "a" and "b.," check the "None" box and enter *N/A*.

22. Former partners, officers, directors and shareholders: Under "a" and "b.," check the "None" box and enter *N/A*.

23. Withdrawals from a partnership or distributions by a corporation: Enter *N/A*.

24. Tax consolidation group: Check the "None" box and enter *N/A*.

25. Pension Funds: Check the "None" box and enter *N/A*.

If completed by an individual or individual and spouse: Date and sign. If a joint petition, your spouse must also sign and date. Enter the total number of sheets attached, including continuation sheets, in the next box.

If completed on behalf of a partnership or corporation: Enter *N/A* and the number of continuation sheets used.

Certification and Signature of Non-Attorney Bankruptcy Petition Preparer: Enter *N/A* on the signature line, unless you were assisted by a bankruptcy petition preparer.

Form 7
(12/03)

FORM 7. STATEMENT OF FINANCIAL AFFAIRS

UNITED STATES BANKRUPTCY COURT

_____Northern_____ **DISTRICT OF** _____Illinois_____

In re: __Mary Ellen and John Alan Smith__ , Case No. __(supplied by clerk)__
       (Name)   Debtor   (if known)

STATEMENT OF FINANCIAL AFFAIRS

    This statement is to be completed by every debtor. Spouses filing a joint petition may file a single statement on which the information for both spouses is combined. If the case is filed under chapter 12 or chapter 13, a married debtor must furnish information for both spouses whether or not a joint petition is filed, unless the spouses are separated and a joint petition is not filed. An individual debtor engaged in business as a sole proprietor, partner, family farmer, or self-employed professional, should provide the information requested on this statement concerning all such activities as well as the individual's personal affairs.

    Questions 1 - 18 are to be completed by all debtors. Debtors that are or have been in business, as defined below, also must complete Questions 19 - 25. **If the answer to an applicable question is "None," mark the box labeled "None."** If additional space is needed for the answer to any question, use and attach a separate sheet properly identified with the case name, case number (if known), and the number of the question.

DEFINITIONS

    "In business." A debtor is "in business" for the purpose of this form if the debtor is a corporation or partnership. An individual debtor is "in business" for the purpose of this form if the debtor is or has been, within the six years immediately preceding the filing of this bankruptcy case, any of the following: an officer, director, managing executive, or owner of 5 percent or more of the voting or equity securities of a corporation; a partner, other than a limited partner, of a partnership; a sole proprietor or self-employed.

    "Insider." The term "insider" includes but is not limited to: relatives of the debtor; general partners of the debtor and their relatives; corporations of which the debtor is an officer, director, or person in control; officers, directors, and any owner of 5 percent or more of the voting or equity securities of a corporate debtor and their relatives; affiliates of the debtor and insiders of such affiliates; any managing agent of the debtor. 11 U.S.C. § 101.

---

    1. **Income from employment or operation of business**

None   State the gross amount of income the debtor has received from employment, trade, or profession, or from operation of
☐   the debtor's business from the beginning of this calendar year to the date this case was commenced. State also the gross amounts received during the **two years** immediately preceding this calendar year. (A debtor that maintains, or has maintained, financial records on the basis of a fiscal rather than a calendar year may report fiscal year income. Identify the beginning and ending dates of the debtor's fiscal year.) If a joint petition is filed, state income for each spouse separately. (Married debtors filing under chapter 12 or chapter 13 must state income of both spouses whether or not a joint petition is filed, unless the spouses are separated and a joint petition is not filed.)

                      AMOUNT   SOURCE (if more than one)

                      $8,000.00   Debtor- wages from Centerville Elementary School

                      $9,500.00   Joint debtor- wages from Centerville Car Repair

2

2. Income other than from employment or operation of business

None ☑ State the amount of income received by the debtor other than from employment, trade, profession, or operation of the debtor's business during the **two years** immediately preceding the commencement of this case. Give particulars. If a joint petition is filed, state income for each spouse separately. (Married debtors filing under chapter 12 or chapter 13 must state income for each spouse whether or not a joint petition is filed, unless the spouses are separated and a joint petition is not filed.)

AMOUNT   SOURCE

3. Payments to creditors

None ☐ a. List all payments on loans, installment purchases of goods or services, and other debts, aggregating more than $600 to any creditor, made within **90 days** immediately preceding the commencement of this case. (Married debtors filing under chapter 12 or chapter 13 must include payments by either or both spouses whether or not a joint petition is filed, unless the spouses are separated and a joint petition is not filed.)

NAME AND ADDRESS OF CREDITOR	DATES OF PAYMENTS	AMOUNT PAID	AMOUNT STILL OWING
American Bank 1234 First Ave. Chicago, IL 60606	1/15/04	$550.00	
American Bank 1234 First Ave. Chicago, IL 60606	3/1/04	$400.00	$3,500.00

None ☑ b. List all payments made within **one year** immediately preceding the commencement of this case to or for the benefit of creditors who are or were insiders. (Married debtors filing under chapter 12 or chapter 13 must include payments by either or both spouses whether or not a joint petition is filed, unless the spouses are separated and a joint petition is not filed.)

NAME AND ADDRESS OF CREDITOR   DATE OF   AMOUNT   AMOUNT
AND RELATIONSHIP TO DEBTOR   PAYMENT   PAID   STILL OWING

4. Suits and administrative proceedings, executions, garnishments and attachments

None ☑ a. List all suits and administrative proceedings to which the debtor is or was a party within **one year** immediately preceding the filing of this bankruptcy case. (Married debtors filing under chapter 12 or chapter 13 must include information concerning either or both spouses whether or not a joint petition is filed, unless the spouses are separated and a joint petition is not filed.)

CAPTION OF SUIT   COURT OR AGENCY   STATUS OR
AND CASE NUMBER   NATURE OF PROCEEDING   AND LOCATION   DISPOSITION

None ☑ b. Describe all property that has been attached, garnished or seized under any legal or equitable process within **one year** immediately preceding the commencement of this case. (Married debtors filing under chapter 12 or chapter 13 must include information concerning property of either or both spouses whether or not a joint petition is filed, unless the spouses are separated and a joint petition is not filed.)

NAME AND ADDRESS OF PERSON FOR WHOSE BENEFIT PROPERTY WAS SEIZED	DATE OF SEIZURE	DESCRIPTION AND VALUE OF PROPERTY

5. Repossessions, foreclosures and returns

None ☐ List all property that has been repossessed by a creditor, sold at a foreclosure sale, transferred through a deed in lieu of foreclosure or returned to the seller, within **one year** immediately preceding the commencement of this case. (Married debtors filing under chapter 12 or chapter 13 must include information concerning property of either or both spouses whether or not a joint petition is filed, unless the spouses are separated and a joint petition is not filed.)

NAME AND ADDRESS OF CREDITOR OR SELLER	DATE OF REPOSSESSION, FORECLOSURE SALE, TRANSFER OR RETURN	DESCRIPTION AND VALUE OF PROPERTY
Hunt Ford Motor Company 444 Main Street Centerville, IL 61111	6/19/03	Ford Truck $15,995

6. Assignments and receiverships

None ☑ a. Describe any assignment of property for the benefit of creditors made within **120 days** immediately preceding the commencement of this case. (Married debtors filing under chapter 12 or chapter 13 must include any assignment by either or both spouses whether or not a joint petition is filed, unless the spouses are separated and a joint petition is not filed.)

NAME AND ADDRESS OF ASSIGNEE	DATE OF ASSIGNMENT	TERMS OF ASSIGNMENT OR SETTLEMENT

None ☑ b. List all property which has been in the hands of a custodian, receiver, or court-appointed official within **one year** immediately preceding the commencement of this case. (Married debtors filing under chapter 12 or chapter 13 must include information concerning property of either or both spouses whether or not a joint petition is filed, unless the spouses are separated and a joint petition is not filed.)

NAME AND ADDRESS OF CUSTODIAN	NAME AND LOCATION OF COURT CASE TITLE & NUMBER	DATE OF ORDER	DESCRIPTION AND VALUE OF PROPERTY

7. Gifts

None ☐ List all gifts or charitable contributions made within **one year** immediately preceding the commencement of this case except ordinary and usual gifts to family members aggregating less than $200 in value per individual family member and charitable contributions aggregating less than $100 per recipient. (Married debtors filing under chapter 12 or chapter 13 must include gifts or contributions by either or both spouses whether or not a joint petition is filed, unless the spouses are separated and a joint petition is not filed.)

NAME AND ADDRESS OF PERSON OR ORGANIZATION	RELATIONSHIP TO DEBTOR, IF ANY	DATE OF GIFT	DESCRIPTION AND VALUE OF GIFT
First Church of God Church 34 Main Street Centerville, IL 61111		monthly	cash donation $100.00

8. Losses

None ☑ List all losses from fire, theft, other casualty or gambling within **one year** immediately preceding the commencement of this case **or since the commencement of this case**. (Married debtors filing under chapter 12 or chapter 13 must include losses by either or both spouses whether or not a joint petition is filed, unless the spouses are separated and a joint petition is not filed.)

DESCRIPTION AND VALUE OF PROPERTY	DESCRIPTION OF CIRCUMSTANCES AND, IF LOSS WAS COVERED IN WHOLE OR IN PART BY INSURANCE, GIVE PARTICULARS	DATE OF LOSS

9. Payments related to debt counseling or bankruptcy

None ☑ List all payments made or property transferred by or on behalf of the debtor to any persons, including attorneys, for consultation concerning debt consolidation, relief under the bankruptcy law or preparation of a petition in bankruptcy within **one year** immediately preceding the commencement of this case.

NAME AND ADDRESS OF PAYEE	DATE OF PAYMENT, NAME OF PAYOR IF OTHER THAN DEBTOR	AMOUNT OF MONEY OR DESCRIPTION AND VALUE OF PROPERTY

10. Other transfers

None ☐ List all other property, other than property transferred in the ordinary course of the business or financial affairs of the debtor, transferred either absolutely or as security within **one year** immediately preceding the commencement of this case. (Married debtors filing under chapter 12 or chapter 13 must include transfers by either or both spouses whether or not a joint petition is filed, unless the spouses are separated and a joint petition is not filed.)

NAME AND ADDRESS OF TRANSFEREE, RELATIONSHIP TO DEBTOR	DATE	DESCRIBE PROPERTY TRANSFERRED AND VALUE RECEIVED
William David Smith 567 Elm Street Centerville, IL 61111	1/15/04	Boat and trailer $1,500.00

11. Closed financial accounts

None ☐ List all financial accounts and instruments held in the name of the debtor or for the benefit of the debtor which were closed, sold, or otherwise transferred within **one year** immediately preceding the commencement of this case. Include checking, savings, or other financial accounts, certificates of deposit, or other instruments; shares and share accounts held in banks, credit unions, pension funds, cooperatives, associations, brokerage houses and other financial institutions. (Married debtors filing under chapter 12 or chapter 13 must include information concerning accounts or instruments held by or for either or both spouses whether or not a joint petition is filed, unless the spouses are separated and a joint petition is not filed.)

NAME AND ADDRESS OF INSTITUTION	TYPE OF ACCOUNT, LAST FOUR DIGITS OF ACCOUNT NUMBER, AND AMOUNT OF FINAL BALANCE	AMOUNT AND DATE OF SALE OR CLOSING
Centerville Credit Unoin 567 Broadway Centerville, IL 61111	Checking Account #222222 $12.00	4/05/04

12. Safe deposit boxes

None ☑ List each safe deposit or other box or depository in which the debtor has or had securities, cash, or other valuables within **one year** immediately preceding the commencement of this case. (Married debtors filing under chapter 12 or chapter 13 must include boxes or depositories of either or both spouses whether or not a joint petition is filed, unless the spouses are separated and a joint petition is not filed.)

NAME AND ADDRESS OF BANK OR OTHER DEPOSITORY	NAMES AND ADDRESSES OF THOSE WITH ACCESS TO BOX OR DEPOSITORY	DESCRIPTION OF CONTENTS	DATE OF TRANSFER OR SURRENDER, IF ANY

13. Setoffs

None ☑ List all setoffs made by any creditor, including a bank, against a debt or deposit of the debtor within **90 days** preceding the commencement of this case. (Married debtors filing under chapter 12 or chapter 13 must include information concerning either or both spouses whether or not a joint petition is filed, unless the spouses are separated and a joint petition is not filed.)

NAME AND ADDRESS OF CREDITOR	DATE OF SETOFF	AMOUNT OF SETOFF

14. Property held for another person

None ☐ List all property owned by another person that the debtor holds or controls.

NAME AND ADDRESS OF OWNER	DESCRIPTION AND VALUE OF PROPERTY	LOCATION OF PROPERTY
Jennifer Jones 167 Main Street Centerville, IL 61111	Mountain Bike $350.00	16 Main Street Centerville, IL 61111

6

15. Prior address of debtor

None ☑ If the debtor has moved within the **two years** immediately preceding the commencement of this case, list all premises which the debtor occupied during that period and vacated prior to the commencement of this case. If a joint petition is filed, report also any separate address of either spouse.

ADDRESS   NAME USED   DATES OF OCCUPANCY

16. Spouses and Former Spouses

None ☑ If the debtor resides or resided in a community property state, commonwealth, or territory (including Alaska, Arizona, California, Idaho, Louisiana, Nevada, New Mexico, Puerto Rico, Texas, Washington, or Wisconsin) within the **six-year period** immediately preceding the commencement of the case, identify the name of the debtor's spouse and of any former spouse who resides or resided with the debtor in the community property state.

NAME

17. Environmental Information.

For the purpose of this question, the following definitions apply:

"Environmental Law" means any federal, state, or local statute or regulation regulating pollution, contamination, releases of hazardous or toxic substances, wastes or material into the air, land, soil, surface water, groundwater, or other medium, including, but not limited to, statutes or regulations regulating the cleanup of these substances, wastes, or material.

"Site" means any location, facility, or property as defined under any Environmental Law, whether or not presently or formerly owned or operated by the debtor, including, but not limited to, disposal sites.

"Hazardous Material" means anything defined as a hazardous waste, hazardous substance, toxic substance, hazardous material, pollutant, or contaminant or similar term under an Environmental Law

None ☑ a. List the name and address of every site for which the debtor has received notice in writing by a governmental unit that it may be liable or potentially liable under or in violation of an Environmental Law. Indicate the governmental unit, the date of the notice, and, if known, the Environmental Law:

SITE NAME   NAME AND ADDRESS   DATE OF   ENVIRONMENTAL
AND ADDRESS   OF GOVERNMENTAL UNIT   NOTICE   LAW

None ☑ b. List the name and address of every site for which the debtor provided notice to a governmental unit of a release of Hazardous Material. Indicate the governmental unit to which the notice was sent and the date of the notice.

SITE NAME   NAME AND ADDRESS   DATE OF   ENVIRONMENTAL
AND ADDRESS   OF GOVERNMENTAL UNIT   NOTICE   LAW

None ☑   c. List all judicial or administrative proceedings, including settlements or orders, under any Environmental Law with respect to which the debtor is or was a party. Indicate the name and address of the governmental unit that is or was a party to the proceeding, and the docket number.

NAME AND ADDRESS OF GOVERNMENTAL UNIT	DOCKET NUMBER	STATUS OR DISPOSITION

18. Nature, location and name of business

None ☑   a. If the debtor is an individual, list the names, addresses, taxpayer identification numbers, nature of the businesses, and beginning and ending dates of all businesses in which the debtor was an officer, director, partner, or managing executive of a corporation, partnership, sole proprietorship, or was a self-employed professional within the **six years** immediately preceding the commencement of this case, or in which the debtor owned 5 percent or more of the voting or equity securities within the **six years** immediately preceding the commencement of this case.

   If the debtor is a partnership, list the names, addresses, taxpayer identification numbers, nature of the businesses, and beginning and ending dates of all businesses in which the debtor was a partner or owned 5 percent or more of the voting or equity securities, within the **six years** immediately preceding the commencement of this case.

   If the debtor is a corporation, list the names, addresses, taxpayer identification numbers, nature of the businesses, and beginning and ending dates of all businesses in which the debtor was a partner or owned 5 percent or more of the voting or equity securities within the **six years** immediately preceding the commencement of this case.

NAME	TAXPAYER I.D. NO. (EIN)	ADDRESS	NATURE OF BUSINESS	BEGINNING AND ENDING DATES

None ☑   b. Identify any business listed in response to subdivision a., above, that is "single asset real estate" as defined in 11 U.S.C. § 101.

NAME	ADDRESS

The following questions are to be completed by every debtor that is a corporation or partnership and by any individual debtor who is or has been, within the **six years** immediately preceding the commencement of this case, any of the following: an officer, director, managing executive, or owner of more than 5 percent of the voting or equity securities of a corporation; a partner, other than a limited partner, of a partnership; a sole proprietor or otherwise self-employed.

*(An individual or joint debtor should complete this portion of the statement **only** if the debtor is or has been in business, as defined above, within the six years immediately preceding the commencement of this case. A debtor who has not been in business within those six years should go directly to the signature page.)*

19. Books, records and financial statements

None ☑   a.   List all bookkeepers and accountants who within the **two years** immediately preceding the filing of this bankruptcy case kept or supervised the keeping of books of account and records of the debtor.

           NAME AND ADDRESS   DATES SERVICES RENDERED

None ☑   b.   List all firms or individuals who within the **two years** immediately preceding the filing of this bankruptcy case have audited the books of account and records, or prepared a financial statement of the debtor.

           NAME   ADDRESS   DATES SERVICES RENDERED

None ☑   c.   List all firms or individuals who at the time of the commencement of this case were in possession of the books of account and records of the debtor. If any of the books of account and records are not available, explain.

           NAME   ADDRESS

None ☑   d.   List all financial institutions, creditors and other parties, including mercantile and trade agencies, to whom a financial statement was issued within the **two years** immediately preceding the commencement of this case by the debtor.

           NAME AND ADDRESS   DATE ISSUED

20. Inventories

None ☑   a.   List the dates of the last two inventories taken of your property, the name of the person who supervised the taking of each inventory, and the dollar amount and basis of each inventory.

                                                                                     DOLLAR AMOUNT OF INVENTORY
           DATE OF INVENTORY   INVENTORY SUPERVISOR   (Specify cost, market or other basis)

None ☑   b.   List the name and address of the person having possession of the records of each of the two inventories reported in a., above.

                                                              NAME AND ADDRESSES OF CUSTODIAN
           DATE OF INVENTORY   OF INVENTORY RECORDS

21. **Current Partners, Officers, Directors and Shareholders**

None ☑ a. If the debtor is a partnership, list the nature and percentage of partnership interest of each member of the partnership.

| NAME AND ADDRESS | NATURE OF INTEREST | PERCENTAGE OF INTEREST |

None ☑ b. If the debtor is a corporation, list all officers and directors of the corporation, and each stockholder who directly or indirectly owns, controls, or holds 5 percent or more of the voting or equity securities of the corporation.

| NAME AND ADDRESS | TITLE | NATURE AND PERCENTAGE OF STOCK OWNERSHIP |

22. **Former partners, officers, directors and shareholders**

None ☑ a. If the debtor is a partnership, list each member who withdrew from the partnership within **one year** immediately preceding the commencement of this case.

| NAME | ADDRESS | DATE OF WITHDRAWAL |

None ☑ b. If the debtor is a corporation, list all officers, or directors whose relationship with the corporation terminated within **one year** immediately preceding the commencement of this case.

| NAME AND ADDRESS | TITLE | DATE OF TERMINATION |

23. **Withdrawals from a partnership or distributions by a corporation**

None ☑ If the debtor is a partnership or corporation, list all withdrawals or distributions credited or given to an insider, including compensation in any form, bonuses, loans, stock redemptions, options exercised and any other perquisite during **one year** immediately preceding the commencement of this case.

| NAME & ADDRESS OF RECIPIENT, RELATIONSHIP TO DEBTOR | DATE AND PURPOSE OF WITHDRAWAL | AMOUNT OF MONEY OR DESCRIPTION AND VALUE OF PROPERTY |

24. Tax Consolidation Group.

None ☑ If the debtor is a corporation, list the name and federal taxpayer identification number of the parent corporation of any consolidated group for tax purposes of which the debtor has been a member at any time within the **six-year period** immediately preceding the commencement of the case.

NAME OF PARENT CORPORATION   TAXPAYER IDENTIFICATION NUMBER (EIN)

---

25. Pension Funds.

None ☑ If the debtor is not an individual, list the name and federal taxpayer identification number of any pension fund to which the debtor, as an employer, has been responsible for contributing at any time within the **six-year period** immediately preceding the commencement of the case.

NAME OF PENSION FUND   TAXPAYER IDENTIFICATION NUMBER (EIN)

---

* * * * * *

[If completed by an individual or individual and spouse]

I declare under penalty of perjury that I have read the answers contained in the foregoing statement of financial affairs and any attachments thereto and that they are true and correct.

Date March 13, 2004   Signature Mary Ellen Smith (handwritten signature)
                       of Debtor

Date March 13, 2004   Signature John Alan Smith (handwritten signature)
                       of Joint Debtor
                       (if any)

[If completed on behalf of a partnership or corporation]

I declare under penalty of perjury that I have read the answers contained in the foregoing statement of financial affairs and any attachments thereto and that they are true and correct to the best of my knowledge, information and belief.

Date _____   Signature n/a _____

                      Print Name and Title

[An individual signing on behalf of a partnership or corporation must indicate position or relationship to debtor.]

_____ continuation sheets attached

Penalty for making a false statement: Fine of up to $500,000 or imprisonment for up to 5 years, or both. 18 U.S.C. § 152 and 3571

CERTIFICATION AND SIGNATURE OF NON-ATTORNEY BANKRUPTCY PETITION PREPARER (See 11 U.S.C. § 110)

I certify that I am a bankruptcy petition preparer as defined in 11 U.S.C. § 110, that I prepared this document for compensation, and that I have provided the debtor with a copy of this document.

Printed or Typed Name of Bankruptcy Petition Preparer   Social Security No.
                                                            (Required by 11 U.S.C. § 110(c).)

Address

Names and Social Security numbers of all other individuals who prepared or assisted in preparing this document:

If more than one person prepared this document, attach additional signed sheets conforming to the appropriate Official Form for each person.

X n/a
Signature of Bankruptcy Petition Preparer   Date

A bankruptcy petition preparer's failure to comply with the provisions of title 11 and the Federal Rules of Bankruptcy Procedure may result in fines or imprisonment or both. 18 U.S.C. § 156.

Instructions for the Statement of Social Security Number(s) [Official Form 21]

This form is required in all cases.

1. Name of Debtor: Fill in the debtor's (your) name, last name first, and complete the section regarding your social security number.

2. Name of Joint Debtor: Complete the same for your spouse, if filing jointly. Then your and your spouse (if filing jointly) should sign and date this form.

Form B 21 Official Form 21
(12/03)

UNITED STATES BANKRUPTCY COURT
_____Northern_____ District of _____Illinois_____

n re Mary Ellen and John Alan Smith   ,   Case No. (supplied by clerk)
               Debtor   (If known)

STATEMENT OF SOCIAL SECURITY NUMBER(S)

1. Name of Debtor (enter Last, First, Middle): Smith, Mary Ellen
(Check the appropriate box and, if applicable, provide the required information.)

    /x/ Debtor has a Social Security Number and it is: 5 5 5 - 5 5 - 5 5 5 5
           (If more than one, state all.)
    / / Debtor does not have a Social Security Number.

2. Name of Joint Debtor (enter Last, First, Middle): Smith, John Alan
(Check the appropriate box and, if applicable, provide the required information.)

    /x/ Joint Debtor has a Social Security Number and it is: 8 8 8 - 8 8 - 8 8 8 8
           (If more than one, state all.)
    / / Joint Debtor does not have a Social Security Number.

I declare under penalty of perjury that the foregoing is true and correct.

        X   *Mary Ellen Smith (handwritten signature)*   March 13, 2004
               Signature of Debtor   Date

        X   *John Alan Smith (handwritten signature)*   March 13, 2004
               Signature of Joint Debtor   Date

---

*Joint debtors must provide information for both spouses.
Penalty for making a false statement: Fine of up to $250,000 or up to 5 years imprisonment or both. 18 U.S.C. §§ 152 and 3571.

Instructions for the Chapter 7 Individual Debtor's Statement of Intention (Official Form 8)

This form is required if you have a secured debt (a debt for which you have pledged some type of collateral or which has a lien against it). It is crucial if you wish to keep the collateral and/or eliminate the creditor's claims on the collateral. If you have secured debts, refer to your completed Schedule D. You must separate all debts listed on that schedule into two categories: debts for which you will surrender the collateral and debts for which you wish to keep the collateral. For those debts for which you wish to keep the collateral, there are three additional choices. You may reaffirm the debt; you can claim the property as exempt and redeem the property; or you may claim the property as exempt and seek to eliminate the creditor's lien on the property. Note that you must perform your stated intentions within 45 days of filing Form 8 with the bankruptcy court. If you do not wish to surrender your collateral, you should seek legal advice.

Court Name: Fill in the full name of the judicial district in which you will be filing (as listed on your Voluntary Petition).

In re: Fill in your full name (last name first) that you regularly use to sign checks, etc.

Case No.: Leave this line blank. The court clerk will assign you a case number.

Property to Be Surrendered: Here describe each item of property listed on your Schedule D as collateral which you choose to voluntarily surrender to the bankruptcy court. Use the property descriptions and creditors' names as shown on your Schedule D. Under this option, you are free from the debt entirely; however, you also lose the property. If there is an exemption for the property which is less than the claim against the property, the secured property will generally be surrendered to the bankruptcy trustee and sold. You will receive the amount of the exemption in cash and the remaining proceeds will be used to pay off the secured creditor. If you have no debts listed on Schedule D, enter *N/A* here and skip to the signature line.

Property to Be Retained: If you wish to retain your secured property either by reaffirmation, redemption, or exemption/lien avoidance, you are advised to seek the assistance of a competent attorney. There are additional forms that must be prepared which are beyond the scope of this book. In this section, you list all property on Schedule D that you do not wish to surrender to the court. Describe the property and list the creditor's names as shown on your Schedule D. For each property listed in this section, you must choose to either reaffirm the debt, claim it as exempt and redeem it, or claim it as exempt and seek to avoid any lien against the property. Be very careful not to reaffirm any of your debts without legal advice. In a few judicial districts, there is another option available. You may seek to retain the property by keeping up on your payments, but not reaffirming the debt. The districts which currently allow this are: Colorado, Kansas, Maryland, New Mexico, North Carolina, Oklahoma, Pennsylvania (Western District only), South Carolina, Utah, Virginia, West Virginia, and Wyoming. Consult an attorney if you wish to pursue this option.

Date and Signature of Debtor: Date and sign the form. If filing jointly, spouse should also sign.

Certification of Non-Attorney Bankruptcy Petition Preparer: Enter *N/A*, unless you were assisted by a bankruptcy petition preparer.

Official Form 8
(12/03)

United States Bankruptcy Court
Northern District Of Illinois

In re Mary Ellen and John Alan Smith
        Debtor

Case No. (supplied by clerk)

Chapter 7

CHAPTER 7 INDIVIDUAL DEBTOR'S STATEMENT OF INTENTION

1. I have filed a schedule of assets and liabilities which includes consumer debts secured by property of the estate.

2. I intend to do the following with respect to the property of the estate which secures those consumer debts:

    a. *Property to Be Surrendered.*

Description of Property	Creditor's name
Personal home located at 16 Main Street, Centerville, IL 61111	Centerville Savings and Loan

    b. *Property to Be Retained*   *[Check any applicable statement.]*

Description of Property	Creditor's Name	Property is claimed as exempt	Property will be redeemed pursuant to 11 U.S.C. § 722	Debt will be reaffirmed pursuant to 11 U.S.C. § 524(c)
		☐	☐	☐
		☐	☐	☐

Date: March 13, 2004

Mary Ellen Smith (handwritten signature)
Signature of Debtor

CERTIFICATION OF NON-ATTORNEY BANKRUPTCY PETITION PREPARER (See 11 U.S.C. § 110)

I certify that I am a bankruptcy petition preparer as defined in 11 U.S.C. § 110, that I prepared this document for compensation, and that I have provided the debtor with a copy of this document.

_____
Printed or Typed Name of Bankruptcy Petition Preparer

_____
Social Security No.
(Required by 11 U.S.C. § 110(c).)

_____
Address

Names and Social Security Numbers of all other individuals who prepared or assisted in preparing this document.

If more than one person prepared this document, attach additional signed sheets conforming to the appropriate Official Form for each person.

X n/a
Signature of Bankruptcy Petition Preparer   Date

A bankruptcy petition preparer's failure to comply with the provisions of title 11 and the Federal Rules of Bankruptcy Procedure may result in fines or imprisonment or both. 11 U.S.C. § 110; 18 U.S.C. § 156.

Instructions for the Application to Pay Filing Fee in Installments (Official Form 3)

Page 1

This form is used to request permission to pay your filing fees in installments. You have the right to request this under bankruptcy law. Using this form, you make an initial payment with the filing of your bankruptcy papers and then indicate that you will make up to three further installment payments over a period of up to 120 days in order to pay the filing fee in full. There are a few restrictions, however:

1. You must certify that you are unable to pay the entire fee at one time. Be certain that this request coincides with your description of your current financial situation. If your petition and schedules indicate that you have sufficient cash to pay the filing fee, your request will be denied.

2. If you have already paid an attorney or bankruptcy petition preparer for assistance with your case, you cannot request permission to pay your fee in installments.

3. If your request is granted, you may not pay anyone for any services or assistance related to your bankruptcy until you have first paid your filing fee in full. Additionally, you may not transfer any property to anyone as payment for services in connection with your bankruptcy until your entire filing fee is paid.

Court Name: Fill in the full name of the judicial district in which you will be filing (as listed on your Voluntary Petition).

In re: Fill in your full name (last name first) that you regularly use to sign checks, etc.

Case No.: Leave this line blank. The court clerk will assign you a case number.

Application to Pay Filing Fee in Installments: At the end of "1.," enter the total amount of the filing fee ($209.00). You may request to pay the fee in up to four installments. Under "4.," list first the amount that you will pay either with the filing of the petition itself (check the appropriate box) or within 15 days of filing (list the date in the space shown if you check "On or before"). On the next three lines, indicate the amount that you will pay for each installment and the date on or before which you will pay the installment. The final installment must be paid within 120 days of the filing of your petition, unless you can show the court extraordinary circumstances and they grant you an additional 60 days for final payment (for a total of 180 days).

Signature of Debtor and Date: Sign and date the form. If filing jointly, spouse should also sign.

Certification and Signature of Non-Attorney Bankruptcy Petition Preparer: Enter *N/A*, unless you were assisted by a bankruptcy petition preparer.

Page 2: Order Approving Payment of Filing Fee in Installments

Court Name: Fill in the name and state of the bankruptcy court

In re: Fill in your full name (last name first) that you regularly use to sign checks.

Case No.: Leave this line blank. The court clerk will assign you a number.

Date and Bankruptcy Judge signature: Leave blank. These will be completed by the bankruptcy court judge if your request to pay the fee in installments is approved.

Official Form 3
(12/03)

United States Bankruptcy Court
_____Northern_____ District Of _____Illinois_____

In re Mary Ellen and John Alan Smith , Case No. (supplied by clerk)
Debtor

Chapter 7

APPLICATION TO PAY FILING FEE IN INSTALLMENTS

1. In accordance with Fed. R. Bankr. P. 1006, I apply for permission to pay the Filing Fee amounting to $ __209.00__ in installments.

2. I certify that I am unable to pay the Filing Fee except in installments.

3. I further certify that I have not paid any money or transferred any property to an attorney for services in connection with this case and that I will neither make any payment nor transfer any property for services in connection with this case until the filing fee is paid in full.

4. I propose the following terms for the payment of the Filing Fee.*

   $ _____53.00_____ Check one [✓] With the filing of the petition, or
                                   [ ] On or before _____
   $ _____53.00_____ on or before April 1, 2004
   $ _____53.00_____ on or before April 15, 2004
   $ _____50.00_____ on or before April 30, 2004

* The number of installments proposed shall not exceed four (4), and the final installment shall be payable not later than 120 days after filing the petition. For cause shown, the court may extend the time of any installment, provided the last installment is paid not later than 180 days after filing the petition. Fed. R. Bankr. P. 1006(b)(2).

5. I understand that if I fail to pay any installment when due my bankruptcy case may be dismissed and I may not receive a discharge of my debts.

__n/a_____   _Mary E. Smith (handwritten signature)_   March 13, 2004
Signature of Attorney   Date   Signature of Debtor   Date
                                                   (In a joint case, both spouses must sign.)

_____   _____
Name of Attorney   Signature of Joint Debtor (if any)   Date

CERTIFICATION AND SIGNATURE OF NON-ATTORNEY BANKRUPTCY PETITION PREPARER (See 11 U.S.C. § 110)

I certify that I am a bankruptcy petition preparer as defined in 11 U.S.C. § 110, that I prepared this document for compensation, and that I have provided the debtor with a copy of this document. I also certify that I will not accept money or any other property from the debtor before the filing fee is paid in full.

_____   _____
Printed or Typed Name of Bankruptcy Petition Preparer   Social Security No.
                                                   (Required by 11 U.S.C. § 110(c).)

_____
Address

Names and Social Security numbers of all other individuals who prepared or assisted in preparing this document:

If more than one person prepared this document, attach additional signed sheets conforming to the appropriate Official Form for each person.

x __n/a_____   _____
Signature of Bankruptcy Petition Preparer   Date

A bankruptcy petition preparer's failure to comply with the provisions of title 11 and the Federal Rules of Bankruptcy Procedure may result in fines or imprisonment or both. 11 U.S.C. § 110; 18 U.S.C. § 156.

Official Form 3 continued
(9/97)

United States Bankruptcy Court
<u>   Northern   </u> District Of <u>   Illinois   </u>

In re <u>Mary Ellen and Alan Smith   </u>, Case No. <u> (supplied by clerk) </u>
                  Debtor

Chapter 7

ORDER APPROVING PAYMENT OF FILING FEE IN INSTALLMENTS

       IT IS ORDERED that the debtor(s) may pay the filing fee in installments on the terms proposed in the foregoing application.

       IT IS FURTHER ORDERED that until the filing fee is paid in full the debtor shall not pay any money for services in connection with this case, and the debtor shall not relinquish any property as payment for services in connection with this case.

                                                  BY THE COURT

Date: _____   _____
                                                    United States Bankruptcy Judge

Instructions for the Mailing List of Creditors' Names and Addresses

You will need to prepare a mailing list of all of your creditors' names and addresses in all bankruptcy courts, to be used by the court to provide official notifications to each creditor or security holder that you have listed on your bankruptcy schedules. However, each bankruptcy court has its own specific instructions and forms for preparing mailing lists. Be sure to check with your particular court clerk for any specific instructions for preparing mailing lists and any required verification form to be filed with your list.

CHAPTER 5
Completing Your Bankruptcy

Once you have completed filling in your official bankruptcy forms, you are ready to complete your bankruptcy. There are three basic steps left. First, you must file the original and copies of your complete set of papers with the bankruptcy court in your area and pay the required fees. Next, you will be required to attend a creditors' meeting and surrender any non-exempt property. Finally, you will receive a discharge in bankruptcy which will officially eliminate your dischargeable debts and leave you with full possession of your exempt property. These three steps are not difficult to complete. From start to finish, the entire process will take around four months to complete. You may wish to review the two checklists located at the end of Chapter 2 for an overview of the needed actions and the necessary items to file.

Filing Your Bankruptcy Papers

There are several steps you should take prior to actually filing your papers with the bankruptcy court.

Determine Which Bankruptcy Court: First, you should determine which bankruptcy court is the correct court for you to use. Appendix C contains a listing of the names, addresses, and phone numbers of all of the federal bankruptcy courts. You should file your bankruptcy papers in the federal district where you have lived or conducted your business for the last six months. If you are in doubt as to which court, call and ask the clerk of the bankruptcy court. Although court employees are prohibited from giving you legal advice, they should be able to answer basic informational questions.

Contact the Bankruptcy Court Clerk: You will also need to contact the clerk of your local bankruptcy court to determine if there are any additional local forms which may be required. The official forms in this book are acceptable in all bankruptcy courts in the United States. However, each federal district can also require its own local forms for organizational purposes. These generally consist of cover sheets or other forms to assist the court employees in filing the forms. When you check with the court clerk, you will also need to ask how many copies of your bankruptcy papers will be required. You will generally be required to file the original and at least two sets of photocopies of all of your papers. In addition, you will need to have a copy for yourself. Also, ask the court clerk for a list of the order in which they prefer the papers to be filed. If no particular order is required, file your papers with the cover sheet first and then in the order listed on your cover sheet.

Emergency Filing: If you have decided to pursue an emergency filing, you will only need to file your Voluntary Petition, any additional required local court forms (check with the court clerk), and a complete Mailing List with your creditors' names and addresses with verification. You will also need to either pay the filing fees in full or file an application to pay your filing fee in installments, if you desire. You will have 15 days to file all of the additional required forms. If you miss the 15-day deadline, your case will likely be dismissed and you won't be able to file again for six months. You may also be unable to discharge the debts you owed at the time of your emergency filing. Follow the rest of the instructions for filing your forms.

Check Your Papers Carefully: Go over each of the official documents which you have filled in. Carefully check every item for accuracy, particularly the names and addresses of your creditors. These names and addresses will be used for notifying the creditors of your bankruptcy. If the creditors are not notified properly, your debt to them may not be erased by your bankruptcy. Your creditors must have an opportunity to attend the creditors' meeting or challenge your bankruptcy (although this seldom happens). Also be very certain that you have included every item of property that you own and every debt you owe, regardless how small. Check also that each continuation sheet that you may have used is properly completed. Any required local forms should also be filled in and checked.

Once you have determined that all of your forms are neatly and properly filled in, you should sign and date the originals of each form where indicated. If you are filing jointly, your spouse must also sign the forms. After signing, you should make certain that you have all of the sheets in proper order. Where indicated on each form, note if any continuation sheets are included. Schedules B, D, E, F and your Statement of Financial Affairs have lines on the lower left-hand side of their first page for this information. On your Summary of Schedules, note the number of total pages you are filing.

Make Copies of Your Bankruptcy Papers: You will now need to make several copies of your complete set of bankruptcy papers. Check with the court clerk to determine how many copies are required to be filed. Using your original, you will need to make the required number of copies plus an additional one for yourself. Your additional copy should be taken with you to the court when you file all of your papers. Have the court clerk stamp this copy with a dated "Filed" stamp to indicate that you have filed your bankruptcy papers. All copies and the original of your bankruptcy papers should be two-hole punched at the top. You can have a quick-print shop do the copying and hole punching if you desire. Be certain that you have your forms in the correct order. If you have debts secured by property listed on Schedule D and you are filing a Chapter 7

Individual Debtor's Statement of Intention for those debts, you will need to also make an additional copy of your Chapter 7 Individual Debtor's Statement of Intention for each creditor listed on this form and one for the bankruptcy trustee. Please see "Sending Your Chapter 7 Individual Debtor's Statement of Intention" on the next page for further instructions.

File Your Papers and Pay Your Fees: You should now either mail the papers listed below or go in person to the correct bankruptcy court armed with the following items:

- The complete set of the originals of all of your official bankruptcy forms (except your Chapter 7 Individual Debtor's Statement of Intention)

- The required number of copies of your full set of bankruptcy forms (except your Chapter 7 Individual Debtor's Statement of Intention)

- Your own copy of the full set of bankruptcy forms (except your Chapter 7 Individual Debtor's Statement of Intentions)

- A completed original and the required copies of your Application to Pay Filing Fees in Installments (if you are asking for this)

- A money order or certified bank check for $209.00 made out to the "U.S. Bankruptcy Court." If you are asking for permission to pay your filing fee in installments, make the check out for the downpayment amount which you have listed on your Application to Pay Filing Fees in Installments

Either in person or by mail, ask that the original and copies of your bankruptcy papers be filed. Pay your fee. Ask the court clerk to "File" stamp your own copy of your bankruptcy papers. Request the name and address of the bankruptcy trustee for your case.

Automatic Stay: Once you have filed your bankruptcy papers, the automatic stay goes into effect. The bankruptcy court will notify each of the creditors that you have listed of your filing and of the automatic stay. However, if you are in an emergency situation, you yourself can notify any creditors, collection agencies, landlords, police, or others. To do this, simply make a copy of the file-stamped version of both pages (pages 1 and 2) of your Voluntary Petition (Official Form 1) for each person whom you wish to notify. Using your creditor mailing list, mail a copy of the file-stamped Voluntary Petition to each person whom you wish to immediately notify. This will prevent any further action on their part to evict you, shut off your utilities, harass you, or take any actions to collect on any of your debts. These creditors, however, have the right to ask the bankruptcy court to lift the automatic stay for their particular situation. If they do petition the court to lift the stay, you will be notified by the court.

Sending Your Chapter 7 Individual Debtor's Statement of Intention: If you have any secured debts listed on Schedule D and you have completed a Chapter 7 Individual Debtor's Statement of Intention with regard to those debts, you have one more step to complete in filing your papers. If you did not list any debts on Schedule D, skip the following steps.

You must personally notify each of your secured creditors of your intentions with regard to their debt. To do this, follow these simple steps:

- Within 30 days of filing your papers with the court, you will need to mail a copy of your Chapter 7 Individual Debtor's Statement of Intention to each creditor listed on Schedule D and also to your bankruptcy trustee and complete a Proof of Service by Mail form

- You will need to obtain a Proof of Service by Mail form from your local bankruptcy court which lists the names and addresses of all of the creditors from your Schedule D and of your bankruptcy trustee

- Mail or take your signed original individual debtor's statement of intention and the signed original Proof of Service by Mail to the bankruptcy court within 30 days of filing your other papers. File these two documents with the bankruptcy court clerk and ask the clerk to "file-stamp" your copies of these two forms

The Creditors' Meeting

For you, the next step in your bankruptcy is the creditors' meeting. After you have filed your bankruptcy papers, the court assigns a bankruptcy trustee to handle your case. The trustee sends notices of your bankruptcy, the automatic stay, and a creditors' meeting to all of the creditors which you have listed on your mailing list. You will also be notified of the time and place of this meeting. It will usually be held about a month after the filing of your papers. You must attend this meeting. If you do not, you may be fined, your bankruptcy may be dismissed, and you may be prevented from filing again for six months. Both you and your spouse must attend if you filed jointly. If you have a major schedule conflict, you may be able to contact the court and reschedule the meeting.

Unless you have significant non-exempt assets which can be sold or a creditor suspects you of fraudulent activities with regard to your bankruptcy, creditors rarely attend the meeting. The meeting should take about a half-hour. Generally, at the meeting, the bankruptcy trustee goes over your papers and may question you regarding specific debts or property. The trustee will also likely ask you questions regarding your understanding of bankruptcy. He or she is supposed to be certain that you understand the effect of bankruptcy on your credit, the consequences of a bankruptcy discharge, the availability of other types of bankruptcies, and the effect of reaffirming a debt. If you have read this entire book, you should have no difficulty in answering these questions. Prior to the meeting, review this book and look over your bankruptcy papers so that you will be able to honestly and easily answer any questions regarding your financial circumstances. You should also bring with you any of your financial records that you used to fill in your bankruptcy questionnaire and official forms. The meeting should be relatively brief and businesslike. If you feel that you are being intimidated by the trustee or a creditor, you have the right to stop the meeting and ask for a court hearing.

Within 30 days of your creditors' meeting, the bankruptcy trustee or your creditors can object to your listing certain property as exempt. They must do so in writing and a court hearing will be scheduled. Generally, you need not attend the court hearing unless you wish to contest their claim that the property should not be exempt. Additionally, creditors can specifically object to the discharge of a particular debt. This may be done if they claim it is a non-dischargeable debt or if they feel that you incurred the debt by fraud or dishonesty of some kind. If a creditor challenges the discharge of a particular debt, you will be served court papers informing you of this challenge. If you wish to defend the dischargeability of the debt, you will need to seek the advice of a competent attorney. Finally, a creditor, on rare occasions, can seek to prevent you from obtaining a bankruptcy at all on the basis that you have incurred the bulk of your debts by fraud. If this happens, you will be notified and you should immediately seek the assistance of an attorney skilled in bankruptcy law.

Surrendering Your Property

After your creditors' meeting, your bankruptcy trustee will notify you which of your non-exempt property will have to be surrendered to the court. Excess cash and any valuable property which could be sold to pay your creditors will likely be the only non-exempt property you will need to surrender. You may also be able to negotiate with your trustee to buy back any non-exempt property for cash or trade some of your exempt property for particular non-exempt property which you wish to keep. Most trustees are flexible, as long as they are able to collect property with an equivalent value. You must deal with any secured property (collateral) in the manner in which you have indicated on your Chapter 7 Individual Debtor's Statement of Intention. You have 45 days from the date you filed your bankruptcy papers with the court to complete your stated intentions. If you indicated on your Chapter 7 Individual Debtor's Statement of Intention that you would surrender secured property, it is up to your creditor to repossess the property.

Your Final Discharge

The final step in your bankruptcy will come about three months after your creditors' meeting. Generally, you will be notified by the court of the scheduling of a very brief court hearing. At this quick hearing, the bankruptcy judge will determine that all of the proper steps have been taken and that your bankruptcy should be approved. The judge will then also generally inform you of the effects of bankruptcy. Finally, the judge will issue an order of discharge and your bankruptcy will be over. All of your dischargeable debts will be forever wiped clean. You will receive a final notice of your discharge in the mail a few weeks later. Congratulations.

After Your Bankruptcy

Once your bankruptcy is over, all of the debts listed on your bankruptcy papers that were not successfully challenged by a creditor are wiped out. You are not liable to pay them in any way. Debts that are non-dischargeable are still valid. If a creditor claims you still owe them, write them and state that your bankruptcy has discharged your debt. There are, of course, several other consequences to your bankruptcy:

Your Credit Record: By law, the fact that you have obtained a personal bankruptcy can remain on your credit record for up to 10 years.

Filing Another Bankruptcy: Once you have obtained a personal bankruptcy, you will not be allowed to file another bankruptcy for a period of six years.

Discrimination: All governmental agencies are prohibited from taking action against you based on your bankruptcy. This includes firing you, evicting you, refusing to issue you a license, or other discriminatory actions. In addition, private employers are prohibited from firing you or otherwise discriminating against you because of your bankruptcy.

If You Made a Mistake on Your Bankruptcy Papers: If, after your final discharge, you discover that you have made a mistake on the bankruptcy papers that you filed, you must notify the bankruptcy trustee. This is particularly important if you neglected to include non-exempt property that might have been sold to pay your creditors. The bankruptcy trustee has the power to reopen your case and seek recovery of any non-exempt property that you owned at the time of your discharge and which was not included on your bankruptcy papers. Generally, this will not be done for small amounts of property. If you neglected to list a creditor, unfortunately, the debt you owe to that creditor will not be discharged unless you can show that the creditor actually knew of your bankruptcy in time to file a claim. If the debt is substantial, you may need to seek legal assistance.

If You Receive an Inheritance, Divorce Settlement, or Insurance Proceeds: If within six months of the date when you filed for bankruptcy (not the date of your discharge) you receive or are informed of an inheritance, or divorce or insurance settlement, you must notify your bankruptcy trustee. In the situation of such windfalls that you receive shortly after your bankruptcy, the bankruptcy trustee also has the power to reopen your case and seek to claim such property.

Rebuilding Your Credit: Once you have eliminated your debts through a bankruptcy, you must then begin the process of rebuilding your credit rating. If you have a steady job and are able to build a record of making on-time rental or utility payments, it should take only a few years to be eligible for credit of some kind. The first credit that will generally be available to you will be collateralized consumer loans or credit for consumer goods. Next, within as little as three to four years, credit cards and auto loans may become available. Finally, if you maintain a clear financial record, home mortgages will again be available to you. Be very careful, however, about once again getting into the credit traps which caused your first bankruptcy. Good credit is a valuable asset that can assist you in reaching your goals and achieving a better life. Bankruptcy will have given you a new start on the road to that life.

Appendix A: Federal Bankruptcy Forms

On the following pages, you will find copies of all of the necessary official bankruptcy forms that you will need to complete your personal bankruptcy. These forms should not be removed from this book (particularly if this is a library book!). Instead, you should make photocopies of the forms in this book for your use. You will need to make at least two photocopies of each of the forms. The first copy will be used to make a rough draft of your answers on each form. The final copy will be used to create a clean, legible final version of each completed form. This final draft version will be considered your *original*. On this completed original, you will sign and date each form if necessary before filing it with the bankruptcy court.

In general, you will use every form provided. However, two of the forms (Chapter 7 Individual Debtor's Statement of Intention and the Application to Pay Filing Fees in Installments) are only used if your particular situation warrants their use. Please refer to the instructions for each individual form in Chapter 4. When filling in your copy of these forms, please be careful that your information is listed in the proper columns or on the correct form. Some of these forms are complicated and several forms are very similar. Do not make any stray marks on the forms. Type your information if possible. You may use legible black-ink handwriting to complete them (except the Mailing List of Creditors' Names and Addresses, which you will obtain from your local bankruptcy court clerk and which must be typed).

(Official Form 1) (12/03)

FORM B1	**United States Bankruptcy Court** _____District of_____	**Voluntary Petition**
Name of Debtor (if individual, enter Last, First, Middle):	Name of Joint Debtor (Spouse) (Last, First, Middle):	
All Other Names used by the Debtor in the last 6 years (include married, maiden, and trade names):	All Other Names used by the Joint Debtor in the last 6 years (include married, maiden, and trade names):	
Last four digits of Soc. Sec. No./Complete EIN or other Tax I.D. No. (if more than one, state all):	Last four digits of Soc. Sec.No./Complete EIN or other Tax I.D. No. (if more than one, state all):	
Street Address of Debtor (No. & Street, City, State & Zip Code):	Street Address of Joint Debtor (No. & Street, City, State & Zip Code):	
County of Residence or of the Principal Place of Business:	County of Residence or of the Principal Place of Business:	
Mailing Address of Debtor (if different from street address):	Mailing Address of Joint Debtor (if different from street address):	
Location of Principal Assets of Business Debtor (if different from street address above):		

Information Regarding the Debtor (Check the Applicable Boxes)

Venue (Check any applicable box)
☐ Debtor has been domiciled or has had a residence, principal place of business, or principal assets in this District for 180 days immediately preceding the date of this petition or for a longer part of such 180 days than in any other District.
☐ There is a bankruptcy case concerning debtor's affiliate, general partner, or partnership pending in this District.

Type of Debtor (Check all boxes that apply) ☐ Individual(s) ☐ Railroad ☐ Corporation ☐ Stockbroker ☐ Partnership ☐ Commodity Broker ☐ Other_____ ☐ Clearing Bank	**Chapter or Section of Bankruptcy Code Under Which** **the Petition is Filed** (Check one box) ☐ Chapter 7 ☐ Chapter 11 ☐ Chapter 13 ☐ Chapter 9 ☐ Chapter 12 ☐ Sec. 304 - Case ancillary to foreign proceeding
Nature of Debts (Check one box) ☐ Consumer/Non-Business ☐ Business	**Filing Fee** (Check one box) ☐ Full Filing Fee attached
Chapter 11 Small Business (Check all boxes that apply) ☐ Debtor is a small business as defined in 11 U.S.C. § 101 ☐ Debtor is and elects to be considered a small business under 11 U.S.C. § 1121(e) (Optional)	☐ Filing Fee to be paid in installments (Applicable to individuals only) Must attach signed application for the court's consideration certifying that the debtor is unable to pay fee except in installments. Rule 1006(b). See Official Form No. 3.

Statistical/Administrative Information (Estimates only) | THIS SPACE IS FOR COURT USE ONLY
☐ Debtor estimates that funds will be available for distribution to unsecured creditors.
☐ Debtor estimates that, after any exempt property is excluded and administrative expenses paid, there will be no funds available for distribution to unsecured creditors.

Estimated Number of Creditors
1-15	16-49	50-99	100-199	200-999	1000-over
☐	☐	☐	☐	☐	☐

Estimated Assets
$0 to $50,000	$50,001 to $100,000	$100,001 to $500,000	$500,001 to $1 million	$1,000,001 to $10 million	$10,000,001 to $50 million	$50,000,001 to $100 million	More than $100 million
☐	☐	☐	☐	☐	☐	☐	☐

Estimated Debts
$0 to $50,000	$50,001 to $100,000	$100,001 to $500,000	$500,001 to $1 million	$1,000,001 to $10 million	$10,000,001 to $50 million	$50,000,001 to $100 million	More than $100 million
☐	☐	☐	☐	☐	☐	☐	☐

(Official Form 1) (12/03)   FORM B1, Page 2

Voluntary Petition *(This page must be completed and filed in every case)*	Name of Debtor(s):	
Prior Bankruptcy Case Filed Within Last 6 Years (If more than one, attach additional sheet)		
Location Where Filed:	Case Number:	Date Filed:
Pending Bankruptcy Case Filed by any Spouse, Partner or Affiliate of this Debtor (If more than one, attach additional sheet)		
Name of Debtor:	Case Number:	Date Filed:
District:	Relationship:	Judge:

Signatures

Signature(s) of Debtor(s) (Individual/Joint)

I declare under penalty of perjury that the information provided in this petition is true and correct.
[If petitioner is an individual whose debts are primarily consumer debts and has chosen to file under chapter 7] I am aware that I may proceed under chapter 7, 11, 12 or 13 of title 11, United States Code, understand the relief available under each such chapter, and choose to proceed under chapter 7.
I request relief in accordance with the chapter of title 11, United States Code, specified in this petition.

X _____
Signature of Debtor

X _____
Signature of Joint Debtor

_____
Telephone Number (If not represented by attorney)

_____
Date

Signature of Attorney

X _____
Signature of Attorney for Debtor(s)

_____
Printed Name of Attorney for Debtor(s)

_____
Firm Name

_____
Address

_____
Telephone Number

_____
Date

Signature of Debtor (Corporation/Partnership)

I declare under penalty of perjury that the information provided in this petition is true and correct, and that I have been authorized to file this petition on behalf of the debtor.

The debtor requests relief in accordance with the chapter of title 11, United States Code, specified in this petition.

X _____
Signature of Authorized Individual

_____
Printed Name of Authorized Individual

_____
Title of Authorized Individual

_____
Date

Exhibit A

(To be completed if debtor is required to file periodic reports (e.g., forms 10K and 10Q) with the Securities and Exchange Commission pursuant to Section 13 or 15(d) of the Securities Exchange Act of 1934 and is requesting relief under chapter 11)

☐ Exhibit A is attached and made a part of this petition.

Exhibit B

(To be completed if debtor is an individual whose debts are primarily consumer debts)

I, the attorney for the petitioner named in the foregoing petition, declare that I have informed the petitioner that [he or she] may proceed under chapter 7, 11, 12, or 13 of title 11, United States Code, and have explained the relief available under each such chapter.

X _____
Signature of Attorney for Debtor(s)   Date

Exhibit C

Does the debtor own or have possession of any property that poses or is alleged to pose a threat of imminent and identifiable harm to public health or safety?

☐ Yes, and Exhibit C is attached and made a part of this petition.
☐ No

Signature of Non-Attorney Petition Preparer

I certify that I am a bankruptcy petition preparer as defined in 11 U.S.C. § 110, that I prepared this document for compensation, and that I have provided the debtor with a copy of this document.

_____
Printed Name of Bankruptcy Petition Preparer

_____
Social Security Number (Required by 11 U.S.C. § 110)

_____
Address

Names and Social Security numbers of all other individuals who prepared or assisted in preparing this document:

If more than one person prepared this document, attach additional sheets conforming to the appropriate official form for each person.

X _____
Signature of Bankruptcy Petition Preparer

_____
Date

A bankruptcy petition preparer's failure to comply with the provisions of title 11 and the Federal Rules of Bankruptcy Procedure may result in fines or imprisonment or both 11 U.S.C. §110; 18 U.S.C. §156.

Form B6A
(6/90)

In re _____,   Case No. _____
         Debtor   **(If known)**

SCHEDULE A - REAL PROPERTY

Except as directed below, list all real property in which the debtor has any legal, equitable, or future interest, including all property owned as a co-tenant, community property, or in which the debtor has a life estate. Include any property in which the debtor holds rights and powers exercisable for the debtor's own benefit. If the debtor is married, state whether husband, wife, or both own the property by placing an "H," "W," "J," or "C" in the column labeled "Husband, Wife, Joint, or Community." If the debtor holds no interest in real property, write "None" under "Description and Location of Property."

Do not include interests in executory contracts and unexpired leases on this schedule. List them in Schedule G - Executory Contracts and Unexpired Leases.

If an entity claims to have a lien or hold a secured interest in any property, state the amount of the secured claim. See Schedule D. If no entity claims to hold a secured interest in the property, write "None" in the column labeled "Amount of Secured Claim."

If the debtor is an individual or if a joint petition is filed, state the amount of any exemption claimed in the property only in Schedule C - Property Claimed as Exempt.

DESCRIPTION AND LOCATION OF PROPERTY	NATURE OF DEBTOR'S INTEREST IN PROPERTY	HUSBAND, WIFE, JOINT, OR COMMUNITY	CURRENT MARKET VALUE OF DEBTOR'S INTEREST IN PROPERTY, WITHOUT DEDUCTING ANY SECURED CLAIM OR EXEMPTION	AMOUNT OF SECURED CLAIM

Total▶

(Report also on Summary of Schedules.)

Form B6B
(10/89)

In re _____,   Case No. _____
           Debtor   (If known)

SCHEDULE B - PERSONAL PROPERTY

Except as directed below, list all personal property of the debtor of whatever kind. If the debtor has no property in one or more of the categories, place an "x" in the appropriate position in the column labeled "None." If additional space is needed in any category, attach a separate sheet properly identified with the case name, case number, and the number of the category. If the debtor is married, state whether husband, wife, or both own the property by placing an "H," "W," "J," or "C" in the column labeled "Husband, Wife, Joint, or Community." If the debtor is an individual or a joint petition is filed, state the amount of any exemptions claimed only in Schedule C - Property Claimed as Exempt.

Do not list interests in executory contracts and unexpired leases on this schedule. List them in Schedule G - Executory Contracts and Unexpired Leases.

If the property is being held for the debtor by someone else, state that person's name and address under "Description and Location of Property."

TYPE OF PROPERTY	NONE	DESCRIPTION AND LOCATION OF PROPERTY	HUSBAND, WIFE, JOINT, OR COMMUNITY	CURRENT MARKET VALUE OF DEBTOR'S INTEREST IN PROPERTY, WITHOUT DEDUCTING ANY SECURED CLAIM OR EXEMPTION
1. Cash on hand.				
2. Checking, savings or other financial accounts, certificates of deposit, or shares in banks, savings and loan, thrift, building and loan, and homestead associations, or credit unions, brokerage houses, or cooperatives.				
3. Security deposits with public utilities, telephone companies, landlords, and others.				
4. Household goods and furnishings, including audio, video, and computer equipment.				
5. Books; pictures and other art objects; antiques; stamp, coin, record, tape, compact disc, and other collections or collectibles.				
6. Wearing apparel.				
7. Furs and jewelry.				
8. Firearms and sports, photographic, and other hobby equipment.				
9. Interests in insurance policies. Name insurance company of each policy and itemize surrender or refund value of each.				
10. Annuities. Itemize and name each issuer.				

Form B6B-Cont.
(10/89)

In re _____,   Case No. _____
             Debtor   **(If known)**

SCHEDULE B - PERSONAL PROPERTY
(Continuation Sheet)

TYPE OF PROPERTY	NONE	DESCRIPTION AND LOCATION OF PROPERTY	HUSBAND, WIFE, JOINT, OR COMMUNITY	CURRENT MARKET VALUE OF DEBTOR'S INTEREST IN PROPERTY, WITH-OUT DEDUCTING ANY SECURED CLAIM OR EXEMPTION
11. Interests in IRA, ERISA, Keogh, or other pension or profit sharing plans. Itemize.				
12. Stock and interests in incorporated and unincorporated businesses. Itemize.				
13. Interests in partnerships or joint ventures. Itemize.				
14. Government and corporate bonds and other negotiable and non-negotiable instruments.				
15. Accounts receivable.				
16. Alimony, maintenance, support, and property settlements to which the debtor is or may be entitled. Give particulars.				
17. Other liquidated debts owing debtor including tax refunds. Give particulars.				
18. Equitable or future interests, life estates, and rights or powers exercisable for the benefit of the debtor other than those listed in Schedule of Real Property.				
19. Contingent and noncontingent interests in estate of a decedent, death benefit plan, life insurance policy, or trust.				
20. Other contingent and unliquidated claims of every nature, including tax refunds, counterclaims of the debtor, and rights to setoff claims. Give estimated value of each.				
21. Patents, copyrights, and other intellectual property. Give particulars.				
22. Licenses, franchises, and other general intangibles. Give particulars.				

Form B6B-cont.
(10/89)

In re _____,   Case No. _____
　　　　　Debtor　　　　　　　　　　　　　　　　　　　　　　　　　(If known)

SCHEDULE B - PERSONAL PROPERTY
(Continuation Sheet)

TYPE OF PROPERTY	N O N E	DESCRIPTION AND LOCATION OF PROPERTY	HUSBAND, WIFE, JOINT, OR COMMUNITY	CURRENT MARKET VALUE OF DEBTOR'S INTEREST IN PROPERTY, WITHOUT DEDUCTING ANY SECURED CLAIM OR EXEMPTION
23. Automobiles, trucks, trailers, and other vehicles and accessories.				
24. Boats, motors, and accessories.				
25. Aircraft and accessories.				
26. Office equipment, furnishings, and supplies.				
27. Machinery, fixtures, equipment, and supplies used in business.				
28. Inventory.				
29. Animals.				
30. Crops - growing or harvested. Give particulars.				
31. Farming equipment and implements.				
32. Farm supplies, chemicals, and feed.				
33. Other personal property of any kind not already listed. Itemize.				

_____ continuation sheets attached　　Total▶　　$ _____

(Include amounts from any continuation sheets attached. Report total also on Summary of Schedules.)

Form B6C
(6/90)

In re _____,   Case No. _____
            Debtor   **(If known)**

SCHEDULE C - PROPERTY CLAIMED AS EXEMPT

Debtor elects the exemptions to which debtor is entitled under:
(Check one box)

☐   11 U.S.C. § 522(b)(1):   Exemptions provided in 11 U.S.C. § 522(d). **Note: These exemptions are available only in certain states.**

☐   11 U.S.C. § 522(b)(2):   Exemptions available under applicable nonbankruptcy federal laws, state or local law where the debtor's domicile has been located for the 180 days immediately preceding the filing of the petition, or for a longer portion of the 180-day period than in any other place, and the debtor's interest as a tenant by the entirety or joint tenant to the extent the interest is exempt from process under applicable nonbankruptcy law.

DESCRIPTION OF PROPERTY	SPECIFY LAW PROVIDING EACH EXEMPTION	VALUE OF CLAIMED EXEMPTION	CURRENT MARKET VALUE OF PROPERTY WITHOUT DEDUCTING EXEMPTION

Form B6D
(12/03)

In re _____,   Case No. _____
           Debtor   (If known)

SCHEDULE D - CREDITORS HOLDING SECURED CLAIMS

State the name, mailing address, including zip code and last four digits of any account number of all entities holding claims secured by property of the debtor as of the date of filing of the petition. The complete account number of any account the debtor has with the creditor is useful to the trustee and the creditor and may be provided if the debtor chooses to do so. List creditors holding all types of secured interests such as judgment liens, garnishments, statutory liens, mortgages, deeds of trust, and other security interests. List creditors in alphabetical order to the extent practicable. If all secured creditors will not fit on this page, use the continuation sheet provided.

If any entity other than a spouse in a joint case may be jointly liable on a claim, place an "X" in the column labeled "Codebtor," include the entity on the appropriate schedule of creditors, and complete Schedule H - Codebtors. If a joint petition is filed, state whether husband, wife, both of them, or the marital community may be liable on each claim by placing an "H," "W," "J," or "C" in the column labeled "Husband, Wife, Joint, or Community."

If the claim is contingent, place an "X" in the column labeled "Contingent." If the claim is unliquidated, place an "X" in the column labeled "Unliquidated." If the claim is disputed, place an "X" in the column labeled "Disputed." (You may need to place an "X" in more than one of these three columns.)

Report the total of all claims listed on this schedule in the box labeled "Total" on the last sheet of the completed schedule. Report this total also on the Summary of Schedules.

☐ Check this box if debtor has no creditors holding secured claims to report on this Schedule D.

CREDITOR'S NAME, MAILING ADDRESS INCLUDING ZIP CODE, AND ACCOUNT NUMBER (See instructions above.)	CODEBTOR	HUSBAND, WIFE, JOINT, OR COMMUNITY	DATE CLAIM WAS INCURRED, NATURE OF LIEN, AND DESCRIPTION AND MARKET VALUE OF PROPERTY SUBJECT TO LIEN	CONTINGENT	UNLIQUIDATED	DISPUTED	AMOUNT OF CLAIM WITHOUT DEDUCTING VALUE OF COLLATERAL	UNSECURED PORTION, IF ANY
ACCOUNT NO.			VALUE $					
ACCOUNT NO.			VALUE $					
ACCOUNT NO.			VALUE $					
ACCOUNT NO.			VALUE $					

_____ continuation sheets attached

Subtotal ➡ $ _____
(Total of this page)

Total ➡ $ _____
(Use only on last page)

(Report total also on Summary of Schedules)

Form B6D - Cont.
(12/03)

In re _____,   Case No. _____
                    Debtor   (If known)

SCHEDULE D - CREDITORS HOLDING SECURED CLAIMS
(Continuation Sheet)

CREDITOR'S NAME, MAILING ADDRESS INCLUDING ZIP CODE AND ACCOUNT NUMBER (See instructions.)	CODEBTOR	HUSBAND, WIFE, JOINT, OR COMMUNITY	DATE CLAIM WAS INCURRED, NATURE OF LIEN, AND DESCRIPTION AND MARKET VALUE OF PROPERTY SUBJECT TO LIEN	CONTINGENT	UNLIQUIDATED	DISPUTED	AMOUNT OF CLAIM WITHOUT DEDUCTING VALUE OF COLLATERAL	UNSECURED PORTION, IF ANY
ACCOUNT NO.			VALUE $					
ACCOUNT NO.			VALUE $					
ACCOUNT NO.			VALUE $					
ACCOUNT NO.			VALUE $					
ACCOUNT NO.			VALUE $					

Sheet no. ___ of ___ continuation sheets attached to Schedule of Creditors Holding Secured Claims   Subtotal $ ➡
(Total of this page)
Total $ ➡
(Use only on last page)

(Report total also on Summary of Schedules)

Form B6E
(04/04)

In re _____,   Case No._____
                    Debtor   (if known)

SCHEDULE E - CREDITORS HOLDING UNSECURED PRIORITY CLAIMS

A complete list of claims entitled to priority, listed separately by type of priority, is to be set forth on the sheets provided. Only holders of unsecured claims entitled to priority should be listed in this schedule. In the boxes provided on the attached sheets, state the name, mailing address, including zip code, and last four digits of the account number, if any, of all entities holding priority claims against the debtor or the property of the debtor, as of the date of the filing of the petition. The complete account number of any account the debtor has with the creditor is useful to the trustee and the creditor and may be provided if the debtor chooses to do so.

If any entity other than a spouse in a joint case may be jointly liable on a claim, place an "X" in the column labeled "Codebtor," include the entity on the appropriate schedule of creditors, and complete Schedule H-Codebtors. If a joint petition is filed, state whether husband, wife, both of them or the marital community may be liable on each claim by placing an "H,""W,""J," or "C" in the column labeled "Husband, Wife, Joint, or Community."

If the claim is contingent, place an "X" in the column labeled "Contingent." If the claim is unliquidated, place an "X" in the column labeled "Unliquidated." If the claim is disputed, place an "X" in the column labeled "Disputed." (You may need to place an "X" in more than one of these three columns.)

Report the total of claims listed on each sheet in the box labeled "Subtotal" on each sheet. Report the total of all claims listed on this Schedule E in the box labeled "Total" on the last sheet of the completed schedule. Repeat this total also on the Summary of Schedules.

☐ Check this box if debtor has no creditors holding unsecured priority claims to report on this Schedule E.

TYPES OF PRIORITY CLAIMS (Check the appropriate box(es) below if claims in that category are listed on the attached sheets)

☐ **Extensions of credit in an involuntary case**

Claims arising in the ordinary course of the debtor's business or financial affairs after the commencement of the case but before the earlier of the appointment of a trustee or the order for relief. 11 U.S.C. § 507(a)(2).

☐ **Wages, salaries, and commissions**

Wages, salaries, and commissions, including vacation, severance, and sick leave pay owing to employees and commissions owing to qualifying independent sales representatives up to $4,925* per person earned within 90 days immediately preceding the filing of the original petition, or the cessation of business, whichever occurred first, to the extent provided in 11 U.S.C. § 507(a)(3).

☐ **Contributions to employee benefit plans**

Money owed to employee benefit plans for services rendered within 180 days immediately preceding the filing of the original petition, or the cessation of business, whichever occurred first, to the extent provided in 11 U.S.C. § 507(a)(4).

☐ **Certain farmers and fishermen**

Claims of certain farmers and fishermen, up to $4,925* per farmer or fisherman, against the debtor, as provided in 11 U.S.C. § 507(a)(5).

☐ **Deposits by individuals**

Claims of individuals up to $2,225* for deposits for the purchase, lease, or rental of property or services for personal, family, or household use, that were not delivered or provided. 11 U.S.C. § 507(a)(6).

Form B6E
(04/04)

In re _____, Case No._____
           Debtor   (if known)

☐ **Alimony, Maintenance, or Support**

Claims of a spouse, former spouse, or child of the debtor for alimony, maintenance, or support, to the extent provided in 11 U.S.C. § 507(a)(7).

☐ **Taxes and Certain Other Debts Owed to Governmental Units**

Taxes, customs duties, and penalties owing to federal, state, and local governmental units as set forth in 11 U.S.C. § 507(a)(8).

☐ **Commitments to Maintain the Capital of an Insured Depository Institution**

Claims based on commitments to the FDIC, RTC, Director of the Office of Thrift Supervision, Comptroller of the Currency, or Board of Governors of the Federal Reserve System, or their predecessors or successors, to maintain the capital of an insured depository institution. 11 U.S.C. § 507 (a)(9).

* Amounts are subject to adjustment on April 1, 2007, and every three years thereafter with respect to cases commenced on or after the date of adjustment.

_____ continuation sheets attached

Form B6E - Cont.
(04/04)

In re _____ ,   Case No. _____
            Debtor   (If known)

SCHEDULE E - CREDITORS HOLDING UNSECURED PRIORITY CLAIMS
(Continuation Sheet)

_____
TYPE OF PRIORITY

CREDITOR'S NAME, MAILING ADDRESS INCLUDING ZIP CODE, AND ACCOUNT NUMBER (See instructions.)	CODEBTOR	HUSBAND, WIFE, JOINT, OR COMMUNITY	DATE CLAIM WAS INCURRED AND CONSIDERATION FOR CLAIM	CONTINGENT	UNLIQUIDATED	DISPUTED	AMOUNT OF CLAIM	AMOUNT ENTITLED TO PRIORITY
ACCOUNT NO.								
ACCOUNT NO.								
ACCOUNT NO.								
ACCOUNT NO.								
ACCOUNT NO.								

Sheet no. ___ of ___ sheets attached to Schedule of Creditors Holding Priority Claims

Subtotal ▶ $ _____
(Total of this page)

Total ▶ $ _____
(Use only on last page of the completed Schedule E.)
(Report total also on Summary of Schedules)

Form B6F (12/03)

In re _____ ,   Case No. _____
                         Debtor   **(If known)**

SCHEDULE F- CREDITORS HOLDING UNSECURED NONPRIORITY CLAIMS

State the name, mailing address, including zip code, and last four digits of any account number, of all entities holding unsecured claims without priority against the debtor or the property of the debtor, as of the date of filing of the petition. The complete account number of any account the debtor has with the creditor is useful to the trustee and the creditor and may be provided if the debtor chooses to do so. Do not include claims listed in Schedules D and E. If all creditors will not fit on this page, use the continuation sheet provided.

If any entity other than a spouse in a joint case may be jointly liable on a claim, place an "X" in the column labeled "Codebtor," include the entity on the appropriate schedule of creditors, and complete Schedule H - Codebtors. If a joint petition is filed, state whether husband, wife, both of them, or the marital community maybe liable on each claim by placing an "H," "W," "J," or "C" in the column labeled "Husband, Wife, Joint, or Community."

If the claim is contingent, place an "X" in the column labeled "Contingent." If the claim is unliquidated, place an "X" in the column labeled "Unliquidated." If the claim is disputed, place an "X" in the column labeled "Disputed." (You may need to place an "X" in more than one of these three columns.)

Report total of all claims listed on this schedule in the box labeled "Total" on the last sheet of the completed schedule. Report this total also on the Summary of Schedules.

☐ Check this box if debtor has no creditors holding unsecured claims to report on this Schedule F.

CREDITOR'S NAME, MAILING ADDRESS INCLUDING ZIP CODE, AND ACCOUNT NUMBER (See instructions above.)	CODEBTOR	HUSBAND, WIFE, JOINT, OR COMMUNITY	DATE CLAIM WAS INCURRED AND CONSIDERATION FOR CLAIM. IF CLAIM IS SUBJECT TO SETOFF, SO STATE.	CONTINGENT	UNLIQUIDATED	DISPUTED	AMOUNT OF CLAIM
ACCOUNT NO.							
ACCOUNT NO.							
ACCOUNT NO.							
ACCOUNT NO.							

_____ continuation sheets attached

Subtotal ▶ $ _____

Total ▶ $ _____

(Report also on Summary of Schedules)

Form B6F - Cont.
(12/03)

In re _____,   Case No. _____
            Debtor   (If known)

SCHEDULE F - CREDITORS HOLDING UNSECURED NONPRIORITY CLAIMS
(Continuation Sheet)

CREDITOR'S NAME, MAILING ADDRESS INCLUDING ZIP CODE, AND ACCOUNT NUMBER (See instructions.)	CODEBTOR	HUSBAND, WIFE, JOINT, OR COMMUNITY	DATE CLAIM WAS INCURRED AND CONSIDERATION FOR CLAIM. IF CLAIM IS SUBJECT TO SETOFF, SO STATE.	CONTINGENT	UNLIQUIDATED	DISPUTED	AMOUNT OF CLAIM
ACCOUNT NO.							
ACCOUNT NO.							
ACCOUNT NO.							
ACCOUNT NO							
ACCOUNT NO.							

Sheet no. ___ of ___ sheets attached to Schedule of Creditors Holding Unsecured Nonpriority Claims

Subtotal ▶ $ _____
(Total of this page)

Total ▶ $ _____
(Use only on last page of the completed Schedule F.)
(Report total also on Summary of Schedules)

Form B6G
(10/89)

In re _____,   Case No._____
         Debtor   (if known)

SCHEDULE G - EXECUTORY CONTRACTS AND UNEXPIRED LEASES

Describe all executory contracts of any nature and all unexpired leases of real or personal property. Include any timeshare interests. State nature of debtor's interest in contract, i.e., "Purchaser," "Agent," etc. State whether debtor is the lessor or lessee of a lease. Provide the names and complete mailing addresses of all other parties to each lease or contract described.

NOTE: A party listed on this schedule will not receive notice of the filing of this case unless the party is also scheduled in the appropriate schedule of creditors.

☐ Check this box if debtor has no executory contracts or unexpired leases.

NAME AND MAILING ADDRESS, INCLUDING ZIP CODE, OF OTHER PARTIES TO LEASE OR CONTRACT.	DESCRIPTION OF CONTRACT OR LEASE AND NATURE OF DEBTOR'S INTEREST. STATE WHETHER LEASE IS FOR NONRESIDENTIAL REAL PROPERTY. STATE CONTRACT NUMBER OF ANY GOVERNMENT CONTRACT.

Form B6H
(6/90)

In re _____,   Case No. _____
        Debtor   **(if known)**

SCHEDULE H - CODEBTORS

Provide the information requested concerning any person or entity, other than a spouse in a joint case, that is also liable on any debts listed by debtor in the schedules of creditors. Include all guarantors and co-signers. In community property states, a married debtor not filing a joint case should report the name and address of the nondebtor spouse on this schedule. Include all names used by the nondebtor spouse during the six years immediately preceding the commencement of this case.

☐ Check this box if debtor has no codebtors.

NAME AND ADDRESS OF CODEBTOR	NAME AND ADDRESS OF CREDITOR

Form B6I
(12/03)

In re _____,   Case No._____
            Debtor   (if known)

SCHEDULE I - CURRENT INCOME OF INDIVIDUAL DEBTOR(S)

The column labeled "Spouse" must be completed in all cases filed by joint debtors and by a married debtor in a chapter 12 or 13 case whether or not a joint petition is filed, unless the spouses are separated and a joint petition is not filed.

Debtor's Marital Status:	DEPENDENTS OF DEBTOR AND SPOUSE	
	RELATIONSHIP	AGE

Employment:	DEBTOR	SPOUSE
Occupation		
Name of Employer		
How long employed		
Address of Employer		

Income: (Estimate of average monthly income)   DEBTOR   SPOUSE
Current monthly gross wages, salary, and commissions
   (pro rate if not paid monthly.) $_____ $_____
Estimated monthly overtime $_____ $_____

SUBTOTAL $_____ $_____

   LESS PAYROLL DEDUCTIONS
     a. Payroll taxes and social security $_____ $_____
     b. Insurance $_____ $_____
     c. Union dues $_____ $_____
     d. Other (Specify: _____) $_____ $_____

SUBTOTAL OF PAYROLL DEDUCTIONS $_____ $_____

TOTAL NET MONTHLY TAKE HOME PAY $_____ $_____

Regular income from operation of business or profession or farm $_____ $_____
(attach detailed statement)
Income from real property $_____ $_____
Interest and dividends $_____ $_____
Alimony, maintenance or support payments payable to the debtor for the
debtor's use or that of dependents listed above. $_____ $_____
Social security or other government assistance
(Specify) _____ $_____ $_____
Pension or retirement income $_____ $_____
Other monthly income
(Specify) _____ $_____ $_____
           _____ $_____ $_____

TOTAL MONTHLY INCOME $_____ $_____

TOTAL COMBINED MONTHLY INCOME $_____   (Report also on Summary of Schedules)

Describe any increase or decrease of more than 10% in any of the above categories anticipated to occur within the year following the filing of this document:

Form B6J
(6/90)

In re _____ ,   Case No. _____
                  Debtor   (if known)

SCHEDULE J - CURRENT EXPENDITURES OF INDIVIDUAL DEBTOR(S)

Complete this schedule by estimating the average monthly expenses of the debtor and the debtor's family. Pro rate any payments made bi-weekly, quarterly, semi-annually, or annually to show monthly rate.

☐ Check this box if a joint petition is filed and debtor's spouse maintains a separate household. Complete a separate schedule of expenditures labeled "Spouse."

Rent or home mortgage payment (include lot rented for mobile home)	$ _____
Are real estate taxes included? Yes _____ No _____	
Is property insurance included? Yes _____ No _____	
Utilities Electricity and heating fuel	$ _____
Water and sewer	$ _____
Telephone	$ _____
Other _____	$ _____
Home maintenance (repairs and upkeep)	$ _____
Food	$ _____
Clothing	$ _____
Laundry and dry cleaning	$ _____
Medical and dental expenses	$ _____
Transportation (not including car payments)	$ _____
Recreation, clubs and entertainment, newspapers, magazines, etc.	$ _____
Charitable contributions	$ _____
Insurance (not deducted from wages or included in home mortgage payments)	
Homeowner's or renter's	$ _____
Life	$ _____
Health	$ _____
Auto	$ _____
Other _____	$ _____
Taxes (not deducted from wages or included in home mortgage payments) (Specify) _____	$ _____
Installment payments: (In chapter 12 and 13 cases, do not list payments to be included in the plan)	
Auto	$ _____
Other _____	$ _____
Other _____	$ _____
Alimony, maintenance, and support paid to others	$ _____
Payments for support of additional dependents not living at your home	$ _____
Regular expenses from operation of business, profession, or farm (attach detailed statement)	$ _____
Other _____	$ _____
TOTAL MONTHLY EXPENSES (Report also on Summary of Schedules)	$ _____

[FOR CHAPTER 12 AND 13 DEBTORS ONLY]
Provide the information requested below, including whether plan payments are to be made bi-weekly, monthly, annually, or at some other regular interval.

A. Total projected monthly income	$ _____
B. Total projected monthly expenses	$ _____
C. Excess income (A minus B)	$ _____
D. Total amount to be paid into plan each _____ (interval)	

In re: _____ Case No. _____
           Debtor

CONTINUATION SHEET TO SCHEDULE ____

FORM B6-Cont.
(6/90)

UNITED STATES BANKRUPTCY COURT

_____ District of _____

In re _____,   Case No. _____
　　　　　　　Debtor   (If known)

SUMMARY OF SCHEDULES

Indicate as to each schedule whether that schedule is attached and state the number of pages in each. Report the totals from Schedules A, B, D, E, F, I, and J in the boxes provided. Add the amounts from Schedules A and B to determine the total amount of the debtor's assets. Add the amounts from Schedules D, E, and F to determine the total amount of the debtor's liabilities.

AMOUNTS SCHEDULED

NAME OF SCHEDULE	ATTACHED (YES/NO)	NO. OF SHEETS	ASSETS	LIABILITIES	OTHER
A - Real Property			$		
B - Personal Property			$		
C - Property Claimed as Exempt					
D - Creditors Holding Secured Claims				$	
E - Creditors Holding Unsecured Priority Claims				$	
F - Creditors Holding Unsecured Nonpriority Claims				$	
G - Executory Contracts and Unexpired Leases					
H - Codebtors					
I - Current Income of Individual Debtor(s)					$
J - Current Expenditures of Individual Debtor(s)					$
	Total Number of Sheets of ALL Schedules				
		Total Assets	$		
			Total Liabilities	$	

Official Form 6-Cont.
(12/03)

In re _____ ,   Case No. _____
               Debtor   **(If known)**

DECLARATION CONCERNING DEBTOR'S SCHEDULES

DECLARATION UNDER PENALTY OF PERJURY BY INDIVIDUAL DEBTOR

I declare under penalty of perjury that I have read the foregoing summary and schedules, consisting of _____
                                                                                                   (Total shown on summary page plus 1.)
sheets, and that they are true and correct to the best of my knowledge, information, and belief.

Date _____   Signature: _____
                                                                      Debtor

Date _____   Signature: _____
                                                                 (Joint Debtor, if any)

                                          [If joint case, both spouses must sign.]

CERTIFICATION AND SIGNATURE OF NON-ATTORNEY BANKRUPTCY PETITION PREPARER (See 11 U.S.C. § 110)

I certify that I am a bankruptcy petition preparer as defined in 11 U.S.C. § 110, that I prepared this document for compensation, and that I have provided the debtor with a copy of this document.

_____   _____
Printed or Typed Name of Bankruptcy Petition Preparer   Social Security No.
                                                         (Required by 11 U.S.C. § 110(c).)

_____
Address

Names and Social Security numbers of all other individuals who prepared or assisted in preparing this document:

If more than one person prepared this document, attach additional signed sheets conforming to the appropriate Official Form for each person.

X _____   _____
Signature of Bankruptcy Petition Preparer   Date

A bankruptcy petition preparer's failure to comply with the provisions of title 11 and the Federal Rules of Bankruptcy Procedure may result in fines or imprisonment or both. 11 U.S.C. § 110; 18 U.S.C. § 156.

DECLARATION UNDER PENALTY OF PERJURY ON BEHALF OF A CORPORATION OR PARTNERSHIP

I, the _____ [the president or other officer or an authorized agent of the corporation or a member or an authorized agent of the partnership] of the _____ [corporation or partnership] named as debtor in this case, declare under penalty of perjury that I have read the foregoing summary and schedules, consisting of _____ sheets, and that they are true and correct to the best of my knowledge, information, and belief.   *(Total shown on summary page plus 1.)*

Date _____   Signature: _____

                                                     _____
                                                     [Print or type name of individual signing on behalf of debtor.]

[An individual signing on behalf of a partnership or corporation must indicate position or relationship to debtor.]

Penalty for making a false statement or concealing property: Fine of up to $500,000 or imprisonment for up to 5 years or both. 18 U.S.C. §§ 152 and 3571.

Form 7
(12/03)

FORM 7. STATEMENT OF FINANCIAL AFFAIRS

UNITED STATES BANKRUPTCY COURT

_____ DISTRICT OF _____

In re: _____, Case No. _____
           (Name)   Debtor   (if known)

STATEMENT OF FINANCIAL AFFAIRS

      This statement is to be completed by every debtor. Spouses filing a joint petition may file a single statement on which the information for both spouses is combined. If the case is filed under chapter 12 or chapter 13, a married debtor must furnish information for both spouses whether or not a joint petition is filed, unless the spouses are separated and a joint petition is not filed. An individual debtor engaged in business as a sole proprietor, partner, family farmer, or self-employed professional, should provide the information requested on this statement concerning all such activities as well as the individual's personal affairs.

      Questions 1 - 18 are to be completed by all debtors. Debtors that are or have been in business, as defined below, also must complete Questions 19 - 25. **If the answer to an applicable question is "None," mark the box labeled "None."** If additional space is needed for the answer to any question, use and attach a separate sheet properly identified with the case name, case number (if known), and the number of the question.

DEFINITIONS

      "In business." A debtor is "in business" for the purpose of this form if the debtor is a corporation or partnership. An individual debtor is "in business" for the purpose of this form if the debtor is or has been, within the six years immediately preceding the filing of this bankruptcy case, any of the following: an officer, director, managing executive, or owner of 5 percent or more of the voting or equity securities of a corporation; a partner, other than a limited partner, of a partnership; a sole proprietor or self-employed.

      "Insider." The term "insider" includes but is not limited to: relatives of the debtor; general partners of the debtor and their relatives; corporations of which the debtor is an officer, director, or person in control; officers, directors, and any owner of 5 percent or more of the voting or equity securities of a corporate debtor and their relatives; affiliates of the debtor and insiders of such affiliates; any managing agent of the debtor. 11 U.S.C. § 101.

---

    1. Income from employment or operation of business

None   State the gross amount of income the debtor has received from employment, trade, or profession, or from operation of
☐   the debtor's business from the beginning of this calendar year to the date this case was commenced. State also the gross amounts received during the **two years** immediately preceding this calendar year. (A debtor that maintains, or has maintained, financial records on the basis of a fiscal rather than a calendar year may report fiscal year income. Identify the beginning and ending dates of the debtor's fiscal year.) If a joint petition is filed, state income for each spouse separately. (Married debtors filing under chapter 12 or chapter 13 must state income of both spouses whether or not a joint petition is filed, unless the spouses are separated and a joint petition is not filed.)

                AMOUNT   SOURCE (if more than one)

2

2. **Income other than from employment or operation of business**

None ☐ State the amount of income received by the debtor other than from employment, trade, profession, or operation of the debtor's business during the **two years** immediately preceding the commencement of this case. Give particulars. If a joint petition is filed, state income for each spouse separately. (Married debtors filing under chapter 12 or chapter 13 must state income for each spouse whether or not a joint petition is filed, unless the spouses are separated and a joint petition is not filed.)

AMOUNT   SOURCE

3. **Payments to creditors**

None ☐ a. List all payments on loans, installment purchases of goods or services, and other debts, aggregating more than $600 to any creditor, made within **90 days** immediately preceding the commencement of this case. (Married debtors filing under chapter 12 or chapter 13 must include payments by either or both spouses whether or not a joint petition is filed, unless the spouses are separated and a joint petition is not filed.)

NAME AND ADDRESS OF CREDITOR	DATES OF PAYMENTS	AMOUNT PAID	AMOUNT STILL OWING

None ☐ b. List all payments made within **one year** immediately preceding the commencement of this case to or for the benefit of creditors who are or were insiders. (Married debtors filing under chapter 12 or chapter 13 must include payments by either or both spouses whether or not a joint petition is filed, unless the spouses are separated and a joint petition is not filed.)

NAME AND ADDRESS OF CREDITOR AND RELATIONSHIP TO DEBTOR	DATE OF PAYMENT	AMOUNT PAID	AMOUNT STILL OWING

4. **Suits and administrative proceedings, executions, garnishments and attachments**

None ☐ a. List all suits and administrative proceedings to which the debtor is or was a party within **one year** immediately preceding the filing of this bankruptcy case. (Married debtors filing under chapter 12 or chapter 13 must include information concerning either or both spouses whether or not a joint petition is filed, unless the spouses are separated and a joint petition is not filed.)

CAPTION OF SUIT AND CASE NUMBER	NATURE OF PROCEEDING	COURT OR AGENCY AND LOCATION	STATUS OR DISPOSITION

None ☐   b.   Describe all property that has been attached, garnished or seized under any legal or equitable process within **one year** immediately preceding the commencement of this case. (Married debtors filing under chapter 12 or chapter 13 must include information concerning property of either or both spouses whether or not a joint petition is filed, unless the spouses are separated and a joint petition is not filed.)

NAME AND ADDRESS OF PERSON FOR WHOSE BENEFIT PROPERTY WAS SEIZED	DATE OF SEIZURE	DESCRIPTION AND VALUE OF PROPERTY

5. Repossessions, foreclosures and returns

None ☐ List all property that has been repossessed by a creditor, sold at a foreclosure sale, transferred through a deed in lieu of foreclosure or returned to the seller, within **one year** immediately preceding the commencement of this case. (Married debtors filing under chapter 12 or chapter 13 must include information concerning property of either or both spouses whether or not a joint petition is filed, unless the spouses are separated and a joint petition is not filed.)

NAME AND ADDRESS OF CREDITOR OR SELLER	DATE OF REPOSSESSION, FORECLOSURE SALE, TRANSFER OR RETURN	DESCRIPTION AND VALUE OF PROPERTY

6. Assignments and receiverships

None ☐   a.   Describe any assignment of property for the benefit of creditors made within **120 days** immediately preceding the commencement of this case. (Married debtors filing under chapter 12 or chapter 13 must include any assignment by either or both spouses whether or not a joint petition is filed, unless the spouses are separated and a joint petition is not filed.)

NAME AND ADDRESS OF ASSIGNEE	DATE OF ASSIGNMENT	TERMS OF ASSIGNMENT OR SETTLEMENT

None ☐   b.   List all property which has been in the hands of a custodian, receiver, or court-appointed official within **one year** immediately preceding the commencement of this case. (Married debtors filing under chapter 12 or chapter 13 must include information concerning property of either or both spouses whether or not a joint petition is filed, unless the spouses are separated and a joint petition is not filed.)

NAME AND ADDRESS OF CUSTODIAN	NAME AND LOCATION OF COURT CASE TITLE & NUMBER	DATE OF ORDER	DESCRIPTION AND VALUE OF PROPERTY

7. Gifts

None ☐ List all gifts or charitable contributions made within **one year** immediately preceding the commencement of this case except ordinary and usual gifts to family members aggregating less than $200 in value per individual family member and charitable contributions aggregating less than $100 per recipient. (Married debtors filing under chapter 12 or chapter 13 must include gifts or contributions by either or both spouses whether or not a joint petition is filed, unless the spouses are separated and a joint petition is not filed.)

NAME AND ADDRESS OF PERSON OR ORGANIZATION	RELATIONSHIP TO DEBTOR, IF ANY	DATE OF GIFT	DESCRIPTION AND VALUE OF GIFT

8. Losses

None ☐ List all losses from fire, theft, other casualty or gambling within **one year** immediately preceding the commencement of this case **or since the commencement of this case**. (Married debtors filing under chapter 12 or chapter 13 must include losses by either or both spouses whether or not a joint petition is filed, unless the spouses are separated and a joint petition is not filed.)

DESCRIPTION AND VALUE OF PROPERTY	DESCRIPTION OF CIRCUMSTANCES AND, IF LOSS WAS COVERED IN WHOLE OR IN PART BY INSURANCE, GIVE PARTICULARS	DATE OF LOSS

9. Payments related to debt counseling or bankruptcy

None ☐ List all payments made or property transferred by or on behalf of the debtor to any persons, including attorneys, for consultation concerning debt consolidation, relief under the bankruptcy law or preparation of a petition in bankruptcy within **one year** immediately preceding the commencement of this case.

NAME AND ADDRESS OF PAYEE	DATE OF PAYMENT, NAME OF PAYOR IF OTHER THAN DEBTOR	AMOUNT OF MONEY OR DESCRIPTION AND VALUE OF PROPERTY

10. Other transfers

None ☐ List all other property, other than property transferred in the ordinary course of the business or financial affairs of the debtor, transferred either absolutely or as security within **one year** immediately preceding the commencement of this case. (Married debtors filing under chapter 12 or chapter 13 must include transfers by either or both spouses whether or not a joint petition is filed, unless the spouses are separated and a joint petition is not filed.)

NAME AND ADDRESS OF TRANSFEREE, RELATIONSHIP TO DEBTOR	DATE	DESCRIBE PROPERTY TRANSFERRED AND VALUE RECEIVED

11. Closed financial accounts

None ☐ List all financial accounts and instruments held in the name of the debtor or for the benefit of the debtor which were closed, sold, or otherwise transferred within **one year** immediately preceding the commencement of this case. Include checking, savings, or other financial accounts, certificates of deposit, or other instruments; shares and share accounts held in banks, credit unions, pension funds, cooperatives, associations, brokerage houses and other financial institutions. (Married debtors filing under chapter 12 or chapter 13 must include information concerning accounts or instruments held by or for either or both spouses whether or not a joint petition is filed, unless the spouses are separated and a joint petition is not filed.)

NAME AND ADDRESS OF INSTITUTION	TYPE OF ACCOUNT, LAST FOUR DIGITS OF ACCOUNT NUMBER, AND AMOUNT OF FINAL BALANCE	AMOUNT AND DATE OF SALE OR CLOSING

12. Safe deposit boxes

None ☐ List each safe deposit or other box or depository in which the debtor has or had securities, cash, or other valuables within **one year** immediately preceding the commencement of this case. (Married debtors filing under chapter 12 or chapter 13 must include boxes or depositories of either or both spouses whether or not a joint petition is filed, unless the spouses are separated and a joint petition is not filed.)

NAME AND ADDRESS OF BANK OR OTHER DEPOSITORY	NAMES AND ADDRESSES OF THOSE WITH ACCESS TO BOX OR DEPOSITORY	DESCRIPTION OF CONTENTS	DATE OF TRANSFER OR SURRENDER, IF ANY

13. Setoffs

None ☐ List all setoffs made by any creditor, including a bank, against a debt or deposit of the debtor within **90 days** preceding the commencement of this case. (Married debtors filing under chapter 12 or chapter 13 must include information concerning either or both spouses whether or not a joint petition is filed, unless the spouses are separated and a joint petition is not filed.)

NAME AND ADDRESS OF CREDITOR	DATE OF SETOFF	AMOUNT OF SETOFF

14. Property held for another person

None ☐ List all property owned by another person that the debtor holds or controls.

NAME AND ADDRESS OF OWNER	DESCRIPTION AND VALUE OF PROPERTY	LOCATION OF PROPERTY

6

15. Prior address of debtor

None ☐ If the debtor has moved within the **two years** immediately preceding the commencement of this case, list all premises which the debtor occupied during that period and vacated prior to the commencement of this case. If a joint petition is filed, report also any separate address of either spouse.

ADDRESS   NAME USED   DATES OF OCCUPANCY

---

16. Spouses and Former Spouses

None ☐ If the debtor resides or resided in a community property state, commonwealth, or territory (including Alaska, Arizona, California, Idaho, Louisiana, Nevada, New Mexico, Puerto Rico, Texas, Washington, or Wisconsin) within the **six-year period** immediately preceding the commencement of the case, identify the name of the debtor's spouse and of any former spouse who resides or resided with the debtor in the community property state.

NAME

---

17. Environmental Information.

For the purpose of this question, the following definitions apply:

"Environmental Law" means any federal, state, or local statute or regulation regulating pollution, contamination, releases of hazardous or toxic substances, wastes or material into the air, land, soil, surface water, groundwater, or other medium, including, but not limited to, statutes or regulations regulating the cleanup of these substances, wastes, or material.

"Site" means any location, facility, or property as defined under any Environmental Law, whether or not presently or formerly owned or operated by the debtor, including, but not limited to, disposal sites.

"Hazardous Material" means anything defined as a hazardous waste, hazardous substance, toxic substance, hazardous material, pollutant, or contaminant or similar term under an Environmental Law

None ☐ a. List the name and address of every site for which the debtor has received notice in writing by a governmental unit that it may be liable or potentially liable under or in violation of an Environmental Law. Indicate the governmental unit, the date of the notice, and, if known, the Environmental Law:

SITE NAME   NAME AND ADDRESS   DATE OF   ENVIRONMENTAL
AND ADDRESS   OF GOVERNMENTAL UNIT   NOTICE   LAW

None ☐ b. List the name and address of every site for which the debtor provided notice to a governmental unit of a release of Hazardous Material. Indicate the governmental unit to which the notice was sent and the date of the notice.

SITE NAME   NAME AND ADDRESS   DATE OF   ENVIRONMENTAL
AND ADDRESS   OF GOVERNMENTAL UNIT   NOTICE   LAW

None ☐ c. List all judicial or administrative proceedings, including settlements or orders, under any Environmental Law with respect to which the debtor is or was a party. Indicate the name and address of the governmental unit that is or was a party to the proceeding, and the docket number.

NAME AND ADDRESS OF GOVERNMENTAL UNIT	DOCKET NUMBER	STATUS OR DISPOSITION

18. Nature, location and name of business

None ☐ a. If the debtor is an individual, list the names, addresses, taxpayer identification numbers, nature of the businesses, and beginning and ending dates of all businesses in which the debtor was an officer, director, partner, or managing executive of a corporation, partnership, sole proprietorship, or was a self-employed professional within the **six years** immediately preceding the commencement of this case, or in which the debtor owned 5 percent or more of the voting or equity securities within the **six years** immediately preceding the commencement of this case.

If the debtor is a partnership, list the names, addresses, taxpayer identification numbers, nature of the businesses, and beginning and ending dates of all businesses in which the debtor was a partner or owned 5 percent or more of the voting or equity securities, within the **six years** immediately preceding the commencement of this case.

If the debtor is a corporation, list the names, addresses, taxpayer identification numbers, nature of the businesses, and beginning and ending dates of all businesses in which the debtor was a partner or owned 5 percent or more of the voting or equity securities within the **six years** immediately preceding the commencement of this case.

NAME	TAXPAYER I.D. NO. (EIN)	ADDRESS	NATURE OF BUSINESS	BEGINNING AND ENDING DATES

None ☐ b. Identify any business listed in response to subdivision a., above, that is "single asset real estate" as defined in 11 U.S.C. § 101.

NAME	ADDRESS

The following questions are to be completed by every debtor that is a corporation or partnership and by any individual debtor who is or has been, within the **six years** immediately preceding the commencement of this case, any of the following: an officer, director, managing executive, or owner of more than 5 percent of the voting or equity securities of a corporation; a partner, other than a limited partner, of a partnership; a sole proprietor or otherwise self-employed.

*(An individual or joint debtor should complete this portion of the statement **only** if the debtor is or has been in business, as defined above, within the six years immediately preceding the commencement of this case. A debtor who has not been in business within those six years should go directly to the signature page.)*

8

19. Books, records and financial statements

None ☐ a. List all bookkeepers and accountants who within the **two years** immediately preceding the filing of this bankruptcy case kept or supervised the keeping of books of account and records of the debtor.

NAME AND ADDRESS   DATES SERVICES RENDERED

None ☐ b. List all firms or individuals who within the **two years** immediately preceding the filing of this bankruptcy case have audited the books of account and records, or prepared a financial statement of the debtor.

NAME   ADDRESS   DATES SERVICES RENDERED

None ☐ c. List all firms or individuals who at the time of the commencement of this case were in possession of the books of account and records of the debtor. If any of the books of account and records are not available, explain.

NAME   ADDRESS

None ☐ d. List all financial institutions, creditors and other parties, including mercantile and trade agencies, to whom a financial statement was issued within the **two years** immediately preceding the commencement of this case by the debtor.

NAME AND ADDRESS   DATE ISSUED

20. Inventories

None ☐ a. List the dates of the last two inventories taken of your property, the name of the person who supervised the taking of each inventory, and the dollar amount and basis of each inventory.

DATE OF INVENTORY   INVENTORY SUPERVISOR   DOLLAR AMOUNT OF INVENTORY
                                             (Specify cost, market or other basis)

None ☐ b. List the name and address of the person having possession of the records of each of the two inventories reported in a., above.

DATE OF INVENTORY   NAME AND ADDRESSES OF CUSTODIAN
                                            OF INVENTORY RECORDS

9

21. Current Partners, Officers, Directors and Shareholders

None ☐   a.   If the debtor is a partnership, list the nature and percentage of partnership interest of each member of the partnership.

       NAME AND ADDRESS   NATURE OF INTEREST   PERCENTAGE OF INTEREST

None ☐   b.   If the debtor is a corporation, list all officers and directors of the corporation, and each stockholder who directly or indirectly owns, controls, or holds 5 percent or more of the voting or equity securities of the corporation.

       NAME AND ADDRESS   TITLE   NATURE AND PERCENTAGE OF STOCK OWNERSHIP

22. Former partners, officers, directors and shareholders

None ☐   a.   If the debtor is a partnership, list each member who withdrew from the partnership within **one year** immediately preceding the commencement of this case.

       NAME   ADDRESS   DATE OF WITHDRAWAL

None ☐   b.   If the debtor is a corporation, list all officers, or directors whose relationship with the corporation terminated within **one year** immediately preceding the commencement of this case.

       NAME AND ADDRESS   TITLE   DATE OF TERMINATION

23. Withdrawals from a partnership or distributions by a corporation

None ☐   If the debtor is a partnership or corporation, list all withdrawals or distributions credited or given to an insider, including compensation in any form, bonuses, loans, stock redemptions, options exercised and any other perquisite during **one year** immediately preceding the commencement of this case.

NAME & ADDRESS OF RECIPIENT, RELATIONSHIP TO DEBTOR   DATE AND PURPOSE OF WITHDRAWAL   AMOUNT OF MONEY OR DESCRIPTION AND VALUE OF PROPERTY

24. Tax Consolidation Group.

None ☐ If the debtor is a corporation, list the name and federal taxpayer identification number of the parent corporation of any consolidated group for tax purposes of which the debtor has been a member at any time within the **six-year period** immediately preceding the commencement of the case.

NAME OF PARENT CORPORATION   TAXPAYER IDENTIFICATION NUMBER (EIN)

25. Pension Funds.

None ☐ If the debtor is not an individual, list the name and federal taxpayer identification number of any pension fund to which the debtor, as an employer, has been responsible for contributing at any time within the **six-year period** immediately preceding the commencement of the case.

NAME OF PENSION FUND   TAXPAYER IDENTIFICATION NUMBER (EIN)

* * * * *

[If completed by an individual or individual and spouse]

I declare under penalty of perjury that I have read the answers contained in the foregoing statement of financial affairs and any attachments thereto and that they are true and correct.

Date _____   Signature _____
                                  of Debtor

Date _____   Signature _____
                                  of Joint Debtor
                                  (if any)

_____

[If completed on behalf of a partnership or corporation]

I declare under penalty of perjury that I have read the answers contained in the foregoing statement of financial affairs and any attachments thereto and that they are true and correct to the best of my knowledge, information and belief.

Date _____   Signature _____

                                 _____
                                 Print Name and Title

[An individual signing on behalf of a partnership or corporation must indicate position or relationship to debtor.]

_____ continuation sheets attached

Penalty for making a false statement: Fine of up to $500,000 or imprisonment for up to 5 years, or both. 18 U.S.C. § 152 and 3571

CERTIFICATION AND SIGNATURE OF NON-ATTORNEY BANKRUPTCY PETITION PREPARER (See 11 U.S.C. § 110)

I certify that I am a bankruptcy petition preparer as defined in 11 U.S.C. § 110, that I prepared this document for compensation, and that I have provided the debtor with a copy of this document.

_____   _____
Printed or Typed Name of Bankruptcy Petition Preparer   Social Security No.
                                                           (Required by 11 U.S.C. § 110(c).)

_____
Address

Names and Social Security numbers of all other individuals who prepared or assisted in preparing this document:

If more than one person prepared this document, attach additional signed sheets conforming to the appropriate Official Form for each person.

X_____   _____
Signature of Bankruptcy Petition Preparer   Date

A bankruptcy petition preparer's failure to comply with the provisions of title 11 and the Federal Rules of Bankruptcy Procedure may result in fines or imprisonment or both. 18 U.S.C. § 156.

Form B 21 Official Form 21
(12/03)

UNITED STATES BANKRUPTCY COURT
_____ District of _____

In re _____,   Case No. _____
                  Debtor   **(If known)**

STATEMENT OF SOCIAL SECURITY NUMBER(S)

1. Name of Debtor (enter Last, First, Middle):_____
(Check the appropriate box and, if applicable, provide the required information.)

    / /Debtor has a Social Security Number and it is: ___-__-____
        (If more than one, state all.)
    / /Debtor does not have a Social Security Number.

2. Name of Joint Debtor (enter Last, First, Middle):_____
(Check the appropriate box and, if applicable, provide the required information.)

    / /Joint Debtor has a Social Security Number and it is: ___-__-____
        (If more than one, state all.)
    / /Joint Debtor does not have a Social Security Number.

I declare under penalty of perjury that the foregoing is true and correct.

        X _____
            Signature of Debtor   Date

        X _____
            Signature of Joint Debtor   Date

<u>Joint debtors must provide information for both spouses.</u>
Penalty for making a false statement: Fine of up to $250,000 or up to 5 years imprisonment or both. 18 U.S.C. §§ 152 and 3571.

Official Form 8
(12/03)

United States Bankruptcy Court
_____ District Of _____

In re _____,
            Debtor

Case No. _____

Chapter 7

CHAPTER 7 INDIVIDUAL DEBTOR'S STATEMENT OF INTENTION

1. I have filed a schedule of assets and liabilities which includes consumer debts secured by property of the estate.

2. I intend to do the following with respect to the property of the estate which secures those consumer debts:

    a. *Property to Be Surrendered.*

Description of Property   **Creditor's name**

    b. *Property to Be Retained*   *[Check any applicable statement.]*

Description of Property	Creditor's Name	Property is claimed as exempt	Property will be redeemed pursuant to 11 U.S.C. § 722	Debt will be reaffirmed pursuant to 11 U.S.C. § 524(c)

Date: _____   _____
                                                                                                Signature of Debtor

---

CERTIFICATION OF NON-ATTORNEY BANKRUPTCY PETITION PREPARER (See 11 U.S.C. § 110)

I certify that I am a bankruptcy petition preparer as defined in 11 U.S.C. § 110, that I prepared this document for compensation, and that I have provided the debtor with a copy of this document.

_____   _____
Printed or Typed Name of Bankruptcy Petition Preparer   Social Security No.
                                                                            (Required by 11 U.S.C. § 110(c).)

_____
Address

Names and Social Security Numbers of all other individuals who prepared or assisted in preparing this document.

If more than one person prepared this document, attach additional signed sheets conforming to the appropriate Official Form for each person.

X_____   _____
Signature of Bankruptcy Petition Preparer   Date

A bankruptcy petition preparer's failure to comply with the provisions of title 11 and the Federal Rules of Bankruptcy Procedure may result in fines or imprisonment or both. 11 U.S.C. § 110; 18 U.S.C. § 156.

Official Form 3
(12/03)

United States Bankruptcy Court
_____ District Of _____

In re _____,   Case No. _____
            Debtor
                                          Chapter 7

APPLICATION TO PAY FILING FEE IN INSTALLMENTS

1. In accordance with Fed. R. Bankr. P. 1006, I apply for permission to pay the Filing Fee amounting to $_____ in installments.

2. I certify that I am unable to pay the Filing Fee except in installments.

3. I further certify that I have not paid any money or transferred any property to an attorney for services in connection with this case and that I will neither make any payment nor transfer any property for services in connection with this case until the filing fee is paid in full.

4. I propose the following terms for the payment of the Filing Fee.*

   $ _____   Check one ☐ With the filing of the petition, or
                              ☐ On or before _____

   $ _____   on or before _____

   $ _____   on or before _____

   $ _____   on or before _____

* The number of installments proposed shall not exceed four (4), and the final installment shall be payable not later than 120 days after filing the petition. For cause shown, the court may extend the time of any installment, provided the last installment is paid not later than 180 days after filing the petition. Fed. R. Bankr. P. 1006(b)(2).

5. I understand that if I fail to pay any installment when due my bankruptcy case may be dismissed and I may not receive a discharge of my debts.

_____   _____
Signature of Attorney   Date   Signature of Debtor   Date
                                         (In a joint case, both spouses must sign.)

_____   _____
Name of Attorney   Signature of Joint Debtor (if any)   Date

CERTIFICATION AND SIGNATURE OF NON-ATTORNEY BANKRUPTCY PETITION PREPARER (See 11 U.S.C. § 110)

I certify that I am a bankruptcy petition preparer as defined in 11 U.S.C. § 110, that I prepared this document for compensation, and that I have provided the debtor with a copy of this document. I also certify that I will not accept money or any other property from the debtor before the filing fee is paid in full.

_____   _____
Printed or Typed Name of Bankruptcy Petition Preparer   Social Security No.
                                         (Required by 11 U.S.C. § 110(c).)

_____
Address

Names and Social Security numbers of all other individuals who prepared or assisted in preparing this document:

If more than one person prepared this document, attach additional signed sheets conforming to the appropriate Official Form for each person.

x_____   _____
Signature of Bankruptcy Petition Preparer   Date

A bankruptcy petition preparer's failure to comply with the provisions of title 11 and the Federal Rules of Bankruptcy Procedure may result in fines or imprisonment or both. 11 U.S.C. § 110; 18 U.S.C. § 156.

Official Form 3 continued
(9/97)

United States Bankruptcy Court
_____ District Of _____

In re _____,   Case No. _____
         Debtor

                                     Chapter 7

ORDER APPROVING PAYMENT OF FILING FEE IN INSTALLMENTS

      IT IS ORDERED that the debtor(s) may pay the filing fee in installments on the terms proposed in the foregoing application.

      IT IS FURTHER ORDERED that until the filing fee is paid in full the debtor shall not pay any money for services in connection with this case, and the debtor shall not relinquish any property as payment for services in connection with this case.

      BY THE COURT

Date: _____   _____
                                United States Bankruptcy Judge

Appendix B: State and Federal Bankruptcy Exemptions

On the following pages, you will find an alphabetical state-by-state listing of state bankruptcy exemptions. In addition, at the end of this appendix you will find a listing for federal bankruptcy exemptions and federal non-bankruptcy exemptions. In all states, you can use both the state and federal non-bankruptcy exemptions. In addition, residents of Arkansas, Connecticut, the District of Columbia, Hawaii, Massachusetts, Michigan, Minnesota, New Jersey, New Mexico, Pennsylvania, Rhode Island, South Carolina, Texas, Vermont, Washington, and Wisconsin have a choice. They may choose to use either their state exemptions and the federal non-bankruptcy exemptions or they can choose to use only the federal bankruptcy exemptions as listed at the end of the appendix of state exemptions. If residents of these states choose to use the federal bankruptcy exemptions, they cannot use the state exemptions or the federal non-bankruptcy exemptions. The first item in each listing will explain whether you can use the state exemptions and federal non-bankruptcy exemptions only or can choose between those and the federal bankruptcy exemptions. California residents may choose between two different state exemption systems and can use the federal non-bankruptcy exemptions with either state system. You should read through the entire listing for your state. Using your completed Schedules A: Real Property and B: Personal Property, determine which of your property falls into any of the categories. On a separate worksheet, list the property that you feel is exempt under your state's laws. Then do the same for the federal non-bankruptcy exemptions. If your state does not allow a choice, fill in the property that you have determined is exempt on your Schedule C: Property Claimed as Exempt. If your state allows a choice, make another listing for the federal bankruptcy exemptions. Now, compare the state/federal non-bankruptcy exemption list with the federal bankruptcy exemption list. Decide which exemption list allows you to retain the most property and list that property on Schedule C. In general, all of your property is either personal property or real estate. Real estate includes all land and the buildings or improvements that are permanently attached to the land. All of the rest of your property is considered personal property. Personal property can be divided further into two categories: *tangible property* (property you can see and touch, such as artwork or a car) and *intangible property* (property that represents some type of ownership, such as stocks, bonds, copyrights, etc.). If you are unclear of the meaning of the language in the statute, check the Glossary of Bankruptcy Legal Terms at the end of this book for explanations. In general, each of the listings will indicate exemptions under the following general categories:

Benefits: This listing contains various governmental benefits that are exempt from bankruptcy. This may include workers' compensation, unemployment payments, welfare payments, veterans' benefits and other government benefits. Private benefits are listed under either "Insurance" or "Pensions."

Insurance: Under this listing you will find any insurance-related property, including the cash value of your insurance policies, private annuity and disability proceeds, and various other insurance-based assets.

Miscellaneous: This listing includes those types of property that are not listed elsewhere. This category most often includes property of a business partnership and exemption amounts that may be applied to any property (whether real estate or personal property).

Pensions: Under this list are those items of property that are related to retirement. Various pensions, IRAs, KEOGHs, and other retirement plans are included. Also listed are certain profit-sharing plans that are exempt.

Personal Property: This listing contains all of the personal property that is specifically exempt from bankruptcy. It is under this listing that you will most likely find property that you can keep after your bankruptcy. Every item listed as a state exemption (or federal, if allowed) can be retained.

Real Estate: Listed here are the real estate exemptions. These may also be referred to as homestead exemptions. In general, these allow the exemption of a fixed value amount of the worth of your personal residence. In some states, this amount is very substantial and will allow you to retain your entire house. In other states, the actual size of the property determines the exemption.

Wages: Under this listing are both general and specific wage exemptions for certain professions. Generally, 75 percent of general wages are exempt from creditors. However, check your specific state listing.

> **NOTE FOR SPOUSES**: Most states allow spouses who are filing jointly to each claim a complete set of exemptions. In other words, for joint filers, you can list exemptions for double the amounts that are shown under your state's listing. There are a few exceptions to this. Check your specific state's listings. If in doubt, claim double the exemption amount if filing jointly.

Alabama

Alabama residents cannot use the Federal Bankruptcy Exemptions, but may use the Federal Non-Bankruptcy Exemptions listed at the end of this Appendix and the following state exemptions:

Benefits: Aid to aged, blind, disabled, and families with dependent children (unlimited amount): Alabama Code 38-4-8; Coal miners pneumoconiosis benefits (unlimited amount): Alabama Code 25-5-179; Southeast Asian War POW benefits (unlimited amount): Alabama Code 31-7-2; Unemployment compensation (unlimited amount): Alabama Code 25-4-140; Workers compensation (unlimited amount): Alabama Code 25-5-86.

Insurance: Annuity proceeds (up to $250 per month): Alabama Code 27-14-32; Disability proceeds (up to an average of $250 per month): Alabama Code 27-14-31; Fraternal society benefits (unlimited amount): Alabama Code 27-34-27; Life insurance proceeds if beneficiary is insured's spouse or child (unlimited amount): Alabama Code 6-10-8 & 27-14-29; Life insurance proceeds if policy prohibits use to pay creditors (unlimited amount): Alabama Code 27-15-26; Mutual aid association benefits (unlimited amount): Alabama Code 27-30-25.

Miscellaneous: Property of business partnership (unlimited amount): Alabama Code 10-8-72 (b)(3). (This provision has been repealed effective on January 1, 2001).

Pensions: Judges (payments actually being received): Alabama Code 12-18-10(a-b); Law enforcement officers (unlimited amount): Alabama Code 36-21-77; State employees (unlimited amount): Alabama Code 36-27-28; Teachers (unlimited amount): Alabama Code 16-25-23.

Personal Property: Any personal property not listed below, except life insurance (up to $3,000 total): Alabama Code 6-10-6; Arms, uniforms, and equipment required for military use (unlimited amount): Alabama Code 31-2-78; Books (unlimited amount): Alabama Code 6-10-6; Burial lot (unlimited amount): Alabama Code 6-10-5; Church pew (unlimited amount): Alabama Code 6-10-5; Clothing needed (unlimited amount): Alabama Code 6-10-6; Crops (unlimited amount): Alabama Code 6-9-41; Family portraits or pictures (unlimited amount): Alabama Code 6-10-6.

Real Estate: Real property or mobile home (up to $5,000): Alabama Code 6-10-2; up to 160 acres, husband and wife may double the amount, must file homestead exemption with Probate Court to be effective: Alabama Code 6-10-2.

Wages: 75% of earned but unpaid wages (judge may allow more for low-income debtors): Alabama Code 6-10-7.

Alaska

Alaska residents cannot use the Federal Bankruptcy Exemptions, but may use the Federal Non-Bankruptcy Exemptions listed at the end of this Appendix and the following state exemptions. Amounts may be revised by the state in even-numbered years.

Benefits: Aid to aged, blind, disabled, and families with dependent children (unlimited amount): Alaska Statutes 47.25.210 & 47.25.550; Alaska longevity bonus (unlimited amount): Alaska Statutes 9.38.015(a)(5); Crime victims compensation (unlimited amount): Alaska Statutes 9.38.015 (a)(4); Federally exempt benefits (unlimited amount): Alaska Statutes 9.38.015(a)(6); General relief assistance (unlimited amount): Alaska Statutes 47.25.210; Permanent fund dividends (20% of amount): Alaska Statutes 43.23.065; Tuition credits under an advance college tuition payment contract (unlimited amount): Alaska Statutes 9.38.015(a)(9); Unemployment compensation (unlimited amount): Alaska Statutes 9.38.015(b) & 23.20.405; Workers compensation (unlimited amount): Alaska Statutes 233.30.160.

Insurance: Disability benefits (unlimited amount): Alaska Statutes 9.38.015(b) & 9.38.030 (e)(1), (5); Fraternal society benefits (unlimited amount): Alaska Statutes 21.84.240; Insurance proceeds or recoveries for personal injury or wrongful death (up to wage exemption amount): Alaska Statutes 9.38.030(e)(3) & 9.38.050(a); Unmatured life insurance or annuity contract loan (up to $12,000); Alaska Statutes 9.38.017 & 9.38.025; Life insurance proceeds if beneficiary is insured's spouse or dependent (up to wage exemption amount): Alaska Statutes 9.38.030(e)(4); Medical, surgical, or hospital benefits (unlimited amount): Alaska Statutes 9.38.015(a)(3).

Miscellaneous: Alimony (up to wage exemption amount): Alaska Statutes 9.38.030(e)(2); Child support payments held in an agency (unlimited amount): Alaska Statutes 25.27.095; Liquor licenses (unlimited amount): Alaska Statutes 9.38.015(a)(7); Permits for limited entry into Alaska Fisheries (unlimited amount): Alaska Statutes 9.38.015(a)(8); Property of business partnership (unlimited amount): Alaska Statutes 9.38.100(b).

Pensions: Elected public officers (unpaid benefits only): Alaska Statutes 9.38.015(b); Judicial employees (unpaid benefits only): Alaska Statutes 9.38.015(b); Other pensions (up to wage exemption amount and only for payments being paid): Alaska Statutes 9.38.030(e)(5); Public employees (unpaid benefits only): Alaska Statutes 9.38.015(b) & 39.35.505; Retirement benefits deposited more than 120 days before filing bankruptcy (unlimited amount): Alaska Statutes 9.38,017; Teachers (unpaid benefits only): Alaska Statutes 9.38.015(b).

Personal Property: Books, clothing, family portraits, heirlooms, household goods, and musical instruments (up to $3,600 total): Alaska Statutes 9.38.020(a); Building materials (unlimited amount): Alaska Statutes 34.35.105; Burial plot (unlimited amount): Alaska Statutes 9.38.015(a)(1); Health aids (unlimited amount): Alaska Statutes 9.38.015(a)(2); Implements, books, or tools of a trade (up to $3,360): Alaska Statutes 9.38.020(c); Jewelry (up to $1,200): Alaska Statutes 9.38.020(b); Motor vehicle (up to $3,600, vehicle's market value cannot exceed $20,000): Alaska Statutes 9.38.020(e); Pets (up to $1,200): Alaska Statutes 9.38.020(d); Proceeds for lost, damaged, or destroyed exempt property (up to exemption amount): Alaska Statutes 9.38.060.

Real Estate: Real property used as a residence (up to $64,800): Alaska Statutes 9.38.010.

Wages: If paid weekly, then net earnings up to $420, unless sole wage earner in household, then up to $550; if paid monthly or semi-monthly, then up to $1,680 in cash or liquid assets paid in any month, unless sole wage earner in household, then up to $2,200: Alaska Statutes 9.38.030 (a)(b) & 9.38.050(b).

Arizona

Arizona residents cannot use the Federal Bankruptcy Exemptions, but may use the Federal Non-Bankruptcy Exemptions listed at the end of this Appendix and the following state exemptions. Wife and husband may double all exemption amounts, except real estate exemption.

Benefits: Unemployment compensation (unlimited amount): Arizona Revised Statutes 23-783; Welfare benefits (unlimited amount): Arizona Revised Statutes 46-208; Workers compensation (unlimited amount): Arizona Revised Statutes 23-1068; Compensation for wrongful taking of property (unlimited amount) Arizona Revised Statutes 33-126(A)(7); Compensation for destruction or damage to property and insurance proceeds (up to $25,000): Arizona Revised Statutes 33-126(A)(4); State employee long-term disability benefits: Arizona Revised Statutes 38-791.11; Wrongful death awards: Arizona Revised Statutes 12-592.

Insurance: Fraternal society benefits (unlimited amount): Arizona Revised Statutes 20-877; Group life insurance policy or proceeds (unlimited amount): Arizona Revised Statutes 20-1132; Health, accident, or disability benefits (unlimited amount): Arizona Revised Statutes 33-1126(A)(4); Life insurance cash value (up to $1,000 per dependent, $25,000 total): Arizona Revised Statutes 33-1126(A)(6); Life insurance proceeds (up to $20,000 if beneficiary is spouse or child): Arizona Revised Statutes 33-1126(A)(1); Husband and wife may double: Arizona Revised Statutes 33-1121.01.

Miscellaneous: Property of business partnership (unlimited amount): Arizona Revised Statutes 29-225; Child support or spousal maintenance (alimony): Arizona Revised Statutes 33-1126(A)(3).

Pensions: Board of regents members, faculty, and administration under the jurisdiction of Board of Regents (unlimited amount): Arizona Revised Statutes 15-1628.02(I); Firefighters and police officers (unlimited amount): Arizona Revised Statutes 9-968 & 9-931; Rangers (unlimited amount): Arizona Revised Statutes 41-955; State employees: Arizona Revised Statutes 38-792; Retirement benefits from a qualified plan deposited more than 120 days before filing bankruptcy (unlimited amount): Arizona Revised Statutes 33-1126(C)2.

Personal Property: Appliances, furniture, household goods, and paintings (up to $4,000 total for all listed): Arizona Revised Statutes 33-1123; Arms, uniforms, and equipment required for military use (unlimited amount): Arizona Revised Statutes 33-1130(3); Bank deposit (up to $150 in 1 account, must file notice with bank): Arizona Revised Statutes 33-1126(A)(7); Bible, bicycle, sewing machine, typewriter, burial plot, rifle, pistol, or shotgun (up to $500 total): Arizona Revised Statutes 33-1125; Books (up to $250), clothing (up to $500), wedding and engagement rings (up to $1,000), watch (up to $100), pets, horses, milk cows, and poultry (up to $500), and musical instruments (up to $250): Arizona Revised Statutes 33-1125; Farm machinery and equipment, utensils, seed, feed, grain, and animals (up to $2,500 total): Arizona Revised Statutes 33-1130(2); Food and fuel (amount to last 6 months): Arizona Revised Statutes 33-1124; Health aids (unlimited amount): Arizona Revised Statutes 33-1125; Motor vehicle (up to $5,000; up to $10,000, if disabled): 33-1125(8); Prepaid rent or security deposit (up to $1,000 or 1-1/2 times rent, whichever is less, instead of real estate exemption): Arizona Revised Statutes 33-1126(D); Proceeds for sold or damaged exempt property (up to exemption amount): Arizona Revised Statutes 33-1126(A)(4), (6); Tools, equipment, instruments, and books, except vehicle driven to work (up to $2,500): Arizona Revised Statutes 33-1130(1); Teaching aids of teacher (unlimited amount): Arizona Revised Statutes 33-1127; Pre-arranged funeral trust: Arizona Revised Statutes 32-1391.05.

Real Estate: Real estate, apartment, or mobile home used as residence (up to $100,000); sale proceeds are exempt for 18 months or until new home is purchased, whichever occurs first; must record homestead declaration: Arizona Revised Statutes 33-1101(A), 33-1102.

Wages: Minor child's earnings, unless debt is for child (unlimited amount): Arizona Revised Statutes 33-1126(A)(2); 25% of earned but unpaid wages or pension payments (judge may allow more for low-income debtors): Arizona Revised Statutes 33-1131.

Arkansas

Arkansas residents may use either the Federal Bankruptcy Exemptions listed at the end of this Appendix or the state exemptions listed below. If state exemptions are used, then Federal Non-Bankruptcy Exemptions listed at the end of this Appendix can also be used.

Benefits: Crime victims compensation ($10,000 limit): Arkansas Code Annotated 16-90-716(a)(1); Crime victims compensation for total and permanent disability ($25,000 limit): Arkansas Code Annotated 16-90-716(a)(2); Unemployment compensation (unlimited amount): Arkansas Code Annotated 11-10-109; Workers compensation (unlimited amount): Arkansas Code Annotated 11-9-110.

Insurance: Annuity contract (unlimited amount): Arkansas Code Annotated 23-79-134; Disability benefits (unlimited amount): Arkansas Code Annotated 23-79-133; Fraternal society benefits (unlimited amount): Arkansas Code Annotated 23-74-403; Group life insurance (unlimited amount): Arkansas Code Annotated 23-79-132; Life, health, accident, or disability cash value, or proceeds paid or due (limited to $500 personal property exemption provided by 9-1 and 9-2 of the Arkansas Constitution): Arkansas Code Annotated 16-66-209; Life insurance proceeds if policy prohibits proceeds from being used to pay creditors (unlimited amount): Arkansas Code Annotated 23-79-131; Life insurance proceeds if beneficiary is not the insured (unlimited amount): Arkansas Code Annotated 23-79-131; Mutual life or disability benefits (up to $1,000): Arkansas Code Annotated 23-72-114; Stipulated insurance premiums (unlimited amount): Arkansas Code Annotated 23-71-112.

Miscellaneous: Any property (up to $800 if single, up to $1,250 if married): Arkansas Code Annotated 16-66-218(a)(1); Property of business partnership (unlimited amount): Arkansas Code Annotated 4-42-502 (repealed beginning in 2005).

Pensions: Firefighters (unlimited amount): Arkansas Code Annotated 24-11-814; Police officers (unlimited amount): Arkansas Code Annotated 24-11-417; Firefighters (unlimited amount): Arkansas Code Annotated 24-10-616; IRA deposits (up to $20,000 if deposited at least 1 year before filing for bankruptcy): Arkansas Code Annotated 16-66-218(b)(16); Police officers (unlimited amount): Arkansas Code Annotated 24-10-616; School employees (unlimited amount): Arkansas Code Annotated 24-7-715; State police officers (unlimited amount): Arkansas Code Annotated 24-6-223.

Personal Property: Any personal property (up to $500 if married or head of household, otherwise up to $200): Arkansas Constitution 9-1 & 9-2; Arkansas Code Annotated 16-66-218(b)(1)(2); Burial plot (up to 5 acres, instead of real estate option #2): Arkansas Code Annotated 16-66-207 & 16-66-218(a)(1);

Prepaid funeral trust (unlimited amount) Arkansas Code 23-40-117; Clothing (unlimited amount): Arkansas Constitution 9-1 & 9-2; Implements, books, and tools of a trade (up to $750): Arkansas Code Annotated 16-66-218(a)(4). Motor vehicle (up to $1,200): Arkansas Code Annotated 16-66-218(a)(2); Wedding bands (unlimited amount, diamond cannot exceed ½ carat): Arkansas Code Annotated 16-66-218(a)(3).

Real Estate: Real or personal property used as residence by head of family; if property is up to 1/4 acre in city, town, village, or 80 acres elsewhere (unlimited value is exempt); if property is between 1/4 to 1 acre in city, town, or village, or 80 to 160 acres elsewhere (up to $2,500 is exempt); no homestead may exceed 1 acre in city, town, or village, or 160 acres elsewhere: Arkansas Constitution 9-3, 9-4, & 9-5; Arkansas Code Annotated 16-66-210 & 16-66-218(b)(3).

Wages: Earned but unpaid wages due for 60 days (up to $500 if married or head of household, or up to $200 otherwise): Arkansas Code Annotated 16-66-208 & 16-66-218(b)(6).

California

California residents cannot use the Federal Bankruptcy Exemptions, but may use the Federal Non-Bankruptcy Exemptions listed at the end of this Appendix and one of the following state exemption options only. Married couples cannot double any exemptions under Option #2.

California OPTION #1

Benefits: Aid to aged, blind, disabled, and families with dependent children (unlimited amount): California Code of Civil Procedure 704.170; Financial aid to students (unlimited amount): California Code of Civil Procedure 704.190; Relocation benefits (unlimited amount): California Code of Civil Procedure 704.180; Direct-deposited Social Security and/or public benefit payments (unlimited amount): California Code of Civil Procedure704.080(c); Unemployment benefits (unlimited amount): California Code of Civil Procedure 704.120; Union benefits due to labor dispute (unlimited amount): California Code of Civil Procedure 704.120(b)(5); Workers compensation (unlimited amount): California Code of Civil Procedure 704.160.

Insurance: Disability or health benefits (unlimited amount): California Code of Civil Procedure 704.130; Fidelity bonds (unlimited amount): California Code-Labor 404; Fraternal unemployment benefits (unlimited amount): California Code of Civil Procedure 704.120; Homeowners insurance proceeds up to 6 months after receipt (up to real estate exemption amount): California Code of Civil Procedure 704.720(b); Life insurance proceeds if policy prohibits proceeds from being used to pay creditors (unlimited amount): California Code-Insurance 10171; Matured life insurance benefits (amount needed for support): California Code of Civil Procedure 704.100(c); Unmatured life insurance policy loan value (up to $9,300, husband and wife may double): California Code of Civil Procedure 704.100(b).

Miscellaneous: Business or professional licenses, except liquor licenses (unlimited amount): California Code of Civil Procedure 695.060 & 708.630; Inmate's trust funds (up to $1,000): California Code of Civil Procedure 704.090(a); Inmate's trust account where judgment is for restitution fine or order (up to $300): California Code of Civil Procedure 704.090(b); Property of business partnership (unlimited amount): California Code-Corporations 16504(d).

Pensions: County employees, firefighters, and peace officers (unlimited amount): California Code-Government 31452, 31913, & 32210; Public and private retirement benefits (unlimited amount): California Code of Civil Procedure 704.110 & 704.115, Government 21201.

Personal Property: Appliances, clothing, food, and furnishings (amount needed): California Code of Civil Procedure 704.020; Bank deposits from Social Security (up to $2,000, or $3,000 for husband and wife): California Code of Civil Procedure 704.080; Books, equipment, furnishings, materials, motor vehicle if not claimed otherwise, tools, uniforms, and vessel (up to $5,000 total, up to $10,000 total for both spouses): California Code of Civil Procedure 704.060; Building materials to repair or improve home (up to $2,000): California Code of Civil Procedure 704.030; Burial plot and health aids (unlimited amount): California Code of Civil Procedure 704.050 & 704.200; Jewelry, heirlooms or art (up to $5,000 total): California Code of Civil Procedure 704.040; Motor vehicles or auto insurance proceeds if vehicle lost, damaged, or destroyed (up to $1,900): California Code of Civil Procedure 704.010; Personal injury causes of action or recovery (amount needed for support): California Code of Civil Procedure 704.140; Wrongful death causes of action or recovery (amount needed for support): California Code of Civil Procedure 704.150.

Real Estate: Real or personal property used as residence (up to $50,000 if single and not disabled, up to $75,000 for families if no other member has a homestead; up to $125,000 if: [a] 65 or older, or physically or mentally disabled; [b] 55 or older, single, earn under $15,000, and creditors seek to force the sale of your home; or [c] 55 or older, married, earn under $20,000, and creditors seek to force the sale of your home); proceeds from sale of home exempt for 6 months (husband and wife may not double): California Code of Civil Procedure 704.710, 704.720, & 704.730; California case law.

Wages: Public employee vacation credits (unlimited amount): California Code of Civil Procedure 704.113; 75% of wages paid within 30 days of filing for bankruptcy: California Code of Civil Procedure 704.070.

California OPTION #2:

Benefits: Crime victims compensation (unlimited amount): California Code of Civil Procedure 703.140 (b)(11)(A); Public assistance (unlimited amount): California Code of Civil Procedure 703.140(b)(10)(A); Social Security (unlimited amount): California Code of Civil Procedure 703.140(b)(10)(A); Unemployment compensation (unlimited amount): California Code of Civil Procedure 703.140(b)(10)(A); Veterans benefits (unlimited amount): California Code of Civil Procedure 703.140(b)(10)(B).

Insurance: Disability benefits (unlimited amount): California Code of Civil Procedure 703.140(b)(10)(C); Life insurance proceeds (up to $9,300): California Code of Civil Procedure 703.140(b)(11)(C); Unmatured life insurance contract (up to $9,300): California Code of Civil Procedure 703.140(b)(8); Unmatured life insurance policy other than credit (unlimited amount): California Code of Civil Procedure 703.140(b)(7).

Miscellaneous: Alimony and child support (amount needed for support): California Code of Civil Procedure 703.140(b)(10)(D); Any property (up to $925): California Code of Civil Procedure 703.140 (b)(5); Unused portion of real estate or burial exemption (can be used with any property): California Code of Civil Procedure 703.140(b)(5).

Pensions: Retirement benefits (amount needed for support): California Code of Civil Procedure 703.140 (b)(10)(E).

Personal Property: Animals, appliances, books, clothing, crops, furnishings, household goods, and musical instruments (up to $450 per item): California Code of Civil Procedure 703.140(b)(3); Burial plot (up to $17,425, instead of real estate exemption): California Code of Civil Procedure 703.140(b)(1); Health aids (unlimited amount): California Code of Civil Procedure 703.140 (b)(9); Implements, books, and tools of a trade (up to $1,750): California Code of Civil Procedure 703.140(b)(6); Jewelry (up to $1,150): California Code of Civil Procedure 703.140(b)(4); Motor vehicle (up to $2,775): California Code of Civil Procedure 703.140 (b)(2); Personal injury recoveries (up to $17,425, but not pain and suffering or pecuniary loss): California Code of Civil Procedure 703.140(b)(11)(D), (E); Wrongful death recoveries (amount needed for support): California Code of Civil Procedure 703.140(b)(11)(B).

Real Estate: Real or personal property, including co-op, used as residence (up to $17,425); unused portion of real estate exemption may be applied to any property: California Code of Civil Procedure 703.140(b)(1).

Wages: No exemption.

Colorado

Colorado residents cannot use the Federal Bankruptcy Exemptions, but may use the Federal Non-Bankruptcy Exemptions listed at the end of this Appendix and the following state exemptions:

Benefits: Aid to aged, blind, disabled, and families with dependent children (unlimited amount): Colorado Revised Statutes 26-2-131; Crime victims compensation (unlimited amount): Colorado Revised Statutes 13-54-102(1)(q) & 24-41-114; Unemployment compensation (unlimited amount): Colorado Revised

Statutes 8-80-103; Veterans benefits if war veteran (unlimited amount): Colorado Revised Statutes 13-54-102(1)(h); Workers compensation (unlimited amount): Colorado Revised Statutes 8-42-124.
Insurance: Disability benefits (up to $200 per month, entire amount if received as a lump sum): Colorado Revised Statutes 10-16-212; Fraternal society benefits (unlimited amount): Colorado Revised Statutes 10-14-403; Group life insurance policy or proceeds (unlimited amount): Colorado Revised Statutes 10-7-205; Homeowners insurance proceeds for 1 year after received (up to real estate exemption amount): Colorado Revised Statutes 38-41-209; Life insurance cash value or proceeds (up to $50,000): Colorado Revised Statutes 13-54-102(1)(l); Life insurance proceeds if policy prohibits proceeds from being used to pay creditors (unlimited amount): Colorado Revised Statutes 10-7-106.
Miscellaneous: Property of a business partnership (unlimited amount): Colorado Revised Statutes 7-60-125; Income tax credit refund (unlimited amount): Colorado Revised Statutes 13-54-102(1)(o).
Pensions: Firefighters (unlimited amount): Colorado Revised Statutes 31-30-1117; Police officers (unlimited amount): Colorado Revised Statutes 31-30.5-208; Public employees (unlimited amount): Colorado Revised Statutes 24-51-212 & 24-52-105; Retirement benefits, including IRAs (unlimited amount): Colorado Revised Statutes 13-54-102(1)(s); Teachers (unlimited amount): Colorado Revised Statutes 22-64-120; Veterans (unlimited amount): Colorado Revised Statutes 13-54-102(1)(h) & 13-54-104.
Personal Property: Library of professional person (up to $3,000 total): Colorado Revised Statutes 13-54-102(1)(k); Colorado Revised Statutes 13-54-102(1)(g); Business materials, supplies, machines, tools, equipment, or books: Colorado Revised Statutes 13-54-102(1)(i); Clothing (up to $1,500): Colorado Revised Statutes 13-54-102(1)(a); Motor vehicles used for work (up to $3,000, up to $6,000 if used to get medical care or if elderly or disabled): Colorado Revised Statutes 13-54-102(j)(1)(ll)(a); Appliances or household goods (up to $3,000): Colorado Revised Statutes 13-54-102(1)(e); Health aids (unlimited amount): Colorado Revised Statutes 13-54-102(1)(p); Livestock, poultry, or other animals and agricultural machinery, equipment, and tools (up to $25,000 total): Colorado Revised Statutes 13-54-102(1)(g); Jewelry and/or watches (up to $1,000): Colorado Revised Statutes 13-54-102(1)(b); Food and fuel (up to $600): Colorado Revised Statutes 13-54-102(1)(f); Personal injury recoveries, unless debt is related to injury (unlimited amount): Colorado Revised Statutes 13-54-102(1)(n); Library, family pictures, and books (up to $1,500): Colorado Revised Statutes 13-54-102 (1)(c); Proceeds for damaged exempt property (up to exemption amount): Colorado Revised Statutes 13-54-102(1)(m); Burial plot (unlimited amount): Colorado Revised Statutes 13-54-102(1)(d); Security deposit (unlimited amount): Colorado Revised Statutes 13-54-102(1)(r); Military equipment owned by member of National Guard (unlimited amount): Colorado Revised Statutes 13-54-102(1)(h.5).
Real Estate: Real property, mobile home, or manufactured home (up to $45,000); proceeds from sale exempt for 1 year after received; must file exemption with county: Colorado Revised Statutes 38-41-201, 38-41-201.6, 38-41-203, 38-41-202, & 38-41-207; Mobile home used as residence (up to $6,000): Colorado Revised Statutes 13-54-102(1)(o)(II).
Wages: 75% of earned but unpaid wages or pension payments; 50% where supporting spouse; 60% if single (judge may allow more for low-income debtors): Colorado Revised Statutes 13-54-104.

Connecticut

Connecticut residents may use either the Federal Bankruptcy Exemptions listed at the end of this Appendix or the state exemptions listed below. If state exemptions are used, then Federal Non-Bankruptcy Exemptions listed at the end of this Appendix can also be used.
Benefits: Aid to aged, blind, disabled, and families with dependent children (unlimited amount): Connecticut General Statutes Annotated 52-352b(d); Crime victims compensation (unlimited amount): Connecticut General Statutes Annotated 52-352b(o) & 54-213; Social Security (unlimited amount): Connecticut General Statutes Annotated 52-352b(g); Unemployment compensation (unlimited amount): Connecticut General Statutes Annotated 31-272(c) & 52-352b(g); Veterans benefits (unlimited amount): Connecticut General Statutes Annotated 52-352b(g); Wages from earnings incentive program (unlimited amount): Connecticut General Statutes Annotated 52-352b(d); Workers compensation (unlimited amount): Connecticut General Statutes Annotated 52-352b(g).

Insurance: Disability benefits paid by association (unlimited amount): Connecticut General Statutes Annotated 52-352b(p); Fraternal society benefits (unlimited amount): Connecticut General Statutes Annotated 38a-637; Health or disability benefits (unlimited amount): Connecticut General Statutes Annotated 52-352b(e); Life insurance proceeds (unlimited amount): Connecticut General Statutes Annotated 38a-453, 454; Unmatured life insurance policy loan value (up to $4,000): Connecticut General Statutes Annotated 52-352b(s).

Miscellaneous: Alimony (up to amount of wage exemption): Connecticut General Statutes Annotated 52-352b(n); Animals and livestock feed for farm partnership (with at least 50% same family members): Connecticut General Statutes Annotated 52-352d; Any property (up to $1,000): Connecticut General Statutes Annotated 52-352b(r); Child support (unlimited amount): Connecticut General Statutes Annotated 52-352b(h); Liquor licenses (unlimited amount): Connecticut General Statutes Annotated 30-14.

Pensions: Municipal employees (unlimited amount): Connecticut General Statutes Annotated 7-446; Probate judges and employees (unlimited amount): Connecticut General Statutes Annotated 45a-48; Retirement benefits (amounts being received): Connecticut General Statutes Annotated 52-352b(m); State employees (unlimited amount): Connecticut General Statutes Annotated 5-171 & 5-192w; Teachers (unlimited amount): Connecticut General Statutes Annotated 10-183q.

Personal Property: Appliances, food, clothing, furniture, and bedding (amounts needed): Connecticut General Statutes Annotated 52-352b(a); Arms, equipment, uniforms, or musical instruments required for military use (unlimited amount): Connecticut General Statutes Annotated 52-352b(i); Burial plot (unlimited amount): Connecticut General Statutes Annotated 52-352b(c); Health aids (unlimited amount): Connecticut General Statutes Annotated 52-352b(f); Motor vehicle (up to $1,500): Connecticut General Statutes Annotated 52-352b(j); Proceeds for damaged exempt property (up to exemption amount): Connecticut General Statutes Annotated 52-352b(q); Tools, books, instruments, and farm animals (amounts needed): Connecticut General Statutes Annotated 52-352b(b). Utility and security deposits for residence (unlimited amount): Connecticut General Statutes Annotated 52-352b(l); Wedding and engagement rings (unlimited amount): Connecticut General Statutes Annotated 52-352b(k).

Real Estate: Real property, including mobile or manufactured home (up to $75,000): Connecticut General Statutes Annotated 52-352b(t).

Wages: 75% of earned but unpaid wages (judge may allow more for low-income debtors): Connecticut General Statutes Annotated 52-36la(f)(1).

Delaware

Delaware residents cannot use the Federal Bankruptcy Exemptions, but may use the Federal Non-Bankruptcy Exemptions listed at the end of this Appendix and the following state exemptions. Wife and husband may double exemption amounts. Total exemptions are limited to $5,000 if single and $10,000 for a husband and wife: Delaware Code Annotated 10-4914.

Benefits: Aid to aged, blind, disabled, families with dependent children, and general assistance (up to exemption limit): Delaware Code Annotated 31-513 & 31-2309; Unemployment compensation (up to exemption limit): Delaware Code Annotated 19-3374; Workers compensation (up to exemption limit): Delaware Code Annotated 19-2355.

Insurance: Annuity contract proceeds (up to $350 per month): Delaware Code Annotated 18-2728; Group life insurance policy or proceeds (up to exemption limit): Delaware Code Annotated 18-2727; Health or disability benefits (up to exemption limit): Delaware Code Annotated 18-2726; Life insurance proceeds if policy prohibits proceeds from being used to pay creditors (up to exemption limit): Delaware Code Annotated 18-2729; Life insurance proceeds (up to exemption limit): Delaware Code Annotated 18-2725.

Miscellaneous: Property of business partnership (unlimited amount): Delaware Code Annotated 6-15-504(f).

Pensions: Kent County employees (up to exemption limit): Delaware Code Annotated 9-4316; Police and fire officers (up to exemption limit): Delaware Code Annotated 11-8803; State employees (up to exemption limit): Delaware Code Annotated 29-5503; Volunteer firefighters (up to exemption limit): Delaware Code Annotated 16-6653.

Personal Property: Any personal property, except tools of a trade, if debtor is head of family (up to $500): Delaware Code Annotated 10-4903; Bible, books, and family pictures (up to exemption limit): Delaware Code Annotated 10-4902(a); Burial plot (up to exemption limit): Delaware Code Annotated 10-4902(a); Church pew or seat in public place of worship (up to exemption limit): Delaware Code Annotated 10-4902(a); Clothing, includes jewelry (up to exemption limit): Delaware Code Annotated 10-4902(a); Pianos and leased organs (up to exemption limit): Delaware Code Annotated 10-4902(d); Property with a fair market value not exceeding $5,000: Delaware Code Annotated 10-4914; Sewing machines (up to exemption limit): Delaware Code Annotated 10-4902(c); Tools, implements, and fixtures (up to $75 in New Castle and Sussex Counties, up to $50 in Kent County): Delaware Code Annotated 10-4902(b).
Real Estate: No exemption.
Wages: 85% of earned but unpaid wages: Delaware Code Annotated 10-4913.

District Of Columbia (Washington D.C.)

District of Columbia residents may use either the Federal Bankruptcy Exemptions listed at the end of this Appendix or the district exemptions listed below. If district exemptions are used, then Federal Non-Bankruptcy Exemptions at the end of this Appendix may also be used.
Benefits: Aid to aged, blind, disabled, families with dependent children, and general assistance (unlimited amount): District of Columbia Code 4-215.01; Crime victims compensation (unlimited amount): District of Columbia Code 3-427, 4-507(e), & 15-501(a)(11)(A); Wrongful death award: District of Columbia Code 15-501(a)(11)(B); Disability, illness, or unemployment compensation (unlimited amount): District of Columbia Code 5-501(a)(7)(C); Unemployment compensation (unlimited amount) District of Columbia Code 51-118(b); Workers compensation (unlimited amount): District of Columbia Code 32-1517; Social Security benefits (unlimited amount): District of Columbia Code 5-501(a)(7)(A); Veteran's benefits (unlimited amount): District of Columbia Code 5-501(a)(7)(B).
Insurance: Disability benefits: District of Columbia Code 31-4716.01; Fraternal society benefits (unlimited amount): District of Columbia Code 31-5315; Group life insurance policy or proceeds (unlimited amount): District of Columbia Code 31-4717; Life insurance proceeds if policy prohibits proceeds from being used to pay creditors (unlimited amount): District of Columbia Code 31-4719; Unmatured life insurance policy, other than a credit life insurance contract (unlimited amount): District of Columbia Code 15-501(a)5; Life insurance proceeds: District of Columbia Code 31-4716; Life insurance proceeds from a person whom the debtor was a dependent of (amount reasonably necessary for support): District of Columbia Code 15-501(a)(11)(C); Other insurance proceeds (up to $60 per month, for 2 months, if head of family, then up to $200 per month): District of Columbia Code 15-503(a) & (b); Payments for pain and suffering, actual loss, or future earnings: District of Columbia Code 15-501(a)(11)(D) & (E).
Miscellaneous: Alimony, support, or separate maintenance (amount reasonably necessary for support): District of Columbia Code 15-501(a)(7)(D).
Pensions: Payment under a stock, bonus, pension, profit-sharing, annuity, or similar plan or contract on account of disability, death, age, or length of service, unless established by a relative when the debtor was employed by the relative and does not qualify under IRS sections 401(a) or 403(b) (amount reasonably necessary for support): District of Columbia Code 15-501(a)(7)(E); Benefits under a retirement plan qualified under IRS sections 401(a), 403(a) or (b), 408, 408(A), 414(d) or (e) [*Note*: there are other complex provisions regarding pension plans. Check Code directly]: District of Columbia Code 15-501(a)(9); Judges (unlimited amount): District of Columbia Code 11-1570(f); Public school teachers (unlimited amount): District of Columbia Code 38-2001.17 & 38-2021.17.
Personal Property: Household furnishings, household goods, wearing apparel, appliances, books, crops, or musical instruments (up to $425 per item and $8,625 total): District of Columbia Code 5-501(a)(2); Professionally prescribed health aids: District of Columbia Code 5-501(a)(6); Books and family pictures (up to $400): District of Columbia Code 15-501(a)(8); Clothing (up to $300): District of Columbia Code 15-503(b); Cooperative association holdings (up to $50): District of Columbia Code 29-928; Provisions for support, such as food, utilities, etc. (amount to last 3 months): District of Columbia Code 15-501(a)(12), (4); Library, furniture, and tools of professional person or artist (up to $300): District

of Columbia Code 15-501(a)(13); Implements, professional books, or tools of a trade or business of debtor or dependent (up to $1,625): District of Columbia Code 15-501(a)(4); Mechanic's tools (up to $200): District of Columbia Code 503(b); Motor vehicle (up to $2,575): District of Columbia Code 15-501(a)(1); Residential condominium deposit (unlimited amount): District of Columbia Code 42-1904.09; Cemetery or burial funds (unlimited amount): District of Columbia Code 27-111; Seal and documents of notary public (unlimited amount): District of Columbia Code 1-1206; any other property (up to $850, plus up to $8,075 additional property if you do not use the real estate exemption listed below): District of Columbia Code 15-501(a)(3).

Real Estate: Any residence or property in a cooperative that is used as a residence of debtor or debtor's dependent or a burial plot of debtor or dependent (unlimited amount): District of Columbia Code 15-501(a)(14).

Wages: 25% of earned but unpaid wages or the amount by which his or her disposable wages for that week exceed 30 times the federal minimum hourly wage, whichever is less is the amount subject to use by creditors; in other words, 75% of the wages are exempt up 30 times minimum hourly wage (judge may allow more for low-income debtors): District of Columbia Code 16-572; Non-wage earnings, including insurance, annuity, pension, or retirement benefits (up to $60 per month for 2 months; if head of family, then up to $200 per month for 2 months): District of Columbia Code 15-503(a) & (b); the wages of any person not residing in the District of Columbia who does not earn the majority of wages in the District (exempt up to limits allowed in home state): District of Columbia Code 15-503(c).

Florida

Florida residents cannot use the Federal Bankruptcy Exemptions, but may use the Federal Non-Bankruptcy Exemptions listed at the end of this Appendix and the following state exemptions:

Benefits: Crime victims compensation unless for injury incurred during the crime (unlimited amount): Florida Statutes Annotated 960.14; Public assistance (unlimited amount): Florida Statutes Annotated 222.201; Social Security (unlimited amount): Florida Statutes Annotated 222.201; Unemployment compensation (unlimited amount): Florida Statutes Annotated 222.201 & 443.051(2), (3); Veterans benefits (unlimited amount): Florida Statutes Annotated 222.201 & 744.626; Workers compensation (unlimited amount): Florida Statutes Annotated 440.22.

Insurance: Annuity contract proceeds (unlimited amount): Florida Statutes Annotated 222.14; Death benefits if not payable to the deceased's estate (unlimited amount): Florida Statutes Annotated 222.13; Disability or illness benefits (unlimited amount): Florida Statutes Annotated 222.18; Fraternal society benefits (unlimited amount): Florida Statutes Annotated 632.619; Life insurance cash surrender value (unlimited amount): Florida Statutes Annotated 222.14.

Miscellaneous: Alimony and child support (amount needed for support): Florida Statutes Annotated 222.201; Damages to employees for injuries in hazardous occupations (unlimited amount): Florida Statutes Annotated 769.05; Property of business partnership (unlimited amount): Florida Statutes Annotated 620.8501.

Pensions: County officers or employees (unlimited amount): Florida Statutes Annotated 122.15; Federal employee pension payments (amounts needed for support and received at least 3 months before filing for bankruptcy): Florida Statutes Annotated 222.21; Firefighters (unlimited amount): Florida Statutes Annotated 175.241; Police officers (unlimited amount): Florida Statutes Annotated 185.25; Retirement benefits (unlimited amount): Florida Statutes Annotated 222.21(2); State officers or employees (unlimited amount): Florida Statutes Annotated 121.131; Teachers (unlimited amount): Florida Statutes Annotated 238.15.

Personal Property: Health aids (unlimited amount): Florida Statutes Annotated 222.25; Motor vehicle (up to $1,000): Florida Statutes Annotated 222.25.

Real Estate: Real or personal property used as residence including mobile or modular home (unlimited value, property cannot exceed 160 contiguous acres); must file exemption in Circuit Court: Florida Constitution 10-4 & Florida Statutes Annotated 222.01, 222.02, 222.03, & 222.05.

Wages: 100% of wages for heads of family (up to $500 per week either unpaid or paid and deposited into bank account for up to 6 months): Florida Statutes Annotated 222.11.

Georgia

Georgia residents cannot use the Federal Bankruptcy Exemptions, but may use the Federal Non-Bankruptcy Exemptions listed at the end of this Appendix and the following state exemptions:

Benefits: Aid to aged, blind, or disabled (unlimited amount): Code of Georgia Annotated 49-4-35, 49-4-58, 49-4-84, & 44-13-100(a)(2)(C); Crime victims compensation (unlimited amount): Code of Georgia Annotated 44-13-100(a)(11)(A); Local public assistance (unlimited amount): Code of Georgia Annotated 44-13-100(a)(2)(A); Social Security (unlimited amount): Code of Georgia Annotated 44-13-100 (a)(2)(A); Unemployment compensation (unlimited amount): Code of Georgia Annotated 44-13-100(a)(2)(A); Veterans benefits (unlimited amount): Code of Georgia Annotated 44-13-100 (a)(2)(B); Workers compensation (unlimited amount): Code of Georgia Annotated 34-9-84; Compensation for loss of future earnings (up to $7,500): Code of Georgia Annotated 44-13-100(a)(11)(E); Compensation for personal bodily injury (up to $10,000): Code of Georgia Annotated 44-13-100(a)(11)(D) .

Insurance: Annuity contract benefits (unlimited amount): Code of Georgia Annotated 33-28-7; Payments under a pension, annuity, or similar contract (unlimited amount): Code of Georgia Annotated 44-13-100(a)(2)(E); Disability or health benefits (up to $250 per month): Code of Georgia Annotated 33-29-15; Fraternal society benefits (unlimited amount): Code of Georgia Annotated 33-15-62; Group insurance (unlimited amount): Code of Georgia Annotated 33-30-10; Industrial life insurance if policy needed for support (unlimited amount): Code of Georgia Annotated 33-26-5; Life insurance proceeds if policy needed for support (unlimited amount): Code of Georgia Annotated 44-13-100(a)(11)(C); Unmatured life insurance contract (unlimited amount): Code of Georgia Annotated 44-13-100(a)(8); Unmatured life insurance dividends, interest, loan value, or cash value (up to $2,000): Code of Georgia Annotated 44-13-100(a)(9).

Miscellaneous: Alimony or child support (amount needed for support): Code of Georgia Annotated 44-13-100(a)(2)(D); Any property (up to $600 plus any unused portion of real estate exemption): Code of Georgia Annotated 44-13-100(a)(6).

Pensions: Any pensions or retirement benefits (unlimited amount): Code of Georgia Annotated 18-4-22, 44-13-100(a)(2)(E), & 44-13-100(a)(2.1)(C); Employees of non-profit corporations (unlimited amount): Code of Georgia Annotated 44-13-100(a)(2.1)(B); Public employees (unlimited amount): Code of Georgia Annotated 44-13-100 (a)(2.1)(A) & 47-2-332.

Personal Property: Animals, appliances, books, clothing, crops, furnishings, household goods, and musical instruments (up to $200 per item and up to $5,000 total): Code of Georgia Annotated 44-13-100(a)(4); Burial plot (if taken instead of real estate exemption): Code of Georgia Annotated 44-13-100(a)(1); Health aids (unlimited amount): Code of Georgia Annotated 44-13-100(a)(10); Implements, books, or tools of a trade (up to $1,500): Code of Georgia Annotated 44-13-100(a)(7); Jewelry (up to $500): Code of Georgia Annotated 44-13-100(a)(5); Lost future earnings (amount needed for support): Code of Georgia Annotated 44-13-100(a)(11)(E); Motor vehicles (up to $3,500): Code of Georgia Annotated 44-13-100(a)(3); Personal injury recoveries (up to $7,500, but not for pain and suffering): Code of Georgia Annotated 44-13-100(a)(11)(D); Wrongful death recoveries (amount needed for support): Code of Georgia Annotated 44-13-100(a)(11)(B).

Real Estate: Real or personal property used as residence and burial plot (up to $10,000, unused portion of real estate exemption may be used with any property): Code of Georgia Annotated 44-13-100(a)(1) & 44-13-100(a)(6).

Wages: 75% of earned but unpaid wages (judge may allow more for low-income debtors): Code of Georgia Annotated 18-4-20 & 18-4-21.

Hawaii

Hawaii residents may use either the Federal Bankruptcy Exemptions listed at the end of this Appendix or the state exemptions listed below. If state exemptions are used, then Federal Non-Bankruptcy Exemptions at the end of this Appendix may also be used.

Benefits: Public assistance for work done in home or workshop (unlimited amount): Hawaii Revised Statutes 346-33; Unemployment compensation (unlimited amount): Hawaii Revised Statutes 383-163; Unemployment work relief funds (up to $60 per month): Hawaii Revised Statutes 653-4; Workers compensation (unlimited amount): Hawaii Revised Statutes 386-57; Crime victim's compensation and special account to limit commercial exploitation of crimes (unlimited amount): Hawaii Revised Statutes 351-66.

Insurance: Annuity contract if beneficiary is insured's spouse, child, or parent (unlimited amount): Hawaii Revised Statutes 431:10-232(b); Disability benefits (unlimited amount): Hawaii Revised Statutes 431:10-231; Fraternal society benefits (unlimited amount): Hawaii Revised Statutes 432: 2-403; Group life insurance policy or proceeds (unlimited amount): Hawaii Revised Statutes 431:10-233; Life insurance proceeds if policy prohibits proceeds from being used to pay creditors (unlimited amount): Hawaii Revised Statutes 431:10-D:112; Life or health insurance policy for spouse or child (unlimited amount): Hawaii Revised Statutes 431:10-234.

Miscellaneous: Property of business partnership (unlimited amount): Hawaii Revised Statutes 425-125.

Pensions: Firefighters (unlimited amount): Hawaii Revised Statutes 88-169; Police officers (unlimited amount): Hawaii Revised Statutes 88-169; Public officers and employees (unlimited amount): Hawaii Revised Statutes 88-91 & 653-3; Retirement benefits paid in at least 3 years before filing for bankruptcy (unlimited amount): Hawaii Revised Statutes 651-124.

Personal Property: Appliances and furnishings (amounts needed for support): Hawaii Revised Statutes 651-121(1); Books (unlimited amount): Hawaii Revised Statutes 651-121(1); Burial plot not exceeding 250 square feet and tombstones (unlimited amount): Hawaii Revised Statutes 651-121(4); Clothing (unlimited amount): Hawaii Revised Statutes 651-121(1); Jewelry (up to $1,000): Hawaii Revised Statutes 651-121(1); Motor vehicle (up to $2,575): Hawaii Revised Statutes 651-121(2); Proceeds from sold or damaged exempt property within last 6 months (up to exemption amount): Hawaii Revised Statutes 651-121(5); Tools, books, uniforms, furnishings, fishing equipment, motor vehicle, and other personal property (amount needed for work): Hawaii Revised Statutes 651-121(3).

Real Estate: Real estate if used as a residence (up to 1 acre and up to $30,000 for head of family or if over 65, otherwise up to $20,000); sale proceeds exempt for 6 months: Hawaii Revised Statutes 651-91, 651-92(a)(2) & 651-96(a)(1).

Wages: Prisoner's wages (unlimited amount): Hawaii Revised Statutes 353-22; Unpaid wages due for work of past 31 days; Wages due for over 31 days, then 95% of 1st $100, 90% of 2nd $100, and 80% of remainder: Hawaii Revised Statutes 651-121(6) & 652-1.

Idaho

Idaho residents cannot use the Federal Bankruptcy Exemptions, but may use the Federal Non-Bankruptcy Exemptions listed at the end of this Appendix and the following state exemptions:

Benefits: Aid to aged, blind, disabled, and families with dependent children (unlimited amount): Idaho Code 56-223; Federal, state, or local public assistance (unlimited amount): Idaho Code 11-603(4); General assistance (unlimited amount): Idaho Code 56-223; Social Security (unlimited amount): Idaho Code 11-603(3); Unemployment compensation (unlimited amount): Idaho Code 11-603(6); Veterans benefits (unlimited amount): Idaho Code 11-603(3); Workers compensation (unlimited amount): Idaho Code 72-802.

Insurance: Annuity proceeds (up to $1,250 per month): Idaho Code 41-1836; Death or disability benefits (unlimited amount): Idaho Code 11-604(1)(a) & 41-1834; Fraternal society benefits (unlimited amount): Idaho Code 41-3218; Group life insurance benefits (unlimited amount): Idaho Code 41-1835; Homeowners insurance proceeds (up to amount of real estate exemption): Idaho Code 55-1008; Life insurance proceeds if policy prohibits proceeds from being used to pay creditors (unlimited amount): Idaho Code 41-1930; Life insurance proceeds for beneficiary other than the insured (unlimited amount): Idaho Code 11-604(d) & 41-1833; Medical, surgical, or hospital care benefits (unlimited amount): Idaho Code 11-603(5).

Miscellaneous: Alimony or child support (amount needed for support): Idaho Code 11-604(1)(b); Liquor licenses (unlimited amount): Idaho Code 23-514; Motor vehicle financial responsibility deposits: Idaho Code 49-1216.

Pensions: Firefighters (unlimited amount): Idaho Code 72-1422; Police officers (unlimited amount): Idaho Code 50-1517; Public employees (unlimited amount): Idaho Code 59-1317; Retirement benefits (unlimited amount): Idaho Code 55-1011.

Personal Property: Appliances, books, clothing, family portraits, 1 firearm, furnishings, musical instruments, pets, and sentimental heirlooms (up to $500 per item, and up to $5,000 total): Idaho Code 11-605(1); Arms, uniforms, and equipment required for peace officer, national guard, or military personnel (unlimited amount): Idaho Code 11-605(5); Building materials (unlimited amount): Idaho Code 45-514; Burial plot (unlimited amount): Idaho Code 11-603(1); Crops on up to 50 acres (up to $1,000): Idaho Code 11-605(6); Health aids (unlimited amount): Idaho Code 11-603(2); Implements, books, and tools of a trade (up to $1,500): Idaho Code 11-605(3); Interest in any property (up to $800): Idaho Code 11-605(10); Jewelry (up to $1,000): Idaho Code 11-605(2); Motor vehicle (up to $3,000): Idaho Code 11-605(3); Personal injury recoveries (unlimited amount): Idaho Code 11-604(1)(c); Proceeds for damaged exempt property within last 3 months (up to amount of exemption): Idaho Code 11-606; Water rights (up to 160 inches): Idaho Code 11-605(6); Wrongful death recoveries (unlimited amount): Idaho Code 11-604(1)(c).

Real Estate: Real property or mobile home used as residence (up to $50,000); proceeds from sale are exempt for 6 months; must record homestead exemption: Idaho Code 55-1003, 55-1004, & 55-1113.

Wages: 75% of earned but unpaid wages or pension payments (judge may allow more for low-income debtors): Idaho Code 11-207.

Illinois

Illinois residents cannot use the Federal Bankruptcy Exemptions, but may use the Federal Non-Bankruptcy Exemptions listed at the end of this Appendix and the following state exemptions. Wife and husband may double the real estate exemption.

Benefits: Aid to aged, blind, disabled, and families with dependent children (unlimited amount): Illinois Annotated Statutes 305-5/11-3; Crime victims compensation (unlimited amount): Illinois Annotated Statutes 735-5/12-1001(h)(1); Social Security (unlimited amount): Illinois Annotated Statutes 735-5/12-1001(g)(1); Unemployment compensation (unlimited amount): Illinois Annotated Statutes 735-5/12-1001(g)(1), (3); Veterans benefits (unlimited amount): Illinois Annotated Statutes 735-5/12-1001(g)(2); Workers compensation (unlimited amount): Illinois Annotated Statutes 820-305/21; Workers occupational disease compensation (unlimited amount): Illinois Annotated Statutes 820-310/21.

Insurance: Annuity, life insurance proceeds, or cash value if beneficiary is insured's child, parent, spouse, or other dependent (unlimited amount): Illinois Annotated Statutes 215-5/238; Fraternal society benefits (unlimited amount): Illinois Annotated Statutes 215-5/299.1a; Health or disability benefits (unlimited amount): Illinois Annotated Statutes 735-5/12-1001(g)(3); Homeowners insurance proceeds (up to $7,500): Illinois Annotated Statutes 735-5/12-907; Life insurance policy if beneficiary is insured's spouse or child (unlimited amount): Illinois Annotated Statutes 735-5/12-1001(f); Life insurance proceeds if policy prohibits proceeds from being used to pay creditors (unlimited amount): Illinois Annotated Statutes 215-5/238; Life insurance proceeds (amount needed for support): Illinois Annotated Statutes 735-5/12-1001(f)(h)(3).

Miscellaneous: Alimony and child support (needed for support): Illinois Annotated Statutes 735-5/12-1001(g)(4); Any property (up to $2,000): Illinois Annotated Statutes 735-5/12-1001(b); Property of a business partnership (unlimited amount): Illinois Annotated Statutes 805-205/25.

Pensions: Civil service employees (unlimited amount): Illinois Annotated Statutes 40-5/11-223; Correction employees (unlimited amount): Illinois Annotated Statutes 40-5/19-117; Firefighters, disabled firefighters, and widows and children of firefighters (unlimited amount): Illinois Annotated Statutes 40-5/4-135 & 40-5/6-213; General assembly members (unlimited amount): Illinois Annotated Statutes 40-5/2-154; Judges (unlimited amount): Illinois Annotated Statutes 40-5/18-161; Park employees (unlimited amount):

Illinois Annotated Statutes 40-5/12-190; Police officers (unlimited amount): Illinois Annotated Statutes 40-5/3-144.1 & 40-5/5-218; Public, public library, municipal, county, and state employees (unlimited amount): Illinois Annotated Statutes 40-5/7-217(a), 40-5/8-244, 40-5/9-228, 40-5/14-147, & 735-5/12-1006; Retirement benefits (unlimited amount): Illinois Annotated Statutes 735-5/12-1006; Sanitation district employees (unlimited amount): Illinois Annotated Statutes 40-5/13-805; State university employees (unlimited amount): Illinois Annotated Statutes 40-5/15-185; Teachers (unlimited amount): Illinois Annotated Statutes 40-5/16-190 & 40-5/17-151.

Personal Property: Bible, family pictures, and schoolbooks (unlimited amount) and clothing (amount needed): Illinois Annotated Statutes 735-5/12-1001(a); Health aids (unlimited amount): Illinois Annotated Statutes 735-5/12-1001(e); Implements, books, and tools of a trade (up to $750): Illinois Annotated Statutes 735-5/12-1001(d); Motor vehicle (up to $1,200 per person): Illinois Annotated Statutes 735-5/12-1001(c); Personal injury recoveries (up to $7,500): Illinois Annotated Statutes 735-5/12-1001(h)(4); Proceeds from sale of exempt property (up to exemption amount): Illinois Annotated Statutes 735-5/12-1001; Wrongful death recoveries (amount needed for support): Illinois Annotated Statutes 735-5/12-1001(h)(2); Pre-paid cemetery funds (unlimited amount): Illinois Annotated Statutes 225-45/4a & 815-390/16; Liquor permits (unlimited amount): Illinois Annotated Statutes 235-5/6-1; Cemetery care fund: (unlimited amount): Illinois Annotated Statutes 760-100/4.

Real Estate: Real or personal property used as a residence including a farm, building, condominium, co-op, or mobile home (up to $7,500); proceeds from sale are exempt for up to 1 year from sale; must file exemption with county: Illinois Annotated Statutes 735-5/12-901, 735-5/12-902, & 735-5/12-906.

Wages: 85% of earned but unpaid wages (judge may allow more for low-income debtors): Illinois Annotated Statutes 740-170/4.

Indiana

Indiana residents cannot use the Federal Bankruptcy Exemptions, but may use the Federal Non-Bankruptcy Exemptions listed at the end of this Appendix and the following state exemptions. Wife and husband may double the real estate exemption.

Benefits: Crime victims compensation except for treatment of injury incurred during the crime (unlimited amount): Indiana Statutes Annotated 5-2-6.1-38; Unemployment compensation (unlimited amount): Indiana Statutes Annotated 22-4-33-3; Workers compensation (unlimited amount): Indiana Statutes Annotated 22-3-2-17.

Insurance: Fraternal society benefits (unlimited amount): Indiana Statutes Annotated 27-11-6-3; Group life insurance policy (unlimited amount): Indiana Statutes Annotated 27-1-12-29; Life insurance policy, proceeds, or cash value if beneficiary is insured's spouse or dependent (unlimited amount): Indiana Statutes Annotated 27-1-12-14; Life insurance proceeds if policy prohibits proceeds to be used to pay creditors (unlimited amount): Indiana Statutes Annotated 27-2-5-1; Mutual life or accident insurance proceeds (unlimited amount): Indiana Statutes Annotated 27-8-3-23.

Miscellaneous: Any real estate or tangible personal property (up to $4,000): Indiana Statutes Annotated 34-55-10-2(b)(2); Property of a business partnership (unlimited amount): Indiana Statutes Annotated 23-4-1-25.

Pensions: Firefighters (unlimited amount): Indiana Statutes Annotated 36-8-7-22 & 36-8-8-17; Police officers (only unpaid benefits): Indiana Statutes Annotated 36-8-8-17; Retirement benefits (unlimited amount): Indiana Statutes Annotated 5-10.3-8-9; Sheriffs (only unpaid benefits): Indiana Statutes Annotated 36-8-10-19; State teachers (unlimited amount): Indiana Statutes Annotated 21-6.1-5-17; Contributions made to retirement plan; any rollovers of such and any earnings made on such: Indiana Statutes Annotated 34-55-10-2(b)(6)(A), (B), & (C).

Personal Property: Any intangible personal property, except money that is owed to debtor (up to $100): Indiana Statutes Annotated 34-55-10-2(b)(3); Professionally prescribed health aids (unlimited amount): Indiana Statutes Annotated 34-55-10-2(b)(4); National guard uniforms, arms, and equipment (unlimited amount): Indiana Statutes Annotated 10-16-10-3; Medical care savings account: Indiana Statutes Annotated 34-55-10-2(b)(7); Other personal property (see below under "Real Estate").

Real Estate: Real estate or personal property used as residence (up to $7,500; residence plus personal property exemption, not including health aids, cannot exceed $10,000 total): Indiana Statutes Annotated 34-55-10-2(b)(1); Other real estate or tangible personal property (amount up to $4,000) Indiana Statutes Annotated 34-55-10-2(b)(2); Property owned as tenancy-by-the-entireties: Indiana Statutes Annotated 34-55-10-2(b)(5).

Wages: 75% of earned but unpaid wages (judge may allow more for low-income debtors): Indiana Statutes Annotated 24-4.5-5-105.

Iowa

Iowa residents cannot use the Federal Bankruptcy Exemptions, but may use the Federal Non-Bankruptcy Exemptions listed at the end of this Appendix and the following state exemptions:

Benefits: Adopted child assistance (unlimited amount): Iowa Code Annotated 627.19; Aid to Families with Dependent Children (unlimited amount): Iowa Code Annotated 627.6(8)(a); Disability or illness benefits (unlimited amount): Iowa Code Annotated 627.6(8)(c); Local public assistance (unlimited amount): Iowa Code Annotated 627.6(8)(a); Social Security (unlimited amount): Iowa Code Annotated 627.6(8)(a); Unemployment compensation (unlimited amount): Iowa Code Annotated 627.6(8)(a); Veterans benefits (unlimited amount): Iowa Code Annotated 627.6(8)(b); Workers compensation (unlimited amount): Iowa Code Annotated 627.13.

Insurance: Accident, disability, health, illness, or life insurance proceeds (up to $15,000, if paid to a surviving spouse, child, or other dependent): Iowa Code Annotated 627.6(6); Fraternal benefit society benefits: Iowa Code Annotated 512B.18; Employee group insurance policy or proceeds (unlimited amount): Iowa Code Annotated 509.12; Life insurance cash value or proceeds (up to $10,000, if acquired within 2 years of filing for bankruptcy, and if paid to spouse, child, or other dependent): Iowa Code Annotated 627.6(6).

Miscellaneous: Alimony or child support (amount needed for support): Iowa Code Annotated 627.6(8)(d); Liquor licenses (unlimited amount): Iowa Code Annotated 123.38; Property of a business partnership (unlimited amount): Iowa Code Annotated 410.11.

Pensions: Federal government pensions (payments being received): Iowa Code Annotated 627.8; Firefighters or police officers (payments being received): Iowa Code Annotated 410.11; Firefighters (unlimited amount): Iowa Code Annotated 411.13; Other pensions (payments being received): Iowa Code Annotated 627.6(8)(e); Peace officers (unlimited amount): Iowa Code Annotated 97A.12; Police officers (unlimited amount): Iowa Code Annotated 411.13; Public employees (unlimited amount): Iowa Code Annotated 97B.39; Retirement plan savings: Iowa Code Annotated 627.6(8)(f).

Personal Property: Any personal property, including cash (up to $100): Iowa Code Annotated 627.6(13); Appliances, furnishings, and household goods (up to $2,000 total): Iowa Code Annotated 627.6(5); Bibles, books, paintings, pictures, and portraits (up to $1,000 total): Iowa Code Annotated 627.6(3); Burial plot (up to 1 acre): Iowa Code Annotated 627.6(4); Clothing, engagement, or wedding rings (up to $1,000 plus receptacles to hold clothing): Iowa Code Annotated 627.6(1); Farm equipment, including livestock and feed (up to $10,000): Iowa Code Annotated 627.6(11); Health aids (unlimited amount): Iowa Code Annotated 627.6(7); Motor vehicle, musical instruments, and tax refund (up to $5,000 total, only up to $1,000 may be from tax refund): Iowa Code Annotated 627.6(9); Musket, rifle, or shotgun (unlimited amount): Iowa Code Annotated 627.6(2); Non-farm business books, equipment, and tools (up to $10,000): Iowa Code Annotated 627.6(10).

Real Estate: Real property or an apartment used as a residence (unlimited value, property cannot exceed ½ acre in town or city, or 40 acres elsewhere): Iowa Code Annotated 561.2 & 561.16.

Wages: If annual wage income is less than $12,000, then $250 for each judgment creditor, otherwise depending on income made within 1 year: $12,000-$16,000 = $400/creditor; $16,001-$24,000 = $800/creditor; $24,001-$35,000 = $1,500/creditor; $35,001-$50,000 = $2,000/creditor; over $50,000 = 10% of expected earnings: Iowa Code Annotated 642.21; Wages or salary of prisoner (unlimited amount): Iowa Code Annotated 356.29.

Kansas

Kansas residents cannot use the Federal Bankruptcy Exemptions, but may use the Federal Non-Bankruptcy Exemptions listed at the end of this Appendix and the following state exemptions:

Benefits: Social Security, unemployment compensation, aid to families with dependent children, general assistance, and welfare (unlimited amount): 11 United States Code 522(d)(10)(A through E); Crime victims compensation (unlimited amount): Kansas Statutes Annotated 60-2313(a)(5); Workers compensation (unlimited amount): Kansas Statutes Annotated 44-514.

Insurance: Fraternal life insurance benefits (unlimited amount): Kansas Statutes Annotated 60-2313(a)(8); Life insurance cash value if bankruptcy filed at least 1 year after policy issued (unlimited amount): Kansas Statutes Annotated 60-2313(a)(7); Life insurance proceeds if policy prohibits proceeds from being used to pay creditors (unlimited amount): Kansas Statutes Annotated 60-2313(a)(7).

Miscellaneous: Liquor licenses (unlimited amount): Kansas Statutes Annotated 650-2313(a)(6).

Pensions: Elected and appointed officials in cities with populations between 120,000 and 200,000 (unlimited amount): Kansas Statutes Annotated 13-14,102; Federal government pension payments paid within 3 months of filing for bankruptcy (unlimited amount): Kansas Statutes Annotated 60:2308(a); Firefighters (unlimited amount): Kansas Statutes Annotated 12-5005(e); Judges (unlimited amount): Kansas Statutes Annotated 20-2618; Police officers (unlimited amount): Kansas Statutes Annotated 12-5005(e); Public employees (unlimited amount): Kansas Statutes Annotated 74-4923; Retirement benefits (unlimited amount): Kansas Statutes Annotated 60-2308(b); State highway patrol officers (unlimited amount): Kansas Statutes Annotated 74-4978g; State school employees (unlimited amount): Kansas Statutes Annotated 72-5526.

Personal Property: Books, documents, furniture, instruments, equipment, breeding stock, seed, grain, and livestock used in farm business (up to $7,500 total): Kansas Statutes Annotated 60-2304(e); Burial plot or crypt (unlimited amount): Kansas Statutes Annotated 60-2304(d); Clothing (amount to last 1 year): Kansas Statutes Annotated 60-2304(a); Food and fuel (amount to last 1 year): Kansas Statutes Annotated 60-2304(a); Funeral plan prepayments (unlimited amount): Kansas Statutes Annotated 60-2313(a)(10); Cemetery trust fund: Kansas Statutes Annotated 60-2313(a)(9); Household furnishings and equipment (unlimited amount): Kansas Statutes Annotated 60-2304(a); Jewelry (up to $1,000): Kansas Statutes Annotated 60-2304(b); Motor vehicle (up to $20,000; if equipped for disabled person, then unlimited amount): Kansas Statutes Annotated 60-2304(c); National Guard uniforms, arms, and equipment (unlimited amount): Kansas Statutes Annotated 48-245.

Real Estate: Real property or mobile home used as residence (unlimited value, up to 1 acre in town or city, or 160 acres on farm): Kansas Statutes Annotated 60-2301 & Kansas Constitution 15-9.

Wages: 75% of earned but unpaid wages (judge may allow more for low-income debtors): Kansas Statutes Annotated 60-2310.

Kentucky

Kentucky residents cannot use the Federal Bankruptcy Exemptions, but may use the Federal Non-Bankruptcy Exemptions listed at the end of this Appendix and the following state exemptions:

Benefits: Aid to aged, blind, disabled, and families with dependent children (unlimited amount): Kentucky Revised Statutes 205.220; Crime victims compensation (unlimited amount): Kentucky Revised Statutes 427.150(2)(a); Unemployment compensation (unlimited amount): Kentucky Revised Statutes 341.470; Workers compensation (unlimited amount): Kentucky Revised Statutes 342.180.

Insurance: Annuity contract proceeds (up to $350 per month): Kentucky Revised Statutes 304.14-330; Cooperative life or casualty insurance benefits (unlimited amount): Kentucky Revised Statutes 427.110(1); Fraternal society benefits (unlimited amount): Kentucky Revised Statutes 427.110(2); Group life insurance proceeds (unlimited amount): Kentucky Revised Statutes 304.14-320; Health or disability benefits (unlimited amount): Kentucky Revised Statutes 304.14-310; Life insurance policy if beneficiary is a married woman (unlimited amount): Kentucky Revised Statutes 304.14-340; Life insurance proceeds if policy prohibits proceeds from being used to pay creditors (unlimited amount): Kentucky Revised

Statutes 304.14-350; Life insurance proceeds or cash value if beneficiary is someone other than insured (unlimited amount): Kentucky Revised Statutes 304.14-300.
Miscellaneous: Alimony or child support (amount needed for support): Kentucky Revised Statutes 427.150(1); Any property (real estate or personal property [up to $1,000]): Kentucky Revised Statutes 427.160; Property of a business partnership (unlimited amount): Kentucky Revised Statutes 362.270.
Pensions: Firefighters and police officers (unlimited amount): Kentucky Revised Statutes 67A.620, 95.878, 427.120, & 427.125; Other pensions (unlimited amount): Kentucky Revised Statutes 427.150(2)(e); State employees (unlimited amount): Kentucky Revised Statutes 61.690; Teachers (unlimited amount): Kentucky Revised Statutes 161.700; Urban county government employees (unlimited amount): Kentucky Revised Statutes 67A.350.
Personal Property: Burial plot (up to $5,000, instead of real estate exemption): Kentucky Revised Statutes 427.060; Clothing, jewelry, or furnishings (up to $3,000 total): Kentucky Revised Statutes 427.010(1); Health aids (unlimited amount): Kentucky Revised Statutes 427.010(1); Library, equipment, instruments, and furnishings (up to $1,000) and motor vehicle (up to $2,500) of minister, attorney, physician, surgeon, chiropractor, veterinarian, or dentist (vehicle exemption also valid for mechanic or mechanical or electrical equipment servicer): Kentucky Revised Statutes 427.030 & 427.040; Lost earnings payments (amount needed for support): Kentucky Revised Statutes 427.150(2)(d); Medical expenses benefits received under Kentucky motor vehicle reparation law (unlimited amount): Kentucky Revised Statutes 304.39-260; Motor vehicle (up to $2,500): Kentucky Revised Statutes 427.010(1); Personal injury recoveries (up to $7,500, not including pain and suffering or pecuniary loss): Kentucky Revised Statutes 427.150(2)(c); Tools of a non-farmer (up to $300): Kentucky Revised Statutes 427.30; Tools, equipment, livestock, and poultry of a farmer (up to $3,000): Kentucky Revised Statutes 427.010(1); Wrongful death recoveries (unlimited amount): Kentucky Revised Statutes 427.150(2)(b); Prepaid tuition account: Kentucky Revised Statutes Annotated 164A.707.
Real Estate: Real or personal property used as residence (up to $5,000); proceeds from sale are also exempt: Kentucky Revised Statutes 427.060 & 427.090.
Wages: 75% of earned but unpaid wages (judge may allow more for low-income debtors): Kentucky Revised Statutes 427.010(2), (3).

Louisiana

Louisiana residents cannot use the Federal Bankruptcy Exemptions, but may use the Federal Non-Bankruptcy Exemptions listed at the end of this Appendix and the following state exemptions:
Benefits: Aid to aged, blind, disabled, and families with dependent children (unlimited amount): Louisiana Revised Statutes Annotated 46:111; Crime victims compensation (unlimited amount): Louisiana Revised Statutes Annotated 46:1811; Unemployment compensation (unlimited amount): Louisiana Revised Statutes Annotated 23:1693; Workers compensation (unlimited amount): Louisiana Revised Statutes Annotated 23:1205.
Insurance: Fraternal society benefits (unlimited amount): Louisiana Revised Statutes Annotated 22:558; Group insurance policies or proceeds (unlimited amount): Louisiana Revised Statutes Annotated 22:649; Health, accident, or disability proceeds (unlimited amount): Louisiana Revised Statutes Annotated 22:646; Life insurance proceeds (unlimited amount, unless policy was issued within 9 months of bankruptcy filing, then exempt only up to $35,000): Louisiana Revised Statutes Annotated 22:647.
Miscellaneous: Personal Property of a minor child (unlimited amount): Louisiana Revised Statutes Annotated 13:3881A(3) & Louisiana Civil Code 223.
Pensions: Gratuitous payments to an employee or heirs (unlimited amount): Louisiana Revised Statutes Annotated 20:33(2); Retirement benefits (unlimited amount if contribution was made over 1 year before bankruptcy filed): Louisiana Revised Statutes Annotated 13:3881D(1) & 20:33(1).
Personal Property: Arms, bedding, chinaware, clothing, cow (1), family portraits, freezer, glassware, heating and cooling equipment, household pets, linens and bedroom furniture, living room and dining room furniture, military equipment, musical instruments, poultry, pressing irons, refrigerator, sewing machine, silverware (if non-sterling), stove, utensils, washer, and dryer: Louisiana Revised Statutes An-

notated 13:3881A(4); Cemetery plot and monuments (unlimited amount): Louisiana Revised Statutes Annotated 8:313; Engagement and wedding rings (up to $5,000): Louisiana Revised Statutes Annotated 13:3881A(5); Tools, instruments, books, pickup truck (up to 3 tons), auto (non-luxury), or utility trailer (amount needed for work): Louisiana Revised Statutes Annotated 3:3881A(2).

Real Estate: Real estate used as residence (up to $15,000 and up to 160 acres); spouse or child of deceased owner may claim homestead exemption: Louisiana Revised Statutes Annotated 20:1.

Wages: 75% of earned but unpaid wages (judge may allow more for low-income debtors): Louisiana Revised Statutes Annotated 13:3881A(1)(a).

Maine

Maine residents cannot use the Federal Bankruptcy Exemptions, but may use the Federal Non-Bankruptcy Exemptions listed at the end of this Appendix and the following state exemptions:

Benefits: Aid to needy and needy families or dependent children (unlimited amount): Maine Revised Statutes Annotated 22-3180 & 22-3766; Crime victims compensation (unlimited amount): Maine Revised Statutes Annotated 14-4422(14)A; Social Security (unlimited amount): Maine Revised Statutes Annotated 14-4422(13)A; Unemployment compensation (unlimited amount): Maine Revised Statutes Annotated 14-4422(13)A, C; Veterans benefits (unlimited amount): Maine Revised Statutes Annotated 14-4422(13)B; Workers compensation (unlimited amount): Maine Revised Statutes Annotated 24A-2431; Compensation for personal bodily injury (amount up to $12,500): Maine Revised Statutes Annotated 14-4422(14(D).

Insurance: Annuity proceeds (up to $450 per month): Maine Revised Statutes Annotated 24-A-2431; Disability or health insurance proceeds (unlimited amount): Maine Revised Statutes Annotated 14-4422(13)A, C, & 24-A-2429; Fraternal society benefits (unlimited amount): Maine Revised Statutes Annotated 24-A-4118; Group health or life insurance policy or proceeds (unlimited amount): Maine Revised Statutes Annotated 24-A-2430; Life, endowment, annuity, or accident policy or proceeds (unlimited amount): Maine Revised Statutes Annotated 14-4422(14)C & 24-A-2428; Life insurance policy, proceeds, or loan value (up to $4,000): Maine Revised Statutes Annotated 14-4422(11); Unmatured life insurance policy except credit insurance policy (unlimited amount): Maine Revised Statutes Annotated 14-4422(10); Death benefits of police, fire, or emergency personnel who die in the line of duty (unlimited amount): Maine Revised Statutes Annotated 25-1612.

Miscellaneous: Alimony/child support (amount needed for support): Maine Revised Statutes Annotated 14-4422(13)D; Any additional property (up to $400): Maine Revised Statutes Annotated 14-4422(15); Property of a business partnership (unlimited amount): Maine Revised Statutes Annotated 31-305; Maintenance under the Maine Rehabilitation Act (unlimited amount): Maine Revised Statutes Annotated 26-1411-H.

Pensions: Judges, legislators, and state employees (unlimited amount): Maine Revised Statutes Annotated 3-703, 4-1203, & 5-17054; Retirement benefits (unlimited amount): Maine Revised Statutes Annotated 14-4422(13)E.

Personal Property: Animals, appliances, books, clothing, crops, furnishings, household goods, and musical instruments (up to $200 per item): Maine Revised Statutes Annotated 14-4422(3); Boat used in commercial fishing (up to 5 tons): Maine Revised Statutes Annotated 14-4422(9); Burial plot (instead of real estate exemption): Maine Revised Statutes Annotated 14-4422(1); Business books, materials, and stock (up to $5,000): Maine Revised Statutes Annotated 14-4422(5); Cooking or heating stove or furnaces and fuel (unlimited amount and up to 10 cords of wood, 5 tons of coal, or 1,000 gallons of petroleum): Maine Revised Statutes Annotated 14-4422(6)A-C; Food (amount to last 6 months): Maine Revised Statutes Annotated 14-4422(7)A; Health aids (unlimited amount): Maine Revised Statutes Annotated 14-4422(12); Jewelry (up to $750, no limit for wedding/engagement ring): Maine Revised Statutes Annotated 14-4422(4); Lost earnings payments (unlimited amount): Maine Revised Statutes Annotated 14-4422(14)E; Military uniforms, arms, and equipment (unlimited amount): Maine Revised Statutes Annotated 37-B-262; Motor vehicle (up to $5,000): Maine Revised Statutes Annotated 14-4422(2); Personal injury recoveries (up to $12,500, but not pain and suffering): Maine Revised Statutes Annotated 14-4422(14)D; Tools, seeds, fertilizer, and equipment (amount to raise and harvest food for 1 season) and farm implements needed to harvest and raise crops (1 of each type): Maine Revised Statutes An-

notated 14-4422(7-8); Unused portion of real estate exemption (up to $6,000 may be used for animals, appliances, books, clothing, crops, furnishings, household goods, musical instruments, personal injury recoveries, and tools of a trade): Maine Revised Statutes Annotated 14-4422(15); Wrongful death recoveries (unlimited amount): Maine Revised Statutes Annotated 14-4422(14)B.
Real Estate: Real or personal property (including co-op) used as residence and burial plot (up to $25,000, up to $50,000 if debtor lives with any dependent, and up to $60,000 if debtor is over age 60 or physically or mentally disabled); joint debtors may double exemption amount: Maine Revised Statutes Annotated 14-4422(1).
Wages: None.

Maryland

Maryland residents cannot use the Federal Bankruptcy Exemptions, but may use the Federal Non-Bankruptcy Exemptions listed at the end of this Appendix and the following state exemptions:
Benefits: Aid to families with dependent children and general assistance (unlimited amount): Annotated Code of Maryland 88A-73; Crime victims compensation (unlimited amount): Annotated Code of Maryland-CP-11-816; Unemployment compensation (unlimited amount): Annotated Code of Maryland-Labor and Employment-8-106b; Workers compensation (unlimited amount): Annotated Code of Maryland-Labor and Employment-9-732.
Insurance: Disability and health benefits, court awards, and settlements (unlimited amount): Annotated Code of Maryland-Courts and Judicial Proceedings-11-504(b)(2); Fraternal society benefits (unlimited amount): Annotated Code of Maryland-I-8-431; Life insurance or annuity contract proceeds if beneficiary is insured's dependent, child, or spouse (unlimited amount): Annotated Code of Maryland-I-8-115; Medical benefits that are deducted from wages (unlimited amount): Annotated Code of Maryland-Commercial-15-601.1.
Miscellaneous: Any property, including a car or real estate (up to $5,500): Annotated Code of Maryland-Courts and Judicial Proceedings-11-504(b)(5) & (f); Partnership property: Annotated Code of Maryland-C & A-9A-501.
Pensions: State employees (unlimited amount): Annotated Code of Maryland-SP & P-21-502; Retirement benefits, except IRAs (unlimited amount): Annotated Code of Maryland-Courts and Judicial Proceedings-11-504(h); Death benefits for Baltimore city police: Annotated Code of Maryland 24-16-103.
Personal Property: Appliances, books, clothing, furnishings, household goods, and pets (up to $500 total): Annotated Code of Maryland-Courts and Judicial Proceedings-11-504(b)(4); Burial plot (unlimited amount): Annotated Code of Maryland 5-503; Clothing, books, tools, instruments, and appliances (up to $2,500): Annotated Code of Maryland-Courts and Judicial Proceedings-11-504(b)(1); Health aids (unlimited amount): Annotated Code of Maryland-Courts and Judicial Proceedings-11-504(b)(3); Lost future earnings recoveries (unlimited amount): Annotated Code of Maryland-Courts and Judicial Proceedings-11-504(b)(2); Perpetual care fund (unlimited amount): Annotated Code of Maryland-BR-5-602; Pre-paid college trust benefits: Annotated Code of Maryland-E-18-1913.
Real Estate: None, specifically, but may use $5,500 exemption noted under "Miscellaneous" for real estate.
Wages: Earned but unpaid wages (up to the greater of 75% or $145 per week; except in Kent, Caroline, and Queen Anne's of Worcester Counties; up to the greater of 75% of actual wages or 30% of federal minimum wage): Annotated Code of Maryland-Commercial-15-601.1.

Massachusetts

Massachusetts residents may use either the Federal Bankruptcy Exemptions listed at the end of this Appendix or the state exemptions listed below. If state exemptions are used, then the Federal Non-Bankruptcy Exemptions at the end of this Appendix may also be used.
Benefits: Aid to families with dependent children (unlimited amount): Massachusetts General Laws Annotated 118-10; Aid to aged/disabled or public assistance (unlimited amount): Massachusetts General

Laws Annotated 235-34; Unemployment compensation (unlimited amount): Massachusetts General Laws Annotated 151A-36; Veterans benefits (unlimited amount): Massachusetts General Laws Annotated 115-5; Workers compensation (unlimited amount): Massachusetts General Laws Annotated 152-47.

Insurance: Disability benefits (up to $400 per week): Massachusetts General Laws Annotated 175-110A; Fraternal society benefits (unlimited amount): Massachusetts General Laws Annotated 176-22; Group annuity policy or proceeds (unlimited amount): Massachusetts General Laws Annotated 175-132C; Group life insurance policy (unlimited amount): Massachusetts General Laws Annotated 175-135; Life or endowment policy, proceeds, or cash value (unlimited amount): Massachusetts General Laws Annotated 175-125; Life insurance annuity contract if contract states that it is exempt (unlimited amount): Massachusetts General Laws Annotated 175-125; Life insurance policy if beneficiary is married woman (unlimited amount): Massachusetts General Laws Annotated 175-126; Life insurance proceeds if policy prohibits proceeds from being used to pay creditors (unlimited amount): Massachusetts General Laws Annotated 175-119A; Medical malpractice self-insurance (unlimited amount): Massachusetts General Laws Annotated 175F-15.

Miscellaneous: Property of business partnership (unlimited amount): Massachusetts General Laws Annotated 108A-25.

Pensions: Private retirement benefits (unlimited amount): Massachusetts General Laws Annotated 32-41; Public employees (unlimited amount): Massachusetts General Laws Annotated 32-19; Retirement benefits (unlimited amount): Massachusetts General Laws Annotated 235-34A & 246-28; Savings bank employees (unlimited amount): Massachusetts General Laws Annotated 168-41 & 168-44.

Personal Property: Arms, equipment, and uniforms required for military use (unlimited amount): Massachusetts General Laws Annotated 235-34; Beds, bedding, and heating unit (unlimited amount); clothing (amount needed): Massachusetts General Laws Annotated 235-34; Bibles and books (up to $200 total): Massachusetts General Laws Annotated 235-34; Boats, tackle, and nets of a fisherman (up to $500 total): Massachusetts General Laws Annotated 235-34; Burial plots, tombs, and church pew (unlimited amount): Massachusetts General Laws Annotated 235-34; Cash for fuel, heat, water, or light (up to $75 per month): Massachusetts General Laws Annotated 235-34; Cash for rent (up to $200 per month; instead of real estate exemption): Massachusetts General Laws Annotated 235-34; Cash or bank deposits (up to $500): Massachusetts General Laws Annotated 235-34 & 246-28A; Cooperative association shares (up to $100): Massachusetts General Laws Annotated 235-34; Cows (2), sheep (12), swine (2), and hay (4 tons): Massachusetts General Laws Annotated 235-34; Food or cash for food (up to $300): Massachusetts General Laws Annotated 235-34; Furniture (up to $3,000): Massachusetts General Laws Annotated 235-34; Materials used in business (up to $500): Massachusetts General Laws Annotated 235-34; Motor vehicle (up to $700): Massachusetts General Laws Annotated 235-34; Sewing machine (up to $200): Massachusetts General Laws Annotated 235-34; Tools, implements, and fixtures of business (up to $500 total): Massachusetts General Laws Annotated 235-34.

Real Estate: Property used as a residence (up to $300,000; if over 62 or disabled, then up to $300,000) must record homestead declaration before filing bankruptcy: Massachusetts General Laws Annotated 188-1, 188-1A, & 188-2.

Wages: Earned but unpaid wages (up to $125 per week): Massachusetts General Laws Annotated 246-28; Seaman's wages (unlimited amount): Massachusetts General Laws Annotated 246-32(7).

Michigan

Michigan residents may use either the Federal Bankruptcy Exemptions listed at the end of this Appendix or the state exemptions listed below. If state exemptions are used, then the Federal Non-Bankruptcy Exemptions at the end of this Appendix may also be used.

Benefits: Aid to families with dependent children (unlimited amount): Michigan Compiled Laws Annotated 330.1158a; Crime victims compensation (unlimited amount): Michigan Compiled Laws Annotated 18.362; Unemployment compensation (unlimited amount): Michigan Compiled Laws Annotated 421.30; Veterans benefits for war veterans (unlimited amount): Michigan Compiled Laws Annotated 35.926, 35.977 & 35.1027; Welfare benefits (unlimited amount): Michigan Compiled Laws Annotated 400.63; Workers compensation (unlimited amount): Michigan Compiled Laws Annotated 418.821.

Insurance: Disability, mutual life, or health insurance benefits (unlimited amount): Michigan Compiled Laws Annotated 600.6023(1)(f); Fraternal society benefits (unlimited amount): Michigan Compiled Laws Annotated 500.8181; Life, endowment, or annuity proceeds if policy prohibits proceeds from being used to pay creditors (unlimited amount): Michigan Compiled Laws Annotated 500.4054; Employer-sponsored life insurance policy or trust fund (unlimited amount): Michigan Compiled Laws Annotated 500-2210.

Miscellaneous: Property of a business partnership (unlimited amount): Michigan Compiled Laws Annotated 449.25.

Pensions: Firefighters (unlimited amount): Michigan Compiled Laws Annotated 38.559(6); Police officers (unlimited amount): Michigan Compiled Laws Annotated 38.559(6); Retirement benefits (unlimited amount): Michigan Compiled Laws Annotated 600.6023(1)(l); IRAs (unlimited amount): Michigan Compiled Laws Annotated 600.6023 (1)(k); Legislators (unlimited amount): Michigan Compiled Laws Annotated 38.1057; Public school employees (unlimited amount): Michigan Compiled Laws Annotated 38.1346; State employees (unlimited amount): Michigan Compiled Laws Annotated 38.1683.

Personal Property: Arms and equipment required for military use (unlimited amount): Michigan Compiled Laws Annotated 600.6023(1)(a); Appliances, books, furniture, household goods, and utensils (up to $1,000 total): Michigan Compiled Laws Annotated 600.6023(1)(b); Building and loan association shares (up to $1,000 par value, instead of real estate): Michigan Compiled Laws Annotated 600.6023(1)(g); Burial plots or church pew (unlimited amount): Michigan Compiled Laws Annotated 600.6023(1)(c); Clothing (unlimited amount): Michigan Compiled Laws Annotated 600.6023(1)(a); Cows (2), hens (100), roosters (5), sheep (10), swine (5), and feed to last 6 months (head of household only): Michigan Compiled Laws Annotated 600.6023(1)(d); Family pictures (unlimited amount): Michigan Compiled Laws Annotated 600.6023(1)(a); Food and fuel (amount to last 6 months): Michigan Compiled Laws Annotated 600.6023(1)(a); Tools, implements, materials, stock, apparatus, team, motor vehicle, horse, and harness used in a business (up to $1,000 total): Michigan Compiled Laws Annotated 600.6023(1)(e).

Real Estate: Real estate, including condominium unit occupied as homestead (up to $3,500, up to 1 lot in town, village, city, or 40 acres elsewhere): Michigan Compiled Laws Annotated 559.214, 600.6023 (1)(h) & (i) & (j), 600.6023(3), & 600.6027.

Wages: 60% of earned but unpaid wages (head of household only), otherwise 40%; head of household may keep at least $15 per week plus $2 per week per non-spouse dependent; others at least $10 per week: Michigan Compiled Laws Annotated 600.5311.

Minnesota

Minnesota residents may use either the Federal Bankruptcy Exemptions listed at the end of this Appendix or the state exemptions listed below. If state exemptions are used, then Federal Non-Bankruptcy Exemptions at the end of this Appendix may also be used. Certain state exemptions are adjusted for inflation on July 1st of even-numbered years. The exemptions noted below are current as of July 1, 2000. The next scheduled adjustment is July 1, 2004.

Benefits: Aid to families with dependent children, supplemental and general assistance, and supplemental security income (unlimited amount): Minnesota Statutes Annotated 550.37(14); Crime victims compensation (unlimited amount): Minnesota Statutes Annotated 611A.60; Unemployment compensation (unlimited amount): Minnesota Statutes Annotated 268.192; Veterans benefits (unlimited amount): Minnesota Statutes Annotated 550.38; Workers compensation (unlimited amount): Minnesota Statutes Annotated 176.175.

Insurance: Accident or disability insurance proceeds (unlimited amount): Minnesota Statutes Annotated 550.39; Fraternal society benefits (unlimited amount): Minnesota Statutes Annotated 64B.18; Life insurance proceeds if beneficiary is spouse or child of insured (up to $20,000, plus $9,000 per dependent): Minnesota Statutes Annotated 550.37(10); Police, fire, or beneficiary association benefits (unlimited amount): Minnesota Statutes Annotated 550.37(11); Unmatured life insurance contract dividends, interest, or loan value (up to $4,000 if insured is debtor or dependent): Minnesota Statutes Annotated 550.37(23).

Miscellaneous: Property of a business partnership (unlimited amount): Minnesota Statutes Annotated 323.24.

Pensions: Private retirement benefits (unpaid benefits only): Minnesota Statutes Annotated 181B.16; Public employees (unlimited amount): Minnesota Statutes Annotated 353.15; Retirement benefits and IRAs (up to $30,000 in present value): Minnesota Statutes Annotated 550.37(24); State employees (unlimited amount): Minnesota Statutes Annotated 352.96; State troopers (unlimited amount): Minnesota Statutes Annotated 352B.071.

Personal Property: Appliances, furniture, phonographs, radio, and TV (up to $4,500 total): Minnesota Statutes Annotated 550.37(4)(b); Bible, books, and musical instruments (unlimited amount): Minnesota Statutes Annotated 550.37(2); Burial plot and church pew seat (unlimited amount): Minnesota Statutes Annotated 550.37(3); Clothing, food, utensils, and watch (up to $4,500): Minnesota Statutes Annotated 550.37(4)(a); Farm machines, implements, livestock, farm produce, and crops (up to $13,000 total; total farm tools and other tools exemption cannot exceed $13,000): Minnesota Statutes Annotated 550.37(5); Motor vehicle (up to $2,000, up to $36,000 if modified for disability): Minnesota Statutes Annotated 550.37-(12)(a); Personal injury recoveries (unlimited amount): Minnesota Statutes Annotated 550.37(22); Proceeds for damaged exempt property (up to exemption amount): Minnesota Statutes Annotated 550.37(9), (16); Teaching materials of public school teacher (unlimited amount): Minnesota Statutes Annotated 550.37(8); Tools, implements, machines, business furniture, stock-in-trade, and library used in business (up to $5,000 total): Minnesota Statutes Annotated 550.37(6); Wrongful death recoveries (unlimited amount): Minnesota Statutes Annotated 550.37(22).

Real Estate: Real property, mobile home, or manufactured home ($200,000 for non-farmland, $500,000 for farmland, up to ½ acre in city or 160 acres elsewhere): Minnesota Statutes Annotated 510.01, 510.02, & 550.37(12).

Wages: Earned but unpaid wages (unlimited amount if paid within 6 months of returning to work and if debtor has ever received welfare): Minnesota Statutes Annotated 550.37(13); Earnings of a minor child (unlimited amount): Minnesota Statutes Annotated 550.37(15); Wages when supporting a dependent (40%): Minnesota Statutes Annotated 550.136(3)(2)(1); Wages deposited into bank accounts for 20 days after deposit: Minnesota Statutes Annotated 550.37(13); Wages of released inmates paid within 6 months of release (unlimited amount): Minnesota Statutes Annotated 550.37(14); 75% of earned but unpaid wages (judge may allow more for low-income debtors): Minnesota Statutes Annotated 571.922.

Mississippi

Mississippi residents cannot use the Federal Bankruptcy Exemptions, but may use the Federal Non-Bankruptcy Exemptions listed at the end of this Appendix and the following state exemptions:

Benefits: Assistance to aged, blind, and disabled (unlimited amount): Mississippi Code 43-9-19, 43-3-71, & 43-29-15; Crime victims compensation (unlimited amount): Mississippi Code 99-41-23(7); Social Security (unlimited amount): Mississippi Code 25-11-129; Unemployment compensation (unlimited amount): Mississippi Code 71-5-539; Workers compensation (unlimited amount): Mississippi Code 71-3-43.

Insurance: Disability benefits (unlimited amount): Mississippi Code 85-3-1(b)(ii); Fraternal society benefits (unlimited amount): Mississippi Code 83-29-39; Homeowners insurance proceeds (up to $75,000): Mississippi Code 85-3-23; Life insurance cash value (up to $50,000): Mississippi Code 85-3-11; Life insurance proceeds if policy prohibits proceeds from being used to pay creditors (unlimited amount): Mississippi Code 83-7-5.

Miscellaneous: Property of a business partnership (unlimited amount): Mississippi Code 79-12-49(C).

Pensions: Firefighters (unlimited amount): Mississippi Code 21-29-257; Highway patrol officers (unlimited amount): Mississippi Code 25-13-31; IRAs (unlimited amount if deposited over 1 year before filing for bankruptcy): Mississippi Code 85-3-1(b)(iii); Keogh (unlimited amount if deposited over 1 year before filing for bankruptcy): Mississippi Code 85-3-1(b)(iii); Private retirement benefits (unlimited amount to the extent they are tax-deferred): Mississippi Code 71-1-43; Police officers (unlimited amount): Mississippi Code 21-29-257; Public employees retirement and disability benefits (unlimited amount): Mississippi Code 25-11-129; Retirement benefits (unlimited amount if deposited over 1 year before filing for bankruptcy): Mississippi Code 85-3-1(b)(iii); State employees (unlimited amount): Mississippi Code 25-14-5; Teachers (unlimited amount): Mississippi Code 25-11-201(1)(d); Pension, profit-sharing, stock bonus plan, deferred compensation plan, or retirement account (unlimited amount): Mississippi Code 85-3-1(f).

Personal Property: Personal injury recoveries (up to $10,000): Mississippi Code 85-3-17; Proceeds from sale of exempt property (up to exemption amount): Mississippi Code 85-3-1(b)(i); Tangible personal property of any type (up to $10,000): Mississippi Code 85-3-1(a).

Real Estate: Proceeds from real estate insurance (up to exemption amount): Mississippi Code 85-3-23; Property used as residence (up to $75,000 and up to 160 acres): Mississippi Code 85-3-21; Mobile home (up to $20,000): Mississippi Code 85-3-1(e).

Wages: Earned but unpaid wages owed for 30 days; after 30 days, 75% of wages due (judge may allow more for low-income debtors): Mississippi Code 85-3-4.

Missouri

Missouri residents cannot use the Federal Bankruptcy Exemptions, but may use the Federal Non-Bankruptcy Exemptions listed at the end of this Appendix and the following state exemptions:

Benefits: Aid to families with dependent children (unlimited amount): Missouri Annotated Statutes 513.430(10)(a); Social Security (unlimited amount): Missouri Annotated Statutes 513.430(10)(a); Unemployment compensation (unlimited amount): Missouri Annotated Statutes 288.380(10)(1) & 513.430(10)(c); Veterans benefits (unlimited amount): Missouri Annotated Statutes 513.430 (10)(b); Workers compensation (unlimited amount): Missouri Annotated Statutes 287.260; Crime victim's compensation: Missouri Annotated Statutes 595.025.

Insurance: Disability or illness benefits (unlimited amount): Missouri Annotated Statutes 513.430(10)(c); Fraternal society benefits (up to $5,000 if purchased over 6 months before filing for bankruptcy): Missouri Annotated Statutes 513.430(8); Insurance premium proceeds (unlimited amount): Missouri Annotated Statutes 377.090; Life insurance dividends, loan value, or interest (up to $5,000 if purchased over 6 months before filing for bankruptcy): Missouri Annotated Statutes 513.430(8); Life insurance proceeds if policy owned by a woman and insures her husband (unlimited amount): Missouri Annotated Statutes 376.530; Life insurance proceeds if policy owned by unmarried woman and insures her father or brother (unlimited amount): Missouri Annotated Statutes 376.550; Unmatured life insurance policy (unlimited amount): Missouri Annotated Statutes 513.430(7).

Miscellaneous: Alimony or child support (up to $500 per month): Missouri Annotated Statutes 513.430(10)(d); Any property (up to $850 plus $250 per child if head of family, otherwise up to $400): Missouri Annotated Statutes 513.430(3) & 513.440; Property of a business partnership (unlimited amount): Missouri Annotated Statutes 358.250(3).

Pensions: Employees of municipalities (unlimited amount): Missouri Annotated Statutes 71.207; Firefighters (unlimited amount): Missouri Annotated Statutes 87.090, 87.365, & 87.485; Police department employees (unlimited amount): Missouri Annotated Statutes 86.190, 86.353, 86.493, & 86.780; Political officials and employees (unlimited amount): Missouri Annotated Statutes 70.695; Retirement benefits (amount needed for support and only payments being received): Missouri Annotated Statutes 513.430(10)(e); State employees (unlimited amount): Missouri Annotated Statutes 104.540(2); Teachers (unlimited amount): Missouri Annotated Statutes 169.090; Employee benefit spendthrift trust: Missouri Annotated Statutes 456.072.

Personal Property: Animals, appliances, books, clothing, crops, furnishings, household goods, and musical instruments (up to $1,000 total): Missouri Annotated Statutes 513.430(1); Burial grounds (up to 1 acre or $100): Missouri Annotated Statutes 214.190; Health aids (unlimited amount): Missouri Annotated Statutes 513.430(9); Implements, books, and tools of a trade (up to $2,000): Missouri Annotated Statutes 513.430(4); Jewelry (up to $500): Missouri Annotated Statutes 513.430(2); Motor vehicle (up to $1,000): Missouri Annotated Statutes 513.430(5); Wrongful death recoveries (unlimited amount): Missouri Annotated Statutes 513.430(11).

Real Estate: Real property (up to $8,000) or mobile home (up to $1,000); joint owners may not double: Missouri Annotated Statutes 513.430(6) & 513.475.

Wages: 75% of earned but unpaid wages (90% if head of family and judge may allow more for low-income debtors): Missouri Annotated Statutes 525.030; Wages of servant or common laborer (up to $90): Missouri Annotated Statutes 513.470.

Montana

Montana residents cannot use the Federal Bankruptcy Exemptions, but may use the Federal Non-Bankruptcy Exemptions listed at the end of this Appendix and the following state exemptions:

Benefits: Aid to aged, blind, disabled, and families with dependent children (unlimited amount): Montana Code Annotated 53-2-607; Crime victims compensation (unlimited amount): Montana Code Annotated 53-9-129; Local public assistance (unlimited amount): Montana Code Annotated 25-13-608(1)(b); Silicosis benefits (unlimited amount): Montana Code Annotated 39-73-110; Social Security (unlimited amount): Montana Code Annotated 25-13-608(1)(b); Unemployment compensation (unlimited amount): Montana Code Annotated 31-2-106(2) & 39-51-3105; Veterans benefits (unlimited amount): Montana Code Annotated 25-13-608 (1)(c); Workers compensation (unlimited amount): Montana Code Annotated 39-71-743.

Insurance: Annuity contract proceeds (up to $350 per month): Montana Code Annotated 33-15-514; Disability, illness, medical, surgical, or hospital proceeds or benefits (unlimited amount): Montana Code Annotated 25-13-608(1)(d) & (f), & 33-15-513; Fraternal society benefits (unlimited amount): Montana Code Annotated 33-7-522; Group life insurance policy or proceeds (unlimited amount): Montana Code Annotated 33-15-512; Hail insurance benefits (unlimited amount): Montana Code Annotated 80-2-245; Life insurance proceeds if policy prohibits proceeds from being used to pay creditors (unlimited amount): Montana Code Annotated 33-20-120; Medical, surgical, or hospital care benefits (unlimited amount): Montana Code Annotated 25-13-608(1)(e); Unmatured life insurance contracts (up to $4,000): Montana Code Annotated 25-13-609(4).

Miscellaneous: Alimony or child support (unlimited amount): Montana Code Annotated 25-13-608(1)(g).

Pensions: Firefighters (unlimited amount): Montana Code Annotated 19-18-612(1); Police officers (unlimited amount): Montana Code Annotated 19-19-504(1); Public employees (unlimited amount): Montana Code Annotated 19-2-1004; Retirement benefits (unlimited amount; amount in excess of 15% of debtor's yearly income must have been deposited over 1 year before filing for bankruptcy): Montana Code Annotated 31-2-106; Teachers (unlimited amount): Montana Code Annotated 19-20-706(2); University system employees (unlimited amount): Montana Code Annotated 19-21-212.

Personal Property: Animals, appliances, books, clothing, crops, firearms, household furnishings, jewelry, musical instruments, and sporting goods (up to $600 per item, $4,500 total): Montana Code Annotated 25-13-609(1); Arms and equipment required for military use (unlimited amount): Montana Code Annotated 25-13-613(b); Burial plot (unlimited amount): Montana Code Annotated 25-13-608(1)(h); Cooperative association shares (up to $500): Montana Code Annotated 35-15-404; Health aids (unlimited amount): Montana Code Annotated 25-13-608(1)(a); Implements, books, and tools of a trade (up to $3,000): Montana Code Annotated 25-13-609(3); Motor vehicle (up to $2,500): Montana Code Annotated 25-13-609(2); Proceeds for damaged or lost exempt property for 6 months after received (up to exemption amount): Montana Code Annotated 25-13-610.

Real Estate: Real property or mobile home used as a residence (up to $100,000); proceeds from sale, condemnation, or insurance are exempt for 18 months; must record homestead declaration before filing for bankruptcy: Montana Code Annotated 70-32-104, 70-32-105, 70-32-201, & 70-32-216.

Wages: 75% of earned but unpaid wages (judge may allow more for low-income debtors): Montana Code Annotated 25-13-614.

Nebraska

Nebraska residents cannot use the Federal Bankruptcy Exemptions, but may use the Federal Non-Bankruptcy Exemptions listed at the end of this Appendix and the following state exemptions:

Benefits: Aid to aged, blind, disabled, poor persons, and families with dependent children (unlimited amount): Revised Statutes of Nebraska 68-1013 & 68-148; Unemployment compensation (unlimited amount): Revised Statutes of Nebraska 48-647; Workers compensation (unlimited amount): Revised Statutes of Nebraska 48-149; Deferred compensation (unlimited amount): Revised Statutes of Nebraska 48-1401.

Insurance: Fraternal society benefits (up to $10,000 loan value): Revised Statutes of Nebraska 44-1089; Life insurance or annuity contract proceeds (up to $10,000 loan value): Revised Statutes of Nebraska 44-371.

Miscellaneous: None.

Pensions: County employees (unlimited amount): Revised Statutes of Nebraska 23-2322; Military disability benefits (up to $2,000): Revised Statutes of Nebraska 25-1559; Retirement benefits (amount needed for support): Revised Statutes of Nebraska 25-1563.01; School employees (unlimited amount): Revised Statutes of Nebraska 79-948; State employees (unlimited amount): Revised Statutes of Nebraska 84-1324.

Personal Property: Any personal property, except wages (up to $2,500 if taken instead of real estate exemption): Revised Statutes of Nebraska 25-1552; Burial plot, crypts, lots, tombs, and vaults (unlimited amount): Revised Statutes of Nebraska 12-517 & 12-605; Clothing (amount needed): Revised Statutes of Nebraska 25-1556; Equipment or tools for professional use (up to $2,400): Revised Statutes of Nebraska 25-1556; Food and fuel (amount to last 6 months): Revised Statutes of Nebraska 25-1556; Furniture, kitchen utensils, computers, books, or musical instruments (up to $1,500): Revised Statutes of Nebraska 25-1556; Health aids (unlimited amount): Revised Statutes of Nebraska 25-1556; Perpetual care funds (unlimited amount): Revised Statutes of Nebraska 12-511; Personal injury recoveries (unlimited amount): Revised Statutes of Nebraska 25-1563.02; Personal possessions (unlimited amount): Revised Statutes of Nebraska 25-1556.

Real Estate: Real estate used as residence (up to $12,500 and up to 2 lots in city or village, 160 acres elsewhere); sale proceeds exempt for 6 months after sale: Revised Statutes of Nebraska 40-101, 40-111, & 40-113.

Wages: Earned but unpaid wages or pension payments (85% for head of family, 75% for others; judge may allow more for low-income debtors): Revised Statutes of Nebraska 25-1558.

Nevada

Nevada residents cannot use the Federal Bankruptcy Exemptions, but may use the Federal Non-Bankruptcy Exemptions listed at the end of this Appendix and the following state exemptions:

Benefits: Aid to aged, blind, disabled, children, and families with dependent children (unlimited amount): Nevada Revised Statutes Annotated 422.291 & 432.036; Industrial insurance [workers compensation] (unlimited amount): Nevada Revised Statutes Annotated 6160.205; Unemployment compensation (unlimited amount): Nevada Revised Statutes Annotated 612.710; Vocational rehabilitation benefits (unlimited amount): Nevada Revised Statutes Annotated 615.270.

Insurance: Annuity contract proceeds (up to $350 per month): Nevada Revised Statutes Annotated 687B.290; Fraternal society benefits (unlimited amount): Nevada Revised Statutes Annotated 695A.220; Group life or health policy or proceeds (amount of life insurance bought not to exceed $1,000 annual premium): Nevada Revised Statutes Annotated 687B.280; Health proceeds (unlimited amount): Nevada Revised Statutes Annotated 687B.270; Life insurance policy or proceeds (unlimited): Nevada Revised Statutes Annotated 21.090(1)(k); Life insurance proceeds if debtor is not the insured (unlimited amount): Nevada Revised Statutes Annotated 687B.260.

Miscellaneous: Alimony or child support (unlimited amount): Nevada Revised Statutes Annotated 21.090(1)(r)(s); Property of a business partnership (unlimited amount): Nevada Revised Statutes Annotated 87.250.

Pensions: Public employees (unlimited amount): Nevada Revised Statutes Annotated 286.670; Retirement benefits (up to $500,000): Nevada Revised Statutes Annotated 21.090(1)(q); Simplified Employee Pension Plan (up to $500,000): Nevada Revised Statutes Annotated 21-090(q)(2); Cash or deferred arrangement (up to $500,00): Nevada Revised Statutes Annotated 21.090(q)(3); Trust forming part of a stock bonus, pension, or profit-sharing plan (up to $500,00): Nevada Revised Statutes Annotated 21.090(q)(4).

Personal Property: Appliances, furniture, home and yard equipment, and household goods (up to $3,000 total): Nevada Revised Statutes Annotated 21.090(1)(b); Arms, uniforms, and equipment required for military use (unlimited amount): Nevada Revised Statutes Annotated 21.090(1)(j); Books (up to $1,500): Nevada Revised Statutes Annotated 21.090(1)(a); Cabin or dwelling of miner or prospector, cars and equipment for mining, and mining claim (up to $4,500): Nevada Revised Statutes Annotated 121.090(1)(e); Farm trucks, stock, tools, equipment, and seed (up to $4,500): Nevada Revised Statutes Annotated 21.090(1)(c); Funeral service money held in trust (unlimited amount): Nevada Revised Statutes Annotated 689.700; Geological specimens, art curiosities, or paleontological remains (unlimited amount, if catalogued and numbered): Nevada Revised Statutes Annotated 21.100; Gun (1 only): Nevada Revised Statutes Annotated 21.090(1)(i); Health aids (unlimited amount): Nevada Revised Statutes Annotated 21.090 (1)(p); Keepsakes and pictures (unlimited amount): Nevada Revised Statutes Annotated 21.090(1)(a); Library, equipment, supplies, tools, and materials for business (up to $4,500): Nevada Revised Statutes Annotated 21.090(1)(d); Motor vehicle (up to $4,500, unlimited amount if equipped for disabled person): Nevada Revised Statutes Annotated 21.090(1)(f), (o).

Real Estate: Real property or mobile home used as a residence (up to $125,000, husband and wife may not double); must record homestead declaration before filing for bankruptcy: Nevada Revised Statutes Annotated 21.090(1) & (m), 115.010, & 115.020.

Wages: 75% of earned but unpaid wages (judge may allow more for low-income debtors): Nevada Revised Statutes Annotated 21.090(1)(g).

New Hampshire

New Hampshire residents cannot use the Federal Bankruptcy Exemptions, but may use the Federal Non-Bankruptcy Exemptions listed at the end of this Appendix and the following state exemptions:

Benefits: Aid to aged, blind, disabled, and families with dependent children (unlimited amount): New Hampshire Revised Statutes Annotated 167:25; Unemployment compensation (unlimited amount): New Hampshire Revised Statutes Annotated 282-A:159; Workers compensation (unlimited amount): New Hampshire Revised Statutes Annotated 281-A:52.

Insurance: Firefighters insurance (unlimited amount): New Hampshire Revised Statutes Annotated 402:69; Fraternal society benefits (unlimited amount): New Hampshire Revised Statutes Annotated 418:24; Homeowners insurance proceeds (up to $5,000): New Hampshire Revised Statutes Annotated 512:21(VIII).

Miscellaneous: Child support (unlimited amount): New Hampshire Revised Statutes Annotated 161-C-11; Jury and witness fees (unlimited amount): New Hampshire Revised Statutes Annotated 512:21(VI); Property of a business partnership (unlimited amount): New Hampshire Revised Statutes Annotated 304A-25.

Pensions: Federal pension (unpaid benefits only): New Hampshire Revised Statutes Annotated 512:21(IV); Firefighters (unlimited amount): New Hampshire Revised Statutes Annotated 102:23; Firemen's retirement (unlimited amount): New Hampshire Revised Statutes Annotated 102:23; Public employees (unlimited amount): New Hampshire Revised Statutes Annotated 100A:26.

Personal Property: Auto (up to $4,000): New Hampshire Revised Statutes Annotated 511:2(XVI); Beds, bedding, and cooking utensils (amount needed): New Hampshire Revised Statutes Annotated 511:2(II);

Bibles and books (up to $800): New Hampshire Revised Statutes Annotated 511:2(VIII); Burial plot or lot, or church pew (unlimited amount): New Hampshire Revised Statutes Annotated 511:2(XIV) & 511:2 (XV); Clothing (amount needed): New Hampshire Revised Statutes Annotated 511:2(1); Cooking and heating stoves, and refrigerator (unlimited amount): New Hampshire Revised Statutes Annotated 511:2 (IV); Cow (1), sheep and fleece (6), and hay (4 tons): New Hampshire Revised Statutes Annotated 511:2 (XI), (XII); Food and fuel (up to $400): New Hampshire Revised Statutes Annotated 511:2(VI); Fowl (up to $300): New Hampshire Revised Statutes Annotated 511:2(XIII); Furniture (up to $3,500): New Hampshire Revised Statutes Annotated 511:2(III); Jewelry (up to $500): New Hampshire Revised Statutes Annotated 511:2(XVII); Pork (1, if already slaughtered): New Hampshire Revised Statutes Annotated 511:2(X); Proceeds for lost or destroyed exempt property (up to exemption amount): New Hampshire Revised Statutes Annotated 512:21(VXIII); Sewing machine (unlimited amount): New Hampshire Revised Statutes Annotated 511:2(V); Tools of a trade (up to $5,000): New Hampshire Revised Statutes Annotated 511:2(IX); Uniforms, arms, and equipment required for military use (unlimited amount): New Hampshire Revised Statutes Annotated 511:2(VII); Yoke of oxen or horse (1, if needed for farming): New Hampshire Revised Statutes Annotated 511:2(XII).

Real Estate: Real property or manufactured housing, if located on land owned by debtor (up to $50,000): New Hampshire Revised Statutes Annotated 480:4.

Wages: Earned but unpaid wage (judge decides amount of exemption): New Hampshire Revised Statutes Annotated 512:21(II); Earned but unpaid wages of spouse (unlimited amount): New Hampshire Revised Statutes Annotated 512:21 (III); Wages of a minor child (unlimited amount): New Hampshire Revised Statutes Annotated 512:21 (III).

New Jersey

New Jersey residents may use either the Federal Bankruptcy Exemptions listed at the end of this Appendix or the state exemptions listed below. If state exemptions are used, then the Federal Non-Bankruptcy Exemptions at the end of this Appendix may also be used.

Benefits: Aid to aged and permanent disability assistance (unlimited amount): New Jersey Statutes Annotated 44:7-35; Crime victims compensation (unlimited amount): New Jersey Statutes Annotated 52:4B-18; Unemployment compensation (unlimited amount): New Jersey Statutes Annotated 43:21-53; Workers compensation (unlimited amount): New Jersey Statutes Annotated 34:15-29.

Insurance: Annuity contract proceeds (up to $500 per month): New Jersey Statutes Annotated 17B:24-7; Civil defense workers disability, death, medical, and hospital benefits (unlimited amount): New Jersey Statutes Annotated A:9-57.6; Group life or health policy or proceeds (unlimited amount): New Jersey Statutes Annotated 17B:24-9; Health or disability benefits (unlimited amount): New Jersey Statutes Annotated 17:18-12 & 17B:24-8; Life insurance proceeds if debtor is not the insured (unlimited amount): New Jersey Statutes Annotated 17B:24-(6b); Life insurance proceeds if policy prohibits proceeds from being used to pay creditors (unlimited amount): New Jersey Statutes Annotated 17B:24-10; Military disability or death benefits (unlimited amount): New Jersey Statutes Annotated 38A:4-8.

Miscellaneous: None.

Pensions: Alcohol beverage control officers (unlimited amount): New Jersey Statutes Annotated 43: 8A-20; City board of health employees (unlimited amount): New Jersey Statutes Annotated 43:18-12; Civil defense workers (unlimited amount): New Jersey Statutes Annotated A:9-57.6; County employees (unlimited amount): New Jersey Statutes Annotated 43:10-57 & 43:10-105; Firefighters (unlimited amount): New Jersey Statutes Annotated 43:16-7; Judges (unlimited amount): New Jersey Statutes Annotated 43:6A-41; Municipal employees (unlimited amount): New Jersey Statutes Annotated 43:13-44; Police officers (unlimited amount): New Jersey Statutes Annotated 43:16-7; Prison employees (unlimited amount): New Jersey Statutes Annotated 43:7-13; Public employees (unlimited amount): New Jersey Statutes Annotated 43:15A-53; Retirement benefits (unlimited amount): New Jersey Statutes Annotated 43:13-9; School district employees (unlimited amount): New Jersey Statutes Annotated 18A:66-116; State police (unlimited amount): New Jersey Statutes Annotated 53:5A-45; Street and water department employees (unlimited amount): New Jersey Statutes Annotated 43:19-17; Teachers (unlimited amount):

New Jersey Statutes Annotated 18A:66-51; Traffic officers (unlimited amount): New Jersey Statutes Annotated 43:16A-17.

Personal Property: Any personal property or stock in corporation (up to $1,000 total): New Jersey Statutes Annotated 2A:17-19; Burial plots (unlimited amount): New Jersey Statutes Annotated 8A:5-10; Clothing (unlimited amount): New Jersey Statutes Annotated 2A:17-19; Furniture and household goods (up to $1,000): New Jersey Statutes Annotated 2A:26-4.

Real Estate: None.

Wages: Military wages or allowances (unlimited amount): New Jersey Statutes Annotated 38A:4-8; 90% of earned but unpaid wages (if income under $7,500; if income over $7,500, judge decides wage exemption amount): New Jersey Statutes Annotated 2A:17-56.

New Mexico

New Mexico residents may use either the Federal Bankruptcy Exemptions listed at the end of this Appendix or the state exemptions listed below. If state exemptions are used, then the Federal Non-Bankruptcy Exemptions at the end of this Appendix may also be used.

Benefits: Aid to families with dependent children and general assistance (unlimited amount): New Mexico Statutes Annotated 27-2-21; Crime victims compensation if paid before July 1, 1993 (unlimited amount until July 1, 2001): New Mexico Statutes Annotated 31-22-15; Occupational disease disability benefits (unlimited amount): New Mexico Statutes Annotated 52-3-37; Unemployment compensation (unlimited amount): New Mexico Statutes Annotated 51-1-37; Workers compensation (unlimited amount): New Mexico Statutes Annotated 52-1-52.

Insurance: Benevolent association benefits (up to $5,000): New Mexico Statutes Annotated 42-10-4; Fraternal society benefits (unlimited amount): New Mexico Statutes Annotated 59A-44-18; Life, accident, health or annuity benefits, or cash value, if beneficiary is a New Mexico citizen (unlimited amount): New Mexico Statutes Annotated 42-10-3 & 42-10-5.

Miscellaneous: Any property (up to $2,000, if taken instead of real estate exemption): New Mexico Statutes Annotated 42-10-10; Ownership in an unincorporated association (unlimited amount): New Mexico Statutes Annotated 53-10-2.

Pensions: Pension or retirement benefits (unlimited amount): New Mexico Statutes Annotated 42-10-1 & 42-10-2; Public school employees (unlimited amount): New Mexico Statutes Annotated 22-11-42.

Personal Property: Any personal property (up to $500): New Mexico Statutes Annotated 42-10-1; Books, furniture, and health equipment (unlimited amount): New Mexico Statutes Annotated 42-10-1 & 42-10-2; Books, implements, and tools of a trade (up to $1,500): New Mexico Statutes Annotated 42-10-1 & 42-10-2; Building materials (unlimited amount): New Mexico Statutes Annotated 48-2-15; Clothing (unlimited amount): New Mexico Statutes Annotated 42-10-1 & 42-10-2; Cooperative association shares (minimum amount needed to be member): New Mexico Statutes Annotated 53-4-28; Health aids (unlimited amount): New Mexico Statutes Annotated 42-10-1 & 42-10-2; Jewelry (up to $2,500): New Mexico Statutes Annotated 42-10-1 & 42-10-2; Materials, tools, and machinery to drill, complete, operate, or repair oil line, gas well, or pipeline (unlimited amount): New Mexico Statutes Annotated 70-4-12; Motor vehicle (up to $4,000): New Mexico Statutes Annotated 42-10-1 & 42-10-2.

Real Estate: Real property (up to $30,000; joint owners may double): New Mexico Statutes Annotated 42-10-9.

Wages: 75% of earned but unpaid wages (judge may allow more for low-income debtors): New Mexico Statutes Annotated 35-12-7.

New York

New York residents cannot use the Federal Bankruptcy Exemptions, but may use the Federal Non-Bankruptcy Exemptions listed at the end of this Appendix and the following state exemptions:

Benefits: Aid to aged, blind, disabled, and families with dependent children (unlimited amount): Consolidated Laws of New York: Debtor and Creditor Article 10-A 282(2)(c); Crime victims compensation (unlimited amount): Consolidated Laws of New York: Debtor and Creditor Article 10-A 282(3)(i); Disability, illness, or unemployment benefits, local public assistance, and social security (unlimited amount): Consolidated Laws of New York: Debtor and Creditor Article 10-A 282(2)(a), (c); Veterans benefits (unlimited amount): Consolidated Laws of New York: Debtor and Creditor Article 10-A 282(2)(b); Workers compensation (unlimited amount): Consolidated Laws of New York: Debtor and Creditor Article 10-A 282(2)(c).

Insurance: Annuity contract benefits (unlimited amount, unless purchased within 6 months of filing for bankruptcy and not tax-deferred, then up to $5,000): Insurance Article 32-3212(d), Consolidated Laws of New York: Debtor and Creditor Article 10-A 283(1); Disability or illness benefits (up to $400 per month): Consolidated Laws of New York: Insurance Article 32-3212(c); Life insurance proceeds if beneficiary is the spouse of the insured (unlimited amount): Consolidated Laws of New York: Insurance Article 32-3212(b)(2); Life insurance proceeds if policy prohibits proceeds from being used to pay creditors (unlimited amount): Consolidated Laws of New York: Estates, Powers, and Trusts Article 7-7-1.5(a)(2).

Miscellaneous: Alimony and child support (amount needed for support): Consolidated Laws of New York: Debtor and Creditor Article 10-A 282(2)(d); New York State College State tuition savings program (100% or an amount not exceeding $10,000): Consolidated Laws of New York: Civil Practice Laws and Rules Article 52-5205(j); Property of a business partnership (unlimited amount): Consolidated Laws of New York: Partnership Article 5-51; Trust fund principal and 90% of income: Consolidated Laws of New York: Civil Practice Laws and Rules Article 52 Section 5205(c), (d).

Pensions: Public retirement benefits (unlimited amount): Consolidated Laws of New York: Insurance 4607; Retirement benefits, IRAs, and Keogh (amount needed for support): Consolidated Laws of New York: Debtor and Creditor 282(2)(e) & Civil Practice Law and Rules Article 52 Sec.5205(c); State employees (unlimited amount): Consolidated Laws of New York: Retirement and Social Security 110.

Personal Property: Bible, books (up to $50), church pew or seat, clothing, cooking utensils, crockery, food (amount to last 60 days), furniture, pet (with food to last 60 days, up to $450), pictures, radio, refrigerator, schoolbooks, sewing machine, stoves and fuel (to last 60 days), tableware, TV, watch (up to $35), and wedding ring (up to $5,000 total, with additional limits as noted): Consolidated Laws of New York: Civil Practice Law and Rules Article 52-5205(1)-(6); Burial plot (up to 1/4 acre): Consolidated Laws of New York: Civil Practice Law and Rules Article 52-5206(f); Cash (the lesser of either $2,500 or $5,000 as an annuity, to be taken instead of real estate): Consolidated Laws of New York: Debtor and Creditor Article 10-A 283(2); Farm machinery, team (with food for 60 days), business furniture, books, and instruments (up to $600 total): Consolidated Laws of New York: Civil Practice Law and Rules Article 52-5205(a)(7); Health aids (unlimited amount): Consolidated Laws of New York: Civil Practice Law and Rules Article 52-5205(h); Lost earnings recoveries (amount needed for support): Consolidated Laws of New York: Debtor and Creditor Article 10-A 282(3)(iv); Motor vehicle (up to $2,400): Consolidated Laws of New York: Debtor and Creditor Article 10-A 282(1); Personal injury recoveries (up to $7,500): Consolidated Laws of New York: Debtor and Creditor Article 10-A 282(3)(iii); Security deposits (unlimited amount): Consolidated Laws of New York: Civil Practice Law and Rules Article 52-5205(g); Uniforms, arms, and equipment required for military use (unlimited amount): Consolidated Laws of New York: Civil Practice Law and Rules Article 52-5205(e); Wrongful death recoveries (amount needed for support): Consolidated Laws of New York: Debtor and Creditor Article 10-A 282(3)(ii).

Real Estate: Real property used as residence including co-op, condo, or mobile home (up to $10,000): Consolidated Laws of New York: Civil Practice Law and Rules Article 52-5206(a).

Wages: 90% of earned but unpaid wages (if received within 60 days of filing for bankruptcy): Consolidated Laws of New York: Civil Practice Law and Rules Article 52-5205(d), (e).

North Carolina

North Carolina residents cannot use the Federal Bankruptcy Exemptions, but may use the Federal Non-Bankruptcy Exemptions listed at the end of this Appendix and the following state exemptions:

Benefits: Aid to blind, families with dependent children, special adult assistance, and assistance under the Work First Program (unlimited amount): General Statutes of North Carolina 108A-36 & 111-18; Crime victims compensation (unlimited amount): General Statutes of North Carolina 15B-17; Unemployment compensation (unlimited amount): General Statutes of North Carolina 96-17; Workers compensation (unlimited amount): General Statutes of North Carolina 97-21.

Insurance: Employee group life policy or proceeds (unlimited amount): General Statutes of North Carolina 58-58-165; Fraternal society benefits (unlimited amount): General Statutes of North Carolina 58-24-85; Life insurance policy or proceeds (unlimited amount): General Statutes of North Carolina 1C-1601(a)(6).

Miscellaneous: Any property (up to $3,500, if taken instead of real estate or burial plot exemption): General Statutes of North Carolina 1C-1601(a)(2); Property of a business partnership (unlimited amount): General Statutes of North Carolina 59-55.

Pensions: Firefighters and rescue squad workers (unlimited amount): General Statutes of North Carolina 58-86-90; IRAs (unlimited amount): General Statutes of North Carolina 1C-1601(a)(9); Law enforcement officers (unlimited amount): General Statutes of North Carolina 143-166.30(g); Legislators (unlimited amount): General Statutes of North Carolina 120-4.29; Municipal, city, and county employees (unlimited amount): General Statutes of North Carolina 128-31; Teachers and state employees (unlimited amount): General Statutes of North Carolina 135-9 & 135-95.

Personal Property: Animals, appliances, books, clothing, crops, furnishings, household goods, and musical instruments (up to $3,500 total, plus up to $750 additional per dependent, not to exceed $3,000 for dependents): General Statutes of North Carolina 1C-1601(a)(4); Burial plot (up to $10,000, if taken instead of real estate): General Statutes of North Carolina 1C-1601(a)(1); Health aids (unlimited amount): General Statutes of North Carolina 1C-1601 (a)(7); Implements, books, and tools of a trade (up to $750): General Statutes of North Carolina 1C-1601(a)(5); Motor vehicle (up to $1,500): General Statutes of North Carolina 1C-1601 (a)(3); Personal injury recoveries (unlimited amount): General Statutes of North Carolina 1C-1601(a)(8); Wrongful death recoveries (unlimited amount): General Statutes of North Carolina 1C-1601(a)(8).

Real Estate: Real or personal property, including co-op, used as residence (up to $10,000): General Statutes of North Carolina 1C-1601(a)(1).

Wages: Earned but unpaid wages (amount needed for support and if received 60 days before filing for bankruptcy): General Statutes of North Carolina 1-362.

North Dakota

North Dakota residents cannot use the Federal Bankruptcy Exemptions, but may use the Federal Non-Bankruptcy Exemptions listed at the end of this Appendix and the following state exemptions:

Benefits: Aid to families with dependent children (unlimited amount): North Dakota Century Code 28-22-19(3); Armed conflict veterans benefits (unlimited amount): North Dakota Century Code 37-27-06; Crime victims compensation (unlimited amount): North Dakota Century Code 28-22-19(2); Desert Storm veterans benefits (unlimited amount): North Dakota Century Code 37-26-06; Social Security (unlimited amount): North Dakota Century Code 28-22-03.1 (4)(c); Unemployment compensation (unlimited amount): North Dakota Century Code 52-06-30; Workers compensation (unlimited amount): North Dakota Century Code 65-05-29; Old age and survivor insurance program benefits (unlimited amount): North Dakota Century Code 59-09-22; Deferred compensation program benefits for public employees: North Dakota Century Code 54-52.2-06.

Insurance: Fraternal society benefits (unlimited amount): North Dakota Century Code 26.1-15.1-18 & 26.1-33-40; Life insurance if beneficiary is insured's relative and policy was owned over 1 year before filing for bankruptcy (up to $100,000 per policy and up to $200,000 total life insurance and retirement, IRA, or Keogh; unlimited life insurance if needed for support): North Dakota Century Code 28-22-03.1(3); Life insurance proceeds payable to deceased's estate (unlimited amount): North Dakota Century Code 26.1-33-40.

Miscellaneous: None.

Pensions: Disabled veterans benefits, except military retirement pay (unlimited amount): North Dakota Century Code 28-22-03.1(4)(d); Public employees (unlimited amount): North Dakota Century Code 28-22-19(1); Retirement benefits, IRAs, and Keogh (up to $100,000 per plan and up to $200,000 total life insurance and retirement, IRA, or Keogh; unlimited if needed for support): North Dakota Century Code 28-22-03.1(3).

Personal Property: Any personal property (up to $7,500, if taken instead of real estate exemption): North Dakota Century Code 28-22-03 & 28-22-03.1(1); Bible and books (up to $100): North Dakota Century Code 28-22-02(4); Burial plots and church pew (unlimited amount): North Dakota Century Code 28-22-02(2), (3); Crops (amount raised on debtor's land of up to 160 acres; if this exemption is used, debtor may not take advantage of any other alternative exemptions): North Dakota Century Code 28-22-02(8); Food and fuel (amount to last 1 year): North Dakota Century Code 28-22-02(6); Motor vehicle (up to $1,200): North Dakota Century Code 28-22-03.1(2); Personal injury recoveries (up to $7,500; but not for pain and suffering): North Dakota Century Code 28-22-03.1(4)(b); Pictures and clothing (unlimited amount): North Dakota Century Code 28-22-02(1)(5); Wrongful death recoveries (up to $7,500): North Dakota Century Code 28-22-03.1(4)(a); [*Note*: Any non-head of household who does not claim a crops exemption may claim an additional $2,500 of any Personal Property: North Dakota Century Code 28-22-05. Any head of household who does not claim a crops exemption may claim an additional $5,000 of any personal property or all of the following: North Dakota Century Code 28-22-03: Books and musical instruments (up to $1,500): North Dakota Century Code 28-22-04(1); Furniture and bedding (up to $1,000): North Dakota Century Code 28-22-04(2); Library and professional tools (up to $1,000): North Dakota Century Code 28-22-04(4); Livestock and farm implements (up to $4,500): North Dakota Century Code 28-22-04(3); Tools of a mechanic and business inventory (up to $1,000): North Dakota Century Code 28-22-04(4).]

Real Estate: Real property, house trailer, or mobile home used as a residence (up to $80,000); proceeds for sale of exempt real estate are exempt: North Dakota Century Code 28-22-02(10) & 47-18-01.

Wages: 75% of earned but unpaid pensions or wages (judge may allow more for low-income debtors): North Dakota Century Code 32-09.1-03.

Ohio

Ohio residents cannot use the Federal Bankruptcy Exemptions, but may use the Federal Non-Bankruptcy Exemptions listed at the end of this Appendix and the following state exemptions:

Benefits: Aid to families with dependent children and public assistance benefits (unlimited amount): Ohio Revised Code 2329.66(A)(9)(d), 5107.12, & 5108.08; Crime victims compensation (unlimited amount if received during 12 months before filing for bankruptcy): Ohio Revised Code 2329.66(A)(12)(a) & 2743.66; Disability assistance payments (unlimited amount): Ohio Revised Code 2329.66 (A)(9)(e) & 5115.07; Living maintenance benefits (unlimited amount): Ohio Revised Code 2329.66 (A)(16) & 3304.19; Tuition credit (unlimited amount): Ohio Revised Code 2329.66(A)(16); Unemployment compensation (unlimited amount): Ohio Revised Code 2329.66 (A)(9)(c) & 4141.32; Workers compensation (unlimited amount): Ohio Revised Code 2329.66(A) (9)(b) & 4123.67.

Insurance: Benevolent society benefits (up to $5,000): Ohio Revised Code 2329.63 & 2329.66(A)(6)(a); Disability benefits (up to $600 per month): Ohio Revised Code 2329.66 (A)(6)(e) & 3923.19; Fraternal society benefits (unlimited amount): Ohio Revised Code 2329.66 (A)(6)(d) & 3921.18; Group life insurance policy or proceeds (unlimited amount): Ohio Revised Code 2329.66(A)(6)(c) & 3917.05; Life, endowment, or annuity contract benefits for spouse, child, or dependent (unlimited amount): Ohio Revised Code 2329.66(A)(6)(b) & 3911.10; Life insurance proceeds for spouse (unlimited amount): Ohio Revised Code 3911.12; Life insurance proceeds if policy prohibits proceeds from being used to pay creditors (unlimited amount): Ohio Revised Code 3911.14.

Miscellaneous: Alimony or child support (amount needed for support): Ohio Revised Code 2329.66 (A)(11); Any property, real estate or personal property (up to $400): Ohio Revised Code 2329.66(A)(17); Property of a business partnership (unlimited amount): Ohio Revised Code 1775.24 & 2329.66 (A)(14).

Pensions: Firefighters and police officers pensions or death benefits (unlimited amount): Ohio Revised Code 742.47 & 2329.66(A)(10)(a); Public employees (unlimited amount): Ohio Revised Code 145.56 & 2329.66 (A)(10)(a); Public school employees (unlimited amount): Ohio Revised Code 3307.71 &

3309.66; Retirement benefits, IRAs, and Keogh (amount needed for support): Ohio Revised Code 2329.66(A)(10)(b), (c); State highway patrol employees (unlimited amount): Ohio Revised Code 2329.66 (A)(10)(a) & 5505.22; Volunteer firefighters dependents (unlimited amount): Ohio Revised Code 146.13 & 2329.66(A)(10)(a).

Personal Property: Animals, appliances, books, crops, firearms, furnishings, household goods, hunting and fishing equipment, jewelry (up to $400 per item and $1,500 total), musical instruments (up to $200 per item), refrigerator and stove (up to $300 each) [total exemption for this category is $2,000 if no real estate exemption is taken]: Ohio Revised Code 2329.66(A)(3), 2329.66(A)(4)(b) & (d), & 2329.66(A)(c) & (d); Bank deposits, cash, money due within 90 days, security deposits, and tax refunds (up to $400 total): Ohio Revised Code 2329.66(4)(a); Beds, bedding, and clothing (up to $200 per item): Ohio Revised Code 2329.66(A)(3); Burial plot (unlimited amount): Ohio Revised Code 517.09 & 2329.66(A)(8); Health aids (unlimited amount): Ohio Revised Code 2329.66(A)(7); Implements, books, and tools of a trade (up to $750): Ohio Revised Code 2329.66(A)(5); Lost future earnings (amount needed for support if received during 12 months before filing for bankruptcy): Ohio Revised Code 2329.66(A)(12)(d); Motor vehicle (up to $1,000): Ohio Revised Code 2329.66(A)(2); Personal injury recoveries (up to $5,000 if received during 12 months before filing for bankruptcy, but not for pain and suffering): Ohio Revised Code 2329.66(A)(12)(c); Wrongful death recoveries (amount needed for support if received during 12 months before filing): Ohio Revised Code 2329.66(A)(12)(b).

Real Estate: Real or personal property used as a residence (up to $5,000): Ohio Revised Code 2329.66(A)(1)(b).

Wages: 75% of earned but unpaid wages that are due for 30 days (judge may allow more for low-income debtors): Ohio Revised Code 2329.66 (A)(13).

Oklahoma

Oklahoma residents cannot use the Federal Bankruptcy Exemptions, but may use the Federal Non-Bankruptcy Exemptions listed at the end of this Appendix and the following state exemptions:

Benefits: Aid to the aged, blind, disabled, and families with dependent children (unlimited amount): Oklahoma Statutes Annotated 56-173; Crime victims compensation (unlimited amount): Oklahoma Statutes Annotated 21-142.13; Social Security (unlimited amount): Oklahoma Statutes Annotated 56-173; Unemployment compensation (unlimited amount): Oklahoma Statutes Annotated 40-2-303; Workers compensation (unlimited amount): Oklahoma Statutes Annotated 85-48.

Insurance: Fraternal society benefits (unlimited amount): Oklahoma Statutes Annotated 36-2718.1; Funeral benefits (if prepaid and placed in trust; unlimited amount): Oklahoma Statutes Annotated 36-6125; Group life policy or proceeds (unlimited amount): Oklahoma Statutes Annotated 36-3632; Limited stock insurance benefits (unlimited amount): Oklahoma Statutes Annotated 36-2510; Mutual benefits (unlimited amount): Oklahoma Statutes Annotated 36-2410.

Miscellaneous: Alimony and child support (unlimited amount): Oklahoma Statutes Annotated 31-1(A)(19); Partnership property (unlimited amount): Oklahoma Statutes Annotated 16-1-Appendix Standard 13.6; Limited liability company property (unlimited amount): Oklahoma Statutes Annotated 16-1-Appendix Standard 14.6.

Pensions: County employees (unlimited amount): Oklahoma Statutes Annotated 19-959; Disabled veterans (unlimited amount): Oklahoma Statutes Annotated 31-7; Firefighters (unlimited amount): Oklahoma Statutes Annotated 11-49-126; Law enforcement employees (unlimited amount): Oklahoma Statutes Annotated 47-2-303.3; Police officers (unlimited amount): Oklahoma Statutes Annotated 11-50-124; Public employees (unlimited amount): Oklahoma Statutes Annotated 74-923; Retirement benefits (unlimited amount): Oklahoma Statutes Annotated 31-1 (A)(20); Tax exempt benefits (unlimited amount): Oklahoma Statutes Annotated 60-328); Funds in individual development account (unlimited amount): Oklahoma Statutes Annotated 31-1(A)(22); Funds in Roth individual retirement account (unlimited amount): Oklahoma Statutes Annotated 31-1(A)(23); Funds in individual education retirement account (unlimited amount): Oklahoma Statutes Annotated 31-1(A)(24).

Personal Property: Books, gun (1), pictures, and portraits (unlimited amount): Oklahoma Statutes Annotated 31-1(A)(7), (14); Bridles and saddles (2 each total): Oklahoma Statutes Annotated 31-1 (A)(12); Burial plots (unlimited amount): Oklahoma Statutes Annotated 31-1(A)(4); Chickens (100), dairy cows and calves under 6 months (5), hogs (10), horses (2), sheep (20), and feed to last 1 year: Oklahoma Statutes Annotated 31-1(A)(10), (11), (15), (16), (17); Clothing (up to $4,000): Oklahoma Statutes Annotated 31-1(A)(8); Farm implements to farm homestead (up to $5,000 total): Oklahoma Statutes Annotated 31-1(A)(5); Tools, books, and business equipment (up to $5,000 total); Oklahoma Statutes Annotated 31-1(A)(6) & (C); Food (amount to last 1 year): Oklahoma Statutes Annotated 31-1(A)(17); Furniture and health aids (unlimited amount): Oklahoma Statutes Annotated 31-1-(A)(3), (9); Motor vehicle (up to $3,000): Oklahoma Statutes Annotated 31-1(A)(13); Personal injury, wrongful death, and workers compensation recoveries (up to $50,000 total; but not punitive damages): Oklahoma Statutes Annotated 31-1(A)(21); Federal earned income tax credit (unlimited amount): Oklahoma Statutes Annotated 31-1(A)(25); Liquor license (unlimited amount): Oklahoma Statutes Annotated 37-532; Statutory support trusts (unlimited amount): Oklahoma Statutes Annotated 6-3010; Prepaid funeral benefits (unlimited amount): Oklahoma Statutes Annotated 36-6125; Prepaid dental plan deposits (unlimited amount): Oklahoma Statutes Annotated 36-6146.

Real Estate: Real property or manufactured home (unlimited value if up to 1/4 acre; if over 1/4 acre, up to $5,000 for up to 1 acre in city, town, or village, or up to 160 acres elsewhere): Oklahoma Statutes Annotated 31-1(A)(1), (2), & 31-2.

Wages: 75% of wages earned in the 90 days before filing for bankruptcy (judge may allow more for hardship): Oklahoma Statutes Annotated 12-1171.1 & 31-1(A)(18).

Oregon

Oregon residents cannot use the Federal Bankruptcy Exemptions, but may use the Federal Non-Bankruptcy Exemptions listed at the end of this Appendix and the following state exemptions:

Benefits: Aid to aged, blind, and disabled (unlimited amount): Oregon Revised Statutes 412.115, 412.610, & 413.130; Civil defense and disaster relief (unlimited amount): Oregon Revised Statutes 401.405; Crime victims compensation (unlimited amount): Oregon Revised Statutes 23.160(1)(j) & 147.325; General assistance (unlimited amount): Oregon Revised Statutes 411.760; Inmates injury benefits (unlimited amount): Oregon Revised Statutes 655.530; Medical assistance (unlimited amount): Oregon Revised Statutes 414.095; Unemployment compensation (unlimited amount): Oregon Revised Statutes 657.855; Vocational rehabilitation (unlimited amount): Oregon Revised Statutes 344.580; Workers compensation (unlimited amount): Oregon Revised Statutes 656.234; Veteran's benefits and loans:): Oregon Revised Statutes 23.160(1)(m).

Insurance: Annuity contract benefits (up to $500 per month): Oregon Revised Statutes 743.049; Fraternal society benefits (unlimited amount): Oregon Revised Statutes 748.207; Group life policy or proceeds not payable to the insured (unlimited amount): Oregon Revised Statutes 743.047; Health or disability proceeds (unlimited amount): Oregon Revised Statutes 743.050; Life insurance proceeds or cash value if debtor is not the insured (unlimited amount): Oregon Revised Statutes 743.046.

Miscellaneous: Alimony and child support (amount needed for support): Oregon Revised Statutes 23.160(1)(i); Liquor licenses (unlimited amount): Oregon Revised Statutes 471.292.

Pensions: Public officials and employees (unlimited amount): Oregon Revised Statutes 237.980, 238.445, & 746.147; Retirement benefits (unlimited amount): Oregon Revised Statutes 746.146; School district employees (unlimited amount): Oregon Revised Statutes 239.261 & 746.148.

Personal Property: Any personal property not listed below (up to $400): Oregon Revised Statutes 23.160(1)(o); Bank deposits (up to $7,500, if from exempt wages or pension): Oregon Revised Statutes 23.166; Books, pictures, and musical instruments (up to $600 total): Oregon Revised Statutes 23.160(1)(a); Burial plot (unlimited amount): Oregon Revised Statutes 65.870; Clothing, jewelry, and personal items (up to $1,800 total): Oregon Revised Statutes 23.160(1)(b); Domestic animals and poultry, with food to last 60 days (up to $1,000): Oregon Revised Statutes 23.160(1)(e); Food and fuel (amount to last 60 days): Oregon Revised Statutes 23.160(1)(f); Furniture, household items, radios, TVs, and utensils (up to $3,000 total): Oregon Revised Statutes 23.160(1)(f); Health aids (unlimited amount): Oregon Revised Statutes 23.160(1)(h); Lost future earnings payments (amount needed for support): Oregon Revised Statutes 23.160(1)(j)(C); Motor vehicle (up to $1,700): Oregon Revised Statutes 23.160(1)(d); Personal injury recoveries (up to $10,000): Oregon Revised Statutes 23.160(1)(k); Compensation for lost future earnings (up to $10,000): Oregon Revised Statutes 23.160(1)(L); Pistol, rifle, or shotgun (up to $1,000): Oregon Revised Statutes 23.200; Proceeds from sale of exempt property (up to exemption amount): Oregon Revised Statutes 23.164; Tools, business equipment, library, and team with food to last 60 days (up to $3,000): Oregon Revised Statutes 23.160(1)(c); Earned income tax credit: Oregon Revised Statutes 23.160(1)(n); Building materials for construction or improvement (unlimited amount): Oregon Revised Statutes 87.075; Tuition savings program account (unlimited amount): Oregon Revised Statutes 348.863; Real estate client's trust account (unlimited amount): Oregon Revised Statutes 696.241; Real estate escrow funds (unlimited amount): Oregon Revised Statutes 696.579; Trust funds maintained by a debt consolidation agency (unlimited amount): Oregon Revised Statutes 697.722.

Real Estate: Real property, mobile home, or houseboat used as a residence (up to $25,000, $33,000 for joint owners, only $23,000 if mobile home, and $30,000 for joint mobile home owners; property may be up to 1 block in town or city or 160 acres elsewhere; sale proceeds are exempt for 1 year if held to purchase another home): Oregon Revised Statutes 23.164, 23.240, & 23.250.

Wages: 75% of earned but unpaid wages (judge may allow more for low-income debtors): Oregon Revised Statutes 23.186; Wages withheld in state employees bond savings accounts: Oregon Revised Statutes 292.070.

Pennsylvania

Pennsylvania residents may use either the Federal Bankruptcy Exemptions listed at the end of this Appendix or the state exemptions listed below. If state exemptions are used, then the Federal Non-Bankruptcy Exemptions at the end of this Appendix may also be used.

Benefits: Unemployment compensation (unlimited amount): Pennsylvania Consolidated Statutes Annotated 42-8124(c)(10) & 43-863; Veterans benefits (unlimited amount): Pennsylvania Consolidated Statutes Annotated 51-20012 & 51-20098; Workers compensation (unlimited amount): Pennsylvania Consolidated Statutes Annotated 42-8124(c)(2).

Insurance: Accident or disability benefits (unlimited amount): Pennsylvania Consolidated Statutes Annotated 42-8124(c)(7); Fraternal society benefits (unlimited amount): Pennsylvania Consolidated Statutes Annotated 42-8124(c)(8); Group life policy or proceeds (unlimited amount): Pennsylvania Consolidated Statutes Annotated 42-8124(c)(5); Insurance annuity policy, cash value, or proceeds if beneficiary is insured's dependent, child, or spouse (unlimited amount): Pennsylvania Consolidated Statutes Annotated 42-8124(c)(6); Insurance or annuity payments, if insured is beneficiary, (up to $100 per month): Pennsylvania Consolidated Statutes Annotated 42-8124(c)(3); Life insurance proceeds if policy prohibits proceeds from being used to pay creditors (unlimited amount): Pennsylvania Consolidated Statutes Annotated 42-8124(c)(4); No-fault automobile insurance proceeds (unlimited amount): Pennsylvania Consolidated Statutes Annotated 42-8124(c)(9).

Miscellaneous: Any property (up to $300): Pennsylvania Consolidated Statutes Annotated 42-8123; Property of a business partnership (unlimited amount): Pennsylvania Consolidated Statutes Annotated 15-8341.

Pensions: City employees (unlimited amount): Pennsylvania Consolidated Statutes Annotated 53-13445, 53-23572, & 53-39383; County employees (unlimited amount): Pennsylvania Consolidated Statutes Annotated 16-4716; Municipal employees (unlimited amount): Pennsylvania Consolidated Statutes Annotated 53-881.115; Police officers (unlimited amount): Pennsylvania Consolidated Statutes Annotated 53-764, 53-776, & 53-23666; Private retirement benefits if deposited for over 1 year before filing for bankruptcy and if policy prohibits proceeds from being used to pay creditors (up to $15,000): Pennsylvania Consolidated Statutes Annotated 42-8124(b); Public school employees (unlimited amount): Pennsylvania Consolidated Statutes Annotated 24-8533; State employees (unlimited amount): Pennsylvania Consolidated Statutes Annotated 71-5953.

Personal Property: Bibles, schoolbooks, and sewing machines (unlimited amount): Pennsylvania Consolidated Statutes Annotated 42-8124(a)(2), (3); Clothing (unlimited amount): Pennsylvania Consolidated Statutes Annotated 42-8124(a)(1); Personal property located at a U.S. government international exhibit (unlimited amount): Pennsylvania Consolidated Statutes Annotated 42-8125; Uniform and equipment required for military use (unlimited amount): Pennsylvania Consolidated Statutes Annotated 42-8124(a)(4).

Real Estate: None.

Wages: Earned but unpaid wages (unlimited amount): Pennsylvania Consolidated Statutes Annotated 42-8127; Wages of abused person or victim: Pennsylvania Consolidated Statutes Annotated 42-8127(F).

Rhode Island

Rhode Island residents may use either the Federal Bankruptcy Exemptions listed at the end of this Appendix or the state exemptions listed below. If state exemptions are used, then the Federal Non-Bankruptcy Exemptions at the end of this Appendix may also be used.

Benefits: Aid to aged, blind, disabled, families with dependent children, and general assistance (unlimited amount): General Laws of Rhode Island 40-5.1-15 & 40-6-14; Disability benefits (unlimited amount): General Laws of Rhode Island 28-41-32; Unemployment compensation (unlimited amount): General Laws of Rhode Island 28-44-58; Veterans disability or death benefits (unlimited amount): General Laws of Rhode Island 30-7-9; Workers compensation (unlimited amount): General Laws of Rhode Island 28-33-27; Crime victim's compensation: General Laws of Rhode Island 12-25.1-3.

Insurance: Accident or sickness proceeds or benefits (unlimited amount): General Laws of Rhode Island 27-18-24; Fraternal society benefits (unlimited amount): General Laws of Rhode Island 27-25-18; Life insurance proceeds if policy prohibits proceeds from being used to pay creditors (unlimited amount): General Laws of Rhode Island 27-4-12; Temporary disability insurance (unlimited amount): General Laws of Rhode Island 28-41-32.

Miscellaneous: Property of business partnership: General Laws of Rhode Island 7-12-36.

Pensions: Firefighters (unlimited amount): General Laws of Rhode Island 9-26-5; IRAs (unlimited amount): General Laws of Rhode Island 9-26-4(11); Police officers (unlimited amount): General Laws of Rhode Island 9-26-5; Private employees (unlimited amount): General Laws of Rhode Island 28-17-4; Retirement benefits (unlimited amount): General Laws of Rhode Island 9-26-4 (12); State and municipal employees (unlimited amount): General Laws of Rhode Island 36-10-34.

Personal Property: Beds, bedding, furniture, and household goods (up to $8,600 total): General Laws of Rhode Island 9-26-4(3); Bibles and books (up to $300): General Laws of Rhode Island 9-26-4(4); Burial plot (unlimited amount): General Laws of Rhode Island 9-26-4(5); Clothing (unlimited amount): General Laws of Rhode Island 9-26-4(1); Cooperative association holdings (up to $50): General Laws of Rhode Island 7-8-25; Debt secured by promissory note (unlimited amount): General Laws of Rhode Island 9-26-4(7); Library of a professional in practice (unlimited amount): General Laws of Rhode Island 9-26-4(2); Tools used for work (up to $1,200): General Laws of Rhode Island 9-26-4(2); Motor vehicle (up to $10,000): General Laws of Rhode Island 9-26-4(13): Jewelry (up to $1,000): General Laws of Rhode Island 9-26-4(14); Prepaid tuition or tuition savings program (unlimited amount): General Laws of Rhode Island 9-26-4(15).

Real Estate: None.

Wages: Earned but unpaid wages (up to $50): General Laws of Rhode Island 9-26-4(8)(iii); Earned but unpaid wages due military member on active duty (unlimited amount): General Laws of Rhode Island 30-7-9; Earned but unpaid wages due seaman (unlimited amount): General Laws of Rhode Island 9-26-4(6); Earned but unpaid wages if debtor received welfare during the year before filing for bankruptcy (unlimited amount): General Laws of Rhode Island 9-26-4(8)(ii); Earnings of a minor child (unlimited amount): General Laws of Rhode Island 9-26-4(9); Wages of spouse (unlimited amount): General Laws of Rhode Island 9-26-4(9); Wages to the needy if paid by a charitable organization (unlimited amount): General Laws of Rhode Island 9-26-4(8).

South Carolina

South Carolina residents may use either the Federal Bankruptcy Exemptions listed at the end of this Appendix or the state exemptions listed below. If state exemptions are used, then the Federal Non-Bankruptcy Exemptions at the end of this Appendix may also be used.

Benefits: Aid to aged, blind, disabled, families with dependent children, and general relief (unlimited amount): Code of Laws of South Carolina 43-5-190; Crime victims compensation (unlimited amount): Code of Laws of South Carolina 15-41-30(11)(A) & 16-3-1300; Local public assistance (unlimited amount): Code of Laws of South Carolina 15-41-30(10)(A); Social Security (unlimited amount): Code of Laws of South Carolina 15-41-30 (10)(A); Unemployment compensation (unlimited amount): Code of Laws of South Carolina 15-41-30(10)(A); Veterans benefits (unlimited amount): Code of Laws of South Carolina 15-41-30(10)(B); Workers compensation (unlimited amount): Code of Laws of South Carolina 42-9-360.

Insurance: Disability, illness, or unemployment benefits (unlimited amount): Code of Laws of South Carolina 15-41-30(10)(C); Life insurance benefits if proceeds left with insurance company: Code of Laws of South Carolina 38-63-40; Life insurance proceeds (up to $4,000): Code of Laws of South Carolina 15-41-30(8) & 15-41-30(11)(C); Unmatured life insurance contract (unlimited amount): Code of Laws of South Carolina 15-41-30(7).

Miscellaneous: Alimony and child support (unlimited amount): Code of Laws of South Carolina 15-41-30 (10)(D); Property of a business partnership (unlimited amount): Code of Laws of South Carolina 33-41-720.

Pensions: Firefighters (unlimited amount): Code of Laws of South Carolina 9-13-230; General assembly members (unlimited amount): Code of Laws of South Carolina 9-9-180; Judges and solicitors (unlimited amount): Code of Laws of South Carolina 9-8-190; Police officers (unlimited amount): Code of Laws of South Carolina 9-11-270; Public employees (unlimited amount): Code of Laws of South Carolina 9-1-1680; Retirement benefits (unlimited amount): Code of Laws of South Carolina 15-41-30(10)(E).

Personal Property: Animals, appliances, books, clothing, crops, furnishings, household goods, and musical instruments (up to $2,500): Code of Laws of South Carolina 15-41-30(3); Burial plot (up to $5,000, if taken instead of real estate exemption): Code of Laws of South Carolina 15-41-30(1); Cash and other liquid assets (up to $1,000, if taken instead of burial or real estate exemption): Code of Laws of South Carolina 15-41-30(5); Health aids (unlimited amount): Code of Laws of South Carolina 15-41-30(9); Implements, books, and tools of a trade (up to $750): Code of Laws of South Carolina 15-41-30(6); Jewelry (up to $500): Code of Laws of South Carolina 15-41-30(4); Motor vehicle (up to $1,200): Code of Laws of South Carolina 15-41-30(2); Personal injury recoveries (unlimited amount): Code of Laws of South Carolina 15-41-30(11)(B); Wrongful death recoveries (unlimited amount): Code of Laws of South Carolina 15-41-30(11)(B).

Real Estate: Real property used as a residence, including a co-op (up to $5,000): Code of Laws of South Carolina 15-41-30(1).

Wages: Earnings from personal service: Code of Laws of South Carolina 15-39-410.

South Dakota

South Dakota residents cannot use the Federal Bankruptcy Exemptions, but may use the Federal Non-Bankruptcy Exemptions listed at the end of this Appendix and the following state exemptions:

Benefits: Aid to families with dependent children and public assistance (unlimited amount): South Dakota Codified Laws 28-7A-18; Unemployment compensation (unlimited amount): South Dakota Codified Laws 61-6-28; Workers compensation (unlimited amount): South Dakota Codified Laws 62-4-42; Crime victim's compensation: South Dakota Codified Laws 23A-28B-24.

Insurance: Annuity contract proceeds (up to $250 per month): South Dakota Codified Laws 58-12-6 & 58-12-8; Endowment or life insurance policy, proceeds, or cash value (up to $20,000): South Dakota Codified Laws 58-12-4; Fraternal society benefits (unlimited amount): South Dakota Codified Laws 58-37A-18; Health benefits (up to $20,000): South Dakota Codified Laws 58-12-4; Life insurance proceeds (if held by insurance company and if policy prohibits proceeds from being used to pay creditors): South Dakota Codified Laws 58-15-70; Life insurance proceeds (up to $10,000, if beneficiary is spouse or child): South Dakota Codified Laws 43-45-6.

Miscellaneous: None.

Pensions: City employees (unlimited amount): South Dakota Codified Laws 9-16-47; Public employees (unlimited amount): South Dakota Codified Laws 3-12-115; Employee retirement benefit (unlimited amount): South Dakota Codified Laws 48-4-16.

Personal Property: Bible and books (up to $200), burial plot, church pew, clothing, and food and fuel to last 1 year (unlimited amount for this category unless noted): South Dakota Codified Laws 43-45-2 & 47-29-25; Head of household exemptions: Any personal property (up to $6,000): South Dakota Codified Laws 43-45-4, 5; Non-head of household exemption: Any personal property (up to $4,000): South Dakota Codified Laws 43-45-4.

Real Estate: Real property, including mobile home (unlimited value, up to 1 acre in town or up to 160 acres elsewhere); limited proceeds from sale are exempt for 1 year (up to $30,000; unlimited if over 70, or unmarried widow or widower: South Dakota Codified Laws 43-31-1, 43-31-2, 43-31-3, 43-31-4, & 45-43-3.

Wages: Wages earned up to 60 days prior to filing for bankruptcy (amount needed for support): South Dakota Codified Laws 15-20-12; Wages of prisoners (unlimited amount): South Dakota Codified Laws 24-8-10.

Tennessee

Tennessee residents cannot use the Federal Bankruptcy Exemptions, but may use the Federal Non-Bankruptcy Exemptions listed at the end of this Appendix and the following state exemptions:

Benefits: Aid to aged, blind, disabled, and families with dependent children (unlimited amount): Tennessee Code Annotated 71-2-216, 71-3-121, 71-4-117, & 71-4-1112; Crime victims compensation (up to $5,000 and up to $15,000 total of all personal injury, wrongful death, and crime victims compensation): Tennessee Code Annotated 26-2-111(2)(A) & 29-13-111; Local public assistance (unlimited amount): Tennessee Code Annotated 26-2-111(1)(A); Social Security (unlimited amount): Tennessee Code Annotated 26-2-111(1)(A); Unemployment compensation (unlimited amount): Tennessee Code Annotated 26-2-111(1)(A); Veterans benefits (unlimited amount): Tennessee Code Annotated 26-2-111(1)(B); Workers compensation (unlimited amount): Tennessee Code Annotated 50-6-223; Uniform relocation assistance program (unlimited amount): Tennessee Code Annotated 13-11-115.

Insurance: Accident, health, or disability benefits (unlimited amount): Tennessee Code Annotated 26-2-110; Annuity contract proceeds if payable to dependent (unlimited amount): Tennessee Code Annotated 56-7-203; Disability or illness benefits (unlimited amount): Tennessee Code Annotated 26-2-111(1)(C); Fraternal society benefits (unlimited amount): Tennessee Code Annotated 56-25-1403; Homeowners insurance proceeds (up to $5,000): Tennessee Code Annotated 26-2-304; Life insurance or annuity (unlimited amount): Tennessee Code Annotated 56-7-203.

Miscellaneous: Alimony and child support (if owed for 30 days before filing for bankruptcy): Tennessee Code Annotated 26-2-111(1)(E)(F).

Pensions: Public employees (unlimited amount): Tennessee Code Annotated 8-36-111; Retirement benefits (unlimited amount): Tennessee Code Annotated 26-2-111 (1)(D); State and local government employees (unlimited amount): Tennessee Code Annotated 26-2-104; Teachers (unlimited amount): Tennessee Code Annotated 49-5-909.

Personal Property: Any personal property (up to $4,000): Tennessee Code Annotated 26-2-102; Bible, clothing, pictures, portraits, schoolbooks, and storage containers (unlimited amount): Tennessee Code Annotated 26-2-103; Burial plot (unlimited value, up to 1 acre): Tennessee Code Annotated 26-2-305 & 46-2-102; Health aids (unlimited amount): Tennessee Code Annotated 26-2-111(5); Implements, books, and tools of a trade (up to $1,900): Tennessee Code Annotated 26-2-111(4); Lost earnings payments:

Tennessee Code Annotated 26-2-111(3); Personal injury recoveries except for pain and suffering (up to $7,500 and up to $15,000 total of all personal injury, wrongful death, and crime victims compensation): Tennessee Code Annotated 26-2-111(2)(B); Wrongful death recoveries (up to $7,500 and up to $15,000 total of all personal injury, wrongful death, and crime victims compensation): Tennessee Code Annotated 26-2-111(2)(C); Scholarship trust fund (unlimited amount): Tennessee Code Annotated 49-4-108; Education system trust fund (unlimited amount): Tennessee Code Annotated 49-7-822 .

Real Estate: Real estate-life estate (see statute) [unlimited amount]: Tennessee Code Annotated 26-2-302; Real property used as a residence (up to $5,000 and $7,500 for joint owners): Tennessee Code Annotated 26-2-301; 2-15 year lease (unlimited amount): Tennessee Code Annotated 26-2-303.

Wages: 75% of earned but unpaid wages, plus $2.50 per week per child (judge may allow more for low-income debtors): Tennessee Code Annotated 26-2-106 & 26-2-107; Wages of debtor deserting family that are in the hands of the family (up to $5,000): Tennessee Code Annotated 26-2-209.

Texas

Texas residents may use either the Federal Bankruptcy Exemptions listed at the end of this Appendix or the state exemptions listed below. If state exemptions are used, then the Federal Non-Bankruptcy Exemptions at the end of this Appendix may also be used.

Benefits: Aid to families with dependent children (unlimited amount): Texas Revised Civil Statutes Annotated, Human Resources 31.040; Medical assistance (unlimited amount): Texas Revised Civil Statutes Annotated, Human Resources 32.036; Unemployment compensation (unlimited amount): Texas Revised Civil Statutes Annotated 5221b-13; Workers compensation (unlimited amount): Texas Revised Civil Statutes Annotated 8308-4.07.

Insurance: Fraternal society benefits (unlimited amount): Texas Revised Civil Statutes Annotated, Insurance Code 885.316; Life, health, accident, or annuity benefits, cash value, or proceeds (see limits under "Personal Property"): Texas Revised Civil Statutes Annotated, Insurance Code 1108.051; Life insurance if beneficiary is debtor or debtor's dependent (unlimited amount): Texas Revised Civil Statutes Annotated 422(a)(12); Texas employee uniform group insurance (unlimited amount): Texas Revised Civil Statutes Annotated, Insurance 1551.011; Texas state college or university employee benefits (unlimited amount): Texas Revised Civil Statutes Annotated, Insurance 3.50-3(9)(a).

Miscellaneous: Alimony (amount needed for support): Texas Revised Civil Statutes Annotated 421(b)(3).

Pensions: County and district employees (unlimited): Texas Revised Civil Statutes Annotated, Government 8115; Firefighters: Texas Revised Civil Statutes Annotated 6243e(5) & 6243e.1(104); Judges (unlimited amount): Texas Revised Civil Statutes Annotated, Government 8115; Municipal employees (unlimited amount): Texas Revised Civil Statutes Annotated 6243g, Government 8115; Police officers (unlimited amount): Texas Revised Civil Statutes Annotated 6243d-1(17), 6243j(20), & 6243g-1(23B); Retirement benefits (unlimited amount if tax-deferred): Texas Revised Civil Statutes Annotated, Property 4221; State employees (unlimited amount): Texas Revised Civil Statutes Annotated, Government 8115; Teachers (unlimited amount): Texas Revised Civil Statutes Annotated, Government 8115.

Personal Property: Athletic and sporting equipment, bicycles, boat, books, cattle (12), clothing, equipment, farming or ranching equipment, firearms (2), food, heirlooms, home furnishings, horses or donkeys (2 and saddle, blanket, and bridle for both), jewelry (up to 25% of total exemption), livestock (60), motor vehicle, pets, poultry (120), and tools (limits on total of all above personal property, life insurance cash value, and unpaid commissions are up to $30,000 or up to $60,000 for head of family): Texas Revised Civil Statutes Annotated, Property 421 & 422; Burial plots (unlimited amount): Texas Revised Civil Statutes Annotated, Property 411; Health aids (unlimited amount): Texas Revised Civil Statutes Annotated, Property 421(b)(2); Prepaid tuition plans (unlimited amount): Texas Revised Civil Statutes Annotated, Education Code 54.639; Higher education savings plans (unlimited amount): Texas Revised Civil Statutes Annotated, Education Code 54.709.

Real Estate: Real property (unlimited value; up to 1 acre in town, village, city, and 200 acres elsewhere; 100 acres limit if single); must file exemption with county; proceeds of sale are exempt for 6 months: Texas Revised Civil Statutes Annotated, Property 412.
Wages: Earned but unpaid wages (unlimited amount): Texas Revised Civil Statutes Annotated, Property 421(b)(1); Unpaid commissions (up to 75%) [see limits under "Personal Property"]: Texas Revised Civil Statutes Annotated Property 421(d).

Utah

Utah residents cannot use the Federal Bankruptcy Exemptions, but may use the Federal Non-Bankruptcy Exemptions listed at the end of this Appendix and the following state exemptions:
Benefits: Unemployment compensation (unlimited amount): Utah Code 35A-4-103; Veterans benefits (unlimited amount): Utah Code 78-23-5(1)(e)(v); Workers compensation (unlimited amount): Utah Code 34A-2-422; Public assistance benefits (unlimited amount): Utah Code 35A-3-112.
Insurance: Disability, illness, medical, or hospital benefits (unlimited amount): Utah Code 78-23-5(1)(c), (d)(iii)(iv); Fraternal society benefits (unlimited amount): Utah Code 31A-9-603; Life insurance policy (cash surrender value up to $5,000) [unlimited amount]: Utah Code 78-23-7; Life insurance proceeds if beneficiary is insured's spouse or dependent (amount needed for support): Utah Code 78-23-6(2).
Miscellaneous: Alimony or child support (amount needed for support): Utah Code 78-23-5 (1)(f) & (k), & 78-23-6(1); Property of a business partnership (unlimited amount): Utah Code 48-1-22(vi)(xi).
Pensions: Any pension (amount needed for support): Utah Code 78-23-6(3); Public employees (unlimited amount): Utah Code 49-11-612; Retirement benefits (unlimited amount): Utah Code 78-23-5(1)(j)(x).
Personal Property: Animals, books, and musical instruments (up to $500 total): Utah Code 78-23-8(1)(c); Appliances and household furnishings (up to $500 total): Utah Code 7823-8(1)(a); Artwork depicting, or done by, family member (unlimited amount): Utah Code 78-23-5(1)(viii); Bed, bedding, carpets, washer, and dryer (unlimited amount): Utah Code 78-23-5(1)(vii); Burial plot (unlimited amount): Utah Code 78-23-5(1)(a); Clothing (unlimited amount, but not furs or jewelry): Utah Code 78-23-5 (1)(vii); Equipment required for military use (unlimited amount): Utah Code 39-1-47; Food and fuel (amount to last 3 months): Utah Code 78-23-5(1)(vii); Health aids (amount needed): Utah Code 78-23-5(1)(ii); Heirlooms or sentimental item (up to $500): Utah Code 78-23-8(1)(d); Implements, books, and tools of a trade (up to $3,500 total): Utah Code 78-23-8(2); Motor vehicle (for business use only and only up to $2,500): Utah Code 78-23-8(3)(b); Personal injury recoveries (unlimited amount): Utah Code 78-23-5(1)(ix); Proceeds for damaged exempt property (up to exemption amount): Utah Code 78-23-9; Refrigerator, freezer, sewing machine, and stove (unlimited amount): Utah Code 78-23-5(1)(vii); Wrongful death recoveries (unlimited amount): Utah Code 78-23-5(1)(ix).
Real Estate: Real property, mobile home used as a residence, or water rights (up to $10,000, if property is jointly owned; each debtor may claim the exemption, but total exemption not to exceed $20,000); must file exemption with county: Utah Code 78-23-3.
Wages: 75% of earned but unpaid wages (judge may allow more for low-income debtors): Utah Code 78C-7-103.

Vermont

Vermont residents may use either the Federal Bankruptcy Exemptions listed at the end of this Appendix or the state exemptions listed below. If state exemptions are used, then the Federal Non-Bankruptcy Exemptions at the end of this Appendix may also be used.
Benefits: Aid to aged, blind, disabled, families with dependent children, and general assistance (unlimited amount): Vermont Statutes Annotated 33-124; Crime victims compensation (amount needed for support): Vermont Statutes Annotated 12-2740(19)(E); Social Security (amount needed for support): Vermont Statutes Annotated 12-2740(19)(A); Unemployment compensation (unlimited amount): Vermont Statutes Annotated 21-1367; Veterans benefits (amount needed for support): Vermont Statutes Annotated 12-2740(19)(B); Workers compensation (unlimited amount): Vermont Statutes Annotated 21-681.

Insurance: Annuity contract benefits (up to $350 per month): Vermont Statutes Annotated 8-3709; Disability or illness benefits (amount needed for support): Vermont Statutes Annotated 8-3707 & 12-2740(19)(C); Fraternal society benefits (unlimited amount): Vermont Statutes Annotated 8-4478; Group life or health benefits (unlimited amount): Vermont Statutes Annotated 8-3708; Health benefits (up to $200 per month): Vermont Statutes Annotated 8-4086; Life insurance proceeds if beneficiary not the insured (unlimited amount): Vermont Statutes Annotated 8-3706; Life insurance proceeds if policy prohibits proceeds from being used to pay creditors (unlimited amount): Vermont Statutes Annotated 8-3705; Life insurance proceeds (unlimited amount): Vermont Statutes Annotated 8-3708 & 12-2740(19)(H); Supplemental disability benefits (unlimited amount): Vermont Statutes Annotated 8-3707; Unmatured life insurance contract (unlimited amount): Vermont Statutes Annotated 12-2740(18).
Miscellaneous: Alimony or child support (amount needed for support): Vermont Statutes Annotated 12-2740(19)(D); Any property (up to $400): Vermont Statutes Annotated 12-2740(7).
Pensions: Any pensions (unlimited amount): Vermont Statutes Annotated 12-2740 (19)(j); IRAs and Keogh (up to $10,000): Vermont Statutes Annotated 12-2740(16); Municipal employees (unlimited amount): Vermont Statutes Annotated 24-5066; State employees (unlimited amount): Vermont Statutes Annotated 3-476; Teachers (unlimited amount): Vermont Statutes Annotated 16-1946.
Personal Property: Animals, appliances, books, clothing, crops, furnishings, goods, and musical instruments (up to $2,500 total): Vermont Statutes Annotated 12-2740(5); Bank deposits (up to $700): Vermont Statutes Annotated 12-2740(15); Books and tools of a trade (up to $5,000 total): Vermont Statutes Annotated 12-2740(2); Farm crops and animals: bees (3 swarms), crops (up to $5,000), chickens (10), cow, goats (2), horses (2), sheep (10), yoke of oxen or steers, and feed to last through winter: Vermont Statutes Annotated 12-2740 (6), (11)-(13); Farm equipment: chains (2), halters (2), harnesses (2), plow, and yoke: Vermont Statutes Annotated 12-2740(14); Firewood (10 cords), coal (5 tons), heating oil (500 gallons), or bottled gas (500 gallons): Vermont Statutes Annotated 12-2740(9)-(10); Freezer, heating unit, refrigerator, sewing machines, stove, and water heater (unlimited amount): Vermont Statutes Annotated 12-2740(8); Health aids (unlimited amount): Vermont Statutes Annotated 12-2740(17); Jewelry (up to $500, unlimited amount for wedding ring): Vermont Statutes Annotated 12-2740(3), (4); Lost future earnings (unlimited amount): Vermont Statutes Annotated 12-2740 (19)(l); Motor vehicles (up to $2,500): Vermont Statutes Annotated 12-2740(1); Personal injury recoveries (unlimited amount): Vermont Statutes Annotated 12-2740(19)(F); Wrongful death recoveries (unlimited amount): Vermont Statutes Annotated 12-2740(19)(G).
Real Estate: Real property or mobile home (up to $75,000): Vermont Statutes Annotated 27-101.
Wages: 75% of earned but unpaid wages (judge may allow more for low-income debtors, unlimited amount if debtor received welfare within 2 months of filing for bankruptcy): Vermont Statutes Annotated 12-3170.

Virginia

Virginia residents cannot use the Federal Bankruptcy Exemptions, but may use the Federal Non-Bankruptcy Exemptions listed at the end of this Appendix and the following state exemptions:
Benefits: Aid to aged, blind, disabled, families with dependent child, and general relief (unlimited amount): Code of Virginia 63.2-506; Crime victims compensation (unlimited amount, except not for debt for treatment of injury incurred during crime): Code of Virginia 19.2-368.12; Unemployment compensation (unlimited amount): Code of Virginia 60.2-600; Workers compensation (unlimited amount): Code of Virginia 65.2-531.
Insurance: Accident or sickness benefits (unlimited amount): Code of Virginia 38.2-3549; Burial benefits (unlimited amount): Code of Virginia 38.2-4021; Cooperative life insurance benefits (unlimited amount): Code of Virginia 38.2-3811; Fraternal society benefits (unlimited amount): Code of Virginia 38.2-4118; Government group life or accident insurance (unlimited amount): Code of Virginia 51.1-510; Group life insurance policy or proceeds (unlimited amount): Code of Virginia 38.2-3339; Sickness benefits (unlimited amount): Code of Virginia 38.2-3549; Retiree's supplemental health insurance benefits (unlimited amount): Code of Virginia: 51.1-1404.
Miscellaneous: Any property for disabled veterans homeowner (up to $2,000): Code of Virginia 34-4.1.

Pensions: City, town, and county employees (unlimited amount): Code of Virginia 51.1-802; Retirement benefits (up to $17,500 per year): Code of Virginia 34-34; 75% of earned but unpaid pension payments (judge may allow more for low-income debtors): Code of Virginia 34-29.

Personal Property: [*Note*: Debtor must be a householder to claim any personal property exemption in Virginia.] Bible (unlimited amount): Code of Virginia 34-26(1); Burial plot (unlimited amount): Code of Virginia 34-26(3); Clothing (up to $1,000): Code of Virginia 34-26(4); Crops (unlimited amount): Code of Virginia 8.01-489; Estate sale proceeds (up to amount of unused real estate exemption): Code of Virginia 34-20; Family portraits and heirlooms (up to $5,000 total): Code of Virginia 34-26(2); Farm equipment: fertilizer (up to $1,000), horses (2), mules (2), with gear, pitchfork, plows (2), rake, tractor (up to $3,000), wagon, drag, harvest cradle, and iron wedges (2): Code of Virginia 34-27; Health aids (unlimited amount): Code of Virginia 34-26(6); Household furnishings (up to $5,000): Code of Virginia 34-26(4)(a); Motor vehicle (up to $2,000): Code of Virginia 34-26(8); Personal injury recoveries or causes of action (unlimited amount): Code of Virginia 34-28.1; Pets (unlimited amount): Code of Virginia 34-26(5); Tools, books, and instruments of trade, including motor vehicles (up to $10,000): Code of Virginia 34-26; Uniforms, arms, and equipment required for military use: Code of Virginia 44-96; Wedding and engagement rings (unlimited amount): Code of Virginia 34-26 (1)(a); Prepaid tuition contracts (unlimited amount): Code of Virginia 23-38.81; Tobacco fund payments (unlimited amount): Code of Virginia 3.1-1111.1.

Real Estate: Real property (up to $5,000 plus $500 per dependent) and homestead for surviving spouse or children (up to $15,000); proceeds from the sale of exempt real estate are also exempt; must file homestead declaration before filing for bankruptcy: Code of Virginia 34-4, 34-6, & 64.1-151.3.

Wages: 75% of earned but unpaid wages (judge may allow more for low-income debtors): Code of Virginia 34-29.

Washington

Washington residents may use either the Federal Bankruptcy Exemptions listed at the end of this Appendix or the state exemptions listed below. If state exemptions are used, then the Federal Non-Bankruptcy Exemptions at the end of this Appendix may also be used.

Benefits: Aid to aged and families with dependent children (unlimited amount): Revised Code of Washington Annotated 74.08.210 & 74.13.070; Crime victims compensation (unlimited amount): Revised Code of Washington Annotated 7.68.070; General assistance (unlimited amount): Revised Code of Washington Annotated 74.04.280; Unemployment compensation (unlimited amount): Revised Code of Washington Annotated 50.40.020; Workers compensation (unlimited amount): Revised Code of Washington Annotated 51.32.040.

Insurance: Annuity contract proceeds (up to $250 per month): Revised Code of Washington Annotated 48.18.430; Disability proceeds or benefits (unlimited amount): Revised Code of Washington Annotated 48.18.400; Fraternal society benefits (unlimited amount): Revised Code of Washington Annotated 48.36A.180; Group life insurance policy or proceeds (unlimited amount): Revised Code of Washington Annotated 48.18.420; Insurance proceeds for destroyed exempt property (up to exemption amount): Revised Code of Washington Annotated 6.15.030; Life insurance proceeds if beneficiary is not the insured (unlimited amount): Revised Code of Washington Annotated 48.18.410.

Miscellaneous: Child support payments (unlimited amount): Revised Code of Washington Annotated 6.15.010(3)(d).

Pensions: City employees (unlimited amount): Revised Code of Washington Annotated 41.28.200; IRAs (unlimited amount): Revised Code of Washington Annotated 6.15.020; Public employees (unlimited amount): Revised Code of Washington Annotated 41.40.052; Retirement benefits (unlimited amount): Revised Code of Washington Annotated 6.15.020; State patrol officers (unlimited amount): Revised Code of Washington Annotated 43.43.310; Volunteer firefighters (unlimited amount): Revised Code of Washington Annotated 41.24.240.

Personal Property: Any personal property (up to $2,000; only $200 may be cash, bank deposits, bonds, stocks, or securities): Revised Code of Washington Annotated 6.15.010(3)(b); Appliances, furniture, home and yard equipment, and household goods (up to $2,700 total): Revised Code of Washington Annotated 6.15.010(3)(a); Books (up to $1,500): Revised Code of Washington Annotated 6.15. 010(2); Burial plots (unlimited amount): Revised Code of Washington Annotated 68.24.220; Clothing (unlimited amount, but only up to $1,000 of furs or jewelry): Revised Code of Washington Annotated 6.15.010(1); Farm equipment: equipment, seed, stock, tools, and vehicles (up to $5,000 total): Revised Code of Washington Annotated 6.15.010(4)(a); Food and fuel (amount needed): Revised Code of Washington Annotated 6.15.010(3)(a); Keepsakes and pictures (unlimited amount): Revised Code of Washington Annotated 6.15.010(2); Library, office equipment, office furniture, and supplies of attorney, clergy, physician, surgeon, or other professional (up to $5,000 total): Revised Code of Washington Annotated 6.15.010(4)(b); Motor vehicle (up to $2,500): Revised Code of Washington Annotated 6.15.010(3)(c); Tools of a trade (up to $5,000): Revised Code of Washington Annotated 6.15.010(4)(c); Professionally prescribed health aids (unlimited amount): Revised Code of Washington Annotated 6.15.010(3)(e); Personal injury awards (up to $16,150): Revised Code of Washington Annotated 6.15.010(3)(f); Building materials for home improvement (unlimited amount): Revised Code of Washington Annotated 60.04.201.

Real Estate: Real property or mobile home (up to $40,000); must file exemption with county: Revised Code of Washington Annotated 6.13.010 & 6.13.030 [*Note*: This exemption is for an unlimited value if for property located in Washington and if debtor is seeking to discharge debt for a state income tax assessed on retirement benefits received while a resident of Washington.]

Wages: 75% of earned but unpaid wages (judge may allow more for low-income debtors): Revised Code of Washington Annotated 6.27.150.

West Virginia

West Virginia residents cannot use the Federal Bankruptcy Exemptions, but may use the Federal Non-Bankruptcy Exemptions listed at the end of this Appendix and the following state exemptions:

Benefits: Aid to aged, blind, disabled, families with dependent children, and general assistance (unlimited amount): West Virginia Code 9-5-1; Crime victims compensation (unlimited amount): West Virginia Code 14-2A-24 & 38-10-4(k)(1); Social Security (unlimited amount): West Virginia Code 38-10-4(j)(1); Unemployment compensation (unlimited amount): West Virginia Code 38-10-4(j)(1); Veterans benefits (unlimited amount): West Virginia Code 38-10-4(j)(2); Workers compensation (unlimited amount): West Virginia Code 23-4-18.

Insurance: Fraternal society benefits (unlimited amount): West Virginia Code 33-23-21; Group life insurance policy or proceeds (unlimited amount): West Virginia Code 33-6-28; Health or disability benefits (unlimited amount): West Virginia Code 38-10-4 (j)(3); Life insurance proceeds (unlimited amount): West Virginia Code 38-10-4(k)(3); Unmatured life insurance contract (unlimited amount; accrued dividend, interest, or loan value up to $8,000, if debtor is the insured or 1 debtor is dependent upon): West Virginia Code 38-10-4(g), (h).

Miscellaneous: Alimony and child support (amount needed for support): West Virginia Code 38-10-4 (j)(4); Any property (up to $800 plus any unused amount of real estate or burial exemption): West Virginia Code 38-10-4(e); Payments made to prepaid tuition trust fund (unlimited amount): West Virginia Code 38-10-4(k)(6).

Pensions: Public employees (unlimited amount): West Virginia Code 5-10-46; Retirement benefits (amount needed for support): West Virginia Code 38-10-4 (j)(5); Teachers (unlimited amount): West Virginia Code 18-7A-30.

Personal Property: Animals, appliances, books, clothing, crops, furnishings, household goods, and musical instruments (up to $400 per item and $8,000 total): West Virginia Code 38-10-4(c); Burial plot (up to $25,000, if taken instead of real estate exemption): West Virginia Code 38-10-4(a); Health aids (unlimited amount): West Virginia Code 38-10-4(i); Implements, books, and tools of a trade (up to $1,500): West Virginia Code 38-10-4(f); Jewelry (up to $1,000): West Virginia Code 38-10-4(d); Lost future earnings payments (amount needed for support): West Virginia Code 38-10-4(k)(5); Motor vehicle (up to $2,400): West Virginia Code 38-10-4(b); Personal injury recoveries (up to $15,000, but not for pain and suffering): West Virginia Code 38-10-4(k)(4); Wrongful death recoveries (amount needed

for support): West Virginia Code 38-10-4(k)(2); Tuition trust fund (unlimited amount): West Virginia Code 38-10-4(k)(6).
Real Estate: Real or personal property used as residence (up to $25,000): West Virginia Code 38-10-4(a).
Wages: 50% of earned but unpaid wages (more possible for low-income debtor): West Virginia Code 38-5A-3.

Wisconsin

Wisconsin residents may use either the Federal Bankruptcy Exemptions listed at the end of this Appendix or the state exemptions listed below. If state exemptions are used, then the Federal Non-Bankruptcy Exemptions at the end of this Appendix may also be used.
Benefits: Aid to families with dependent children and any other social services payments (unlimited amount): Wisconsin Statutes Annotated 49.96; Crime victims compensation (unlimited amount): Wisconsin Statutes Annotated 949.07; Unemployment compensation (unlimited amount): Wisconsin Statutes Annotated 108.13; Veterans benefits (unlimited amount): Wisconsin Statutes Annotated 45.35(8)(b); Workers compensation (unlimited amount): Wisconsin Statutes Annotated 102.27.
Insurance: Federal disability insurance (unlimited amount): Wisconsin Statutes Annotated 815.18(3)(d); Fraternal society benefits (unlimited amount): Wisconsin Statutes Annotated 614.96; Insurance proceeds for exempt property destroyed within 2 years of filing for bankruptcy (up to amount of exemption): Wisconsin Statutes Annotated 815.18(3)(e); Life insurance proceeds if beneficiary was a dependent of the insured (amount needed for support): Wisconsin Statutes Annotated 815.18(3)(i)(1)(a); Life insurance proceeds if held in trust by insurer and if policy prohibits proceeds from being used to pay creditors: Wisconsin Statutes Annotated 632.42; Unmatured life insurance contract (unlimited amount; accrued dividend, interest, or loan value up to $4,000, if debtor is the insured or 1 debtor is dependent upon): Wisconsin Statutes Annotated 815.18(3)(f).
Miscellaneous: Alimony and child support (up to $7,500): Wisconsin Statutes Annotated 815.18(3)(c); Property of a business partnership (unlimited amount): Wisconsin Statutes Annotated 178.21.
Pensions: Firefighters and police officers (unlimited amount): Wisconsin Statutes Annotated 815.18(3)(e) & (f); Military pensions (unlimited amount): Wisconsin Statutes Annotated 815.18 (3)(n); Private or public retirement benefits (amount needed for support): Wisconsin Statutes Annotated 815.18(3)(j); Public employees (unlimited amount): Wisconsin Statutes Annotated 40.08(1).
Personal Property: Animals, appliances, books, clothing, firearms, furnishings, household goods, jewelry, keepsakes, musical instruments, sporting goods, or any other personal property held for personal use (up to $5,000 total): Wisconsin Statutes Annotated 815.18(3)(d); Bank accounts (up to $1,000): Wisconsin Statutes Annotated 815.18(3)(k); Burial plot (unlimited amount): Wisconsin Statutes Annotated 815.18(3)(a); Equipment, inventory, farm products, books, and tools of a trade (up to $7,500 total): Wisconsin Statutes Annotated 815.18(3)(b); Lease or interest in housing co-op (up to real estate exemption amount): Wisconsin Statutes Annotated 1824(6); Lost future earnings recoveries (amount needed for support): Wisconsin Statutes Annotated 815.18(3)(i)(1)(d); Motor vehicles (up to $1,200): Wisconsin Statutes Annotated 815.18(3)(g); Personal injury recoveries (up to $25,000): Wisconsin Statutes Annotated 815.18(3)(i)(1)(c); Wrongful death recoveries (amount needed for support): Wisconsin Statutes Annotated 815.18(3)(i)(1)(b); Fire-fighting equipment belonging to municipality (unlimited amount): Wisconsin Statutes Annotated 815.18(e)(m); State aid to county fairs and agricultural societies (unlimited amount): Wisconsin Statutes Annotated 815.18(d)(f); Tuition trust funds and college savings programs (unlimited amount): Wisconsin Statutes Annotated 14.63 & 14.64.
Real Estate: Real property used, or intended to be used, as a residence, which includes a building, condominium, mobile home, house trailer, or cooperative not less than 1/4 of an acre and not exceeding 40 acres (up to $40,000); proceeds from sale of exempt real estate is exempt for 2 years: Wisconsin Statutes Annotated 815.20.
Wages: 75% of earned but unpaid wages (judge may allow more for low-income debtors): Wisconsin Statutes Annotated 815.18(3)(h); Wages used for the purchase of savings bonds (unlimited amount):

Wisconsin Statutes Annotated 20.921(1)(e); Wages of inmates under work release programs, in county jails, or in county work camps (unlimited amount): Wisconsin Statutes Annotated 303.65, 303.08, & 303.10.

Wyoming

Wyoming residents cannot use the Federal Bankruptcy Exemptions, but may use the Federal Non-Bankruptcy Exemptions listed at the end of this Appendix and the following state exemptions:

Benefits: Aid to families with dependent children and general assistance (unlimited amount): Wyoming Statutes Annotated 42-2-113; Crime victims compensation (unlimited amount): Wyoming Statutes Annotated 1-40-113; Unemployment compensation (unlimited amount): Wyoming Statutes Annotated 27-3-319; Workers compensation (unlimited amount): Wyoming Statutes Annotated 27-14-702.

Insurance: Annuity contract proceeds (up to $350 per month): Wyoming Statutes Annotated 26-15-132; Disability benefits if policy prohibits proceeds from being used to pay creditors (unlimited amount): Wyoming Statutes Annotated 26-15-130; Fraternal society benefits (unlimited amount): Wyoming Statutes Annotated 26-29-218; Group life or disability policy or proceeds (unlimited amount): Wyoming Statutes Annotated 26-15-131; Life insurance proceeds if held in trust by insurer and if policy prohibits proceeds from being used to pay creditors (unlimited amount): Wyoming Statutes Annotated 26-15-133.

Miscellaneous: Liquor and beer licenses (unlimited amount): Wyoming Statutes Annotated 12-4-604.

Pensions: Criminal investigators and highway patrol (unlimited amount): Wyoming Statutes Annotated 9-3-620; Firefighters and police officers (only payments being received): Wyoming Statutes Annotated 15-5-209; Game and fish wardens (unlimited amount): Wyoming Statutes Annotated 9-3-620; Private or public retirement accounts (unlimited amount): Wyoming Statutes Annotated 1-20-110; Public employees (unlimited amount): Wyoming Statutes Annotated 9-3-426.

Personal Property: Bedding, food, furniture, and household articles (up to $2,000 per person in household if 2 or more people, otherwise $2,000): Wyoming Statutes Annotated 1-20-106(a)(iii); Bible, schoolbooks, and pictures (unlimited amount): Wyoming Statutes Annotated 1-20-106(a)(i); Burial plot (unlimited amount): Wyoming Statutes Annotated 1-20-106(a)(ii) & 35-8-104; Clothing and wedding rings (up to $1,000): Wyoming Statutes Annotated 1-20-105; Library and equipment of a professional (up to $2,000): Wyoming Statutes Annotated 1-20-106(b); Motor vehicle (up to $2,400): Wyoming Statutes Annotated 1-20-106 (a)(iv); Pre-paid funeral contracts (unlimited amount): Wyoming Statutes Annotated 26-32-102; Tools, motor vehicle, implements, team, and stock-in-trade used in trade or business (up to $2,400): Wyoming Statutes Annotated 1-20-106(b); Medical savings accounts (unlimited amount): Wyoming Statutes Annotated 1-20-111.

Real Estate: Real property or house trailer used as a residence (up to $10,000, $20,000 for joint owners, only up to $6,000 for house trailer; and up to $12,000 for joint owners of house trailer): Wyoming Statutes Annotated 1-20-101, 1-20-102, & 1-20-104.

Wages: 75% of earned but unpaid wages (judge may allow more for low-income debtors): Wyoming Statutes Annotated 1-15-511; Wages of inmates on work release, in community corrections programs, and correctional industry programs (unlimited amount): Wyoming Statutes Annotated 7-16-308, 7-18-114, & 25-13-107; Wages of National Guard members (unlimited amount): Wyoming Statutes Annotated 19-9-501.

Federal Bankruptcy Exemptions

Federal Bankruptcy Exemptions are only available to residents of the following states: Arkansas, Connecticut, District of Columbia (Washington D.C.), Hawaii, Massachusetts, Michigan, Minnesota, New Jersey, New Mexico, Pennsylvania, Rhode Island, South Carolina, Texas, Vermont, Washington, and Wisconsin. If the debtor elects to use the Federal Bankruptcy Exemptions listed here, he or she cannot use either his or her own state exemptions or the Federal Non-Bankruptcy Exemptions listed at the end of this Appendix. Married couples filing jointly may double the exemption amounts listed.

Benefits: Crime victims compensation (unlimited amount): 11 United States Code 522(d)(11)(A); Public assistance (unlimited amount): 11 United States Code 522(d)(10)(A); Unemployment compensation (unlimited amount): 11 United States Code 522(d)(10)(A); Social Security (unlimited amount): 11 United States Code 522(d)(10)(A); Veterans benefits (unlimited amount): 11 United States Code 522(d)(10)(B).

Insurance: Disability, illness, or unemployment benefits (unlimited amount): 11 United States Code 522(d)(10)(C); Life insurance proceeds (amount needed for support): 11 United States Code 522(d)(11)(C); Life insurance policy loan value, dividends, or interest (up to $9,850): 11 United States Code 522(d)(8); Unmatured life insurance contract (unlimited amount, but not credit insurance policy): 11 United States Code 522(d)(7).

Miscellaneous: Alimony and child support (amount needed for support): 11 United States Code 522(10)(D); Any property (up to $975): 11 United States Code 522(d)(5).

Pensions: Retirement benefits (amount needed for support): 11 United States Code 522(d)(10)(E).

Personal Property: Animals, appliances, books, clothing, crops, furnishings, household goods, and musical instruments (up to $475 per item and up to $9,850 total): 11 United States Code 522(d)(3); One motor vehicle (up to $2,950): 11 United States Code 522(d)(2); Burial plot ($18,450 in lieu of real estate exemption): 11 United States Code 522(d)(1); Health aids (unlimited amount): 11 United States Code 522(d)(9); Implements, books, and tools of a trade (up to $1,850): 11 United States Code 522(d)(6); Jewelry (up to $1,225): 11 United States Code 522(d)(4); Lost earnings payments (unlimited amount): 11 United States Code 522 (d)(11)(E); Personal injury recoveries (up to $18,450, but not for pain and suffering or pecuniary loss): 11 United States Code 522(d)(11)(D); Wrongful death recoveries (amount needed for support): 11 United States Code 522(d)(11)(B).

Real Estate: Real property, co-op, or mobile home (up to $18,450, unused portion of homestead exemption may be used for other property up to $9,250): 11 United States Code 522(d)(1).

Wages: None.

Federal Non-Bankruptcy Exemptions

The following Federal Non-Bankruptcy Exemptions may only be used if the debtor elects to use specific state exemptions. If the debtor elects to use the Federal Bankruptcy Exemptions on the previous page, he or she cannot use the Federal Non-Bankruptcy Exemptions listed here.

Benefits: Government employee death and disability benefits (unlimited amount): 5 United States Code 8130; Harbor workers death and disability benefits (unlimited amount): 33 United States Code 916; Judges survivor benefits (unlimited amount): 28 United States Code 376; Judicial center directors survivor benefits (unlimited amount): 28 United States Code 376; Lighthouse workers survivor benefits (unlimited amount): 33 United States Code 775; Longshoremen death and disability benefits (unlimited amount): 33 United States Code 916; Military service survivor benefits (unlimited amount): 10 United States Code 1450; Supreme Court Chief Justice administrators survivor benefits (unlimited amount): 28 United States Code 376; U.S. court directors survivor benefits (unlimited amount): 28 United States Code 376; War hazard death or injury compensation (unlimited amount): 42 United States Code 1717.

Insurance: Railroad workers unemployment insurance (unlimited amount): 45 United States Code 352(e).

Miscellaneous: Klamath Indian tribe benefits (unlimited amount): 25 United States Code 543 & 545.

Pensions: Civil service employees (unlimited amount): 5 United States Code 8346; Foreign service employees (unlimited amount): 22 United States Code 4060; Military honor roll pensions (unlimited amount): 38 United States Code 562; Military service employees (unlimited amount): 10 United States Code 1440; Social Security (unlimited amount): 42 United States Code 407; Veterans benefits (unlimited amount): 38 United States Code 3101; Veterans medal of honor benefits (unlimited amount): 38 United States Code 562.

Personal Property: Savings account deposits while on permanent military duty outside U.S. (unlimited amount): 10 United States Code 1035; Seamen's clothing (unlimited amount): 46 United States Code 11110.

Real Estate: None.

Wages: 75% of earned but unpaid wages (judge may allow more for low-income debtors): 15 United States Code 1673; Wages of seamen while on a voyage (unlimited amount): 46 United States Code 11111.

Appendix C: Federal Bankruptcy Courts

Alabama
12th & Noble Streets
103 US Courthouse
Anniston AL 36201
Phone: 205-237-5631

1800 5th. Ave. North
Birmingham AL 35203
Phone: 205-731-0850

PO Box 1289
Decatur AL 35601
Phone: 205-353-2817

201 Saint Louis Street
Mobile AL 36602
Phone: 334-441-5391

PO Box 1248
Montgomery AL 36102
Phone: 334-206-6300

PO Box 3226
Tuscaloosa AL 35403
Phone: 205-752-0426

Alaska
605 West 4th Avenue
Suite 138
Anchorage AK 99501
Phone: 907-271-2655

Arizona
US Courthouse
2929 N Central, 9th Floor
PO Box 34151
Phoenix AZ 85067
Phone: 602-620-7500 or
 620-5800

110 South Church Avenue
Suite 8112
Tucson AZ 85701
Phone: 520-620-7459 or
 620-7500

325 19th. Street, Ste. D
Yuma AZ
Phone: 520-783-2288

Arkansas
300 W. 2nd., Ste. 111
Little Rock AR 72201
Phone: 501-918-5506

California
2656 US Courthouse
1130 0 Street
Fresno CA 93721
Phone: 209-498-7217

255 East Temple
Los Angeles CA 90012
Phone: 213-894-6244 or
 894-3118

1130 12th St., Ste. C
Modesto CA 95354
Phone: 209-521-5160

3rd Floor
1300 Clay Street
Oakland CA 94612
Phone: 510-273-7212

501 I St.
Sacramento CA 95814
Phone: 916-498-5564

222 East Carrillo Street
Santa Barbara CA 93101
Phone: 805-897-3870

699 North Arrowhead Avenue
Room 105
San Bernardino CA 92401
Phone: 909-383-5717 or
 383-5742

5-N-26 US Courthouse
940 Front Street, 19th Floor
San Diego CA 92189
Phone: 619-557-5620

PO Box 7341
235 Pine Street
San Francisco CA 94120
Phone: 415-705-3200

280 South First Street
Room 3035
San Jose CA 95113
Phone: 408-291-7286

506 Federal Building
34 Civic Center Plaza
Santa Ana CA 92701
Phone: 714-836-2993

140 Guerneville Road
Building G
Santa Rosa CA 95403
Phone: 707-525-8520 or
 525-8539

Colorado
721 19th Street
Denver CO 80202
Phone: 303-844-4045

Connecticut
US Courthouse
915 Lafayette Boulevard
Bridgeport CT 06604
Phone: 203-579-5808

US Courthouse
450 Main Street
Hartford CT 06103
Phone: 860-240-3675

U.S. Bankruptcy Court
157 Church St., 18th Fl.
New Haven CT 06510
Phone: 203-773-2009

Delaware
824 Market
Wilmington DE 19801
Phone: 302-252-2900

District of Columbia
US Courthouse
4400 U.S. Courthouse Ave.
330 Constitution Ave. NW
Washington DC 20001
Phone: 202-273-0992 or
   273-0042

Florida
Room 310
299 East Broward Blvd.
Fort Lauderdale FL 33301
Phone: 954-769-5700

PO Box 559
311 West Monroe Street
Jacksonville FL 32202
Phone: 904-232-2852

1401 Federal Building
51 SW First Avenue
Miami FL 33130
Phone: 305-536-5216

220 West Garden Street
Suite 700
Pensacola FL 32501
Phone: 904-435-8475

227 North Bronough Street
Suite 3120
Tallahassee FL 32301
Phone: 904-942-8933

U.S. Bankruptcy Court
801 N. Florida Ave.
Tampa FL 33602
Phone: 813-301-5162

701 Clematis Street
335 Federal Building
West Palm Beach FL 33401
Phone: 561-655-6774

Georgia
Suite 1340
75 Spring Street SW
Atlanta GA 30303
Phone: 404-331-6886

PO Box 1487
827 Taylor Street
Augusta GA 30903
Phone: 706-724-2421

PO Box 2147
233 12th Street
Columbus GA 31902
Phone: 706-649-7837

PO Drawer 1957
433 Cherry St.
Macon GA
Phone: 912-752-3506

PO Box 2328
Federal Building
Greenville Street
Newnan GA 30264
Phone: 678-423-3000

PO Box 5231
Federal Building
600 E First Street
Rome GA 30161
Phone: 706-291-5639

PO Box 8347
Savannah GA 31412
Phone: 912-650-4100

Hawaii
1132 Bishop St., Ste. 250L
Honolulu HI 96813
Phone: 808-522-8100, ext. 11

Idaho
550 West Fort Street
Box 042
Federal Building
Boise ID 83724
Phone: 208-334-1074

Illinois
US Courthouse
219 South Dearborn Street
Room 614
Chicago IL 60604
Phone: 312-435-5694

PO Box 657
201 North Vermilion Street
Danville IL 61834
Phone: 217-431-4820

401 S. Missouri
East St. Louis IL 62201-3017
Phone: 219-236-8247

131 Federal Building
100 NE Monroe Street
Peoria IL 61602
Phone: 309-671-7035

211 South Court Street
Rockford IL 61101
Phone: 815-987-4350

226 US Courthouse
600 East Monroe Street
Springfield IL 62701
Phone: 217-492-4551

Indiana
352 Federal Bldg
101 Martin Luther King
  Boulevard
Evansville IN 47708
Phone: 812-465-6440

1188 Federal Building
1300 South Harrison Street
Ft Wayne IN 46802
Phone: 219-420-5100

221 Federal Building
610 Connecticut Street
Gary IN 46402
Phone: 219-881-3335

322 US Courthouse
16 East Ohio Street
Indianapolis IN 46204
Phone: 317-226-6710

121 W. Spring St.
New Albany IN 47150
Phone: 812-948-5254

PO Box 7003
401 South Michigan Street
South Bend IN 46634
Phone: 219-968-2100

203 Post Office Building
30 North 7th Street
Terre Haute IN 47808
Phone: 812-238-1831

Iowa
PO Box 74890
425 2nd Street SE
Cedar Rapids IA 52407
Phone: 319-286-2200 or
  286-2230

320 Sixth St.
Sioux City IA 51101
Phone: 712-233-3939

PO Box 9264
US Courthouse
110 E. Court Ave.
Des Moines IA 50306
Phone: 515-284-6230

Kansas
500 State Avenue
161 US Courthouse
Kansas City KS 66101
Phone: 913-551-6732

240 Federal Building
44 SE Quincy Street Rm. 240
Topeka KS 66683
Phone: 913-295-2750

167 US Courthouse
401 North Market Street
Wichita KS 67202
Phone: 316-269-6486

Kentucky
PO Box 1111
Merrill Lynch Building
100 East Vine Street
Lexington KY 40588
Phone: 606-233-2608

546 US Courthouse
601 West Broadway
Louisville KY 40202
Phone: 502-582-5146

126 U.S. Bankruptcy Court
423 Fredrica St.
Owensboro KY 42301
Phone: 502-683-0221

120 U.S. Bankruptcy Court
241 E. Main St.
Bowling Green KY 42101
Phone: 502-781-1110

U.S. Bankruptcy Court
501 Broadway, Ste. 322
Paducah KY 42001
Phone: 502-443-1337

Louisiana
300 Jackson Street
Alexandria LA 71301
Phone: 318-445-1890

707 Florida St., Ste 119
Baton Rouge LA 70801
Phone: 504-389-0211

Hale Boggs Federal Building
501 Magazine Street
New Orleans LA 70130
Phone: 504-589-7878

205 Federal Building
250 South Union Street
Opelousas LA 70570
Phone: 318-948-3451

300 Fannin Street
US Courthouse
Suite 2201
ShrevePport LA 71101
Phone: 318-676-4267

Maine
202 Harlow St., 3rd. Fl.
Bangor ME 04402
Phone: 207-945-0348

537 Congress Street
Portland ME 04101
Phone: 207-780-3482

Maryland
US Courthouse
101 West Lombard Street
Baltimore MD 21201
Phone: 410-962-2688

Suite 300
6500 Cherry Wood Lane
Greenbelt MD 20770
Phone: 301-344-8018

Massachusetts
1101 Federal Building
10 Causeway Street
Boston MA 02222
Phone: 617-565-6050

Room 211
595 Main Street
Worcester MA 01601
Phone: 508-770-8913

Michigan
211 West Fort Street
21st Floor
Detroit MI 48226
Phone: 313-234-0065

PO Box 3310
110 Michigan Street NW
Grand Rapids MI 49501
Phone: 616-456-2693

202 W. Washington St.
Rm. 314
Marquette MI 49855
Phone: 906-226-2117

U.S. Bankruptcy Court
111 1st., PO Box 911
Bay City MI 48707
Phone: 517-894-8840

U.S. Bankruptcy Clerk
226 West 2nd. St.
Flint MI 48502
Phone: 313-766-5050

Minnesota
416 US Courthouse
515 West 1st Street
Duluth MN 55802
Phone: 218-529-3600

305 US Courthouse
118 South Mill Street
Fergus Falls MN 56537
Phone: 218-739-4671

301 US Courthouse
300 South Fourth Street
Minneapolis MN 55415
Phone: 612-664-5200

200 US Courthouse
316 North Robert Street
Saint Paul MN 55101
Phone: 615-848-1000

Mississippi
PO Drawer 867
205 Federal Building
Arberdeen MS 39730
Phone: 601-369-2596

725 Washington Loop
Room 117
Biloxi MS 39533
Phone: 601-432-5542

PO Drawer 2448
100 East Capitol Street
Room 107
Jackson MS 39225
Phone: 601-965-5301

Missouri
US Courthouse
1800 U.S. Courthouse
400 E. 9th St.
Kansas City MO 64106
Phone: 816-426-3321

1 Metropolitan Square
211 North Broadway
7th Floor
Saint Louis MO 63102
Phone: 314-425-4222

Montana
PO Box 689
Federal Building
400 North Main Street
Butte MT 59701
Phone: 406-782-1043 or
    782-3338

Nebraska
PO Box 428
Downtown Station
215 North 17th Street
New Federal Building
Omaha NE 68101
Phone: 402-221-4687

460 Federal Building
100 Centennial Mall North
Lincoln NE 68508
Phone: 402-437-5100

Nevada
300 Las Vegas Boulevard
    South
Las Vegas NV 89101
Phone: 702-388-6257,
    388-6633, or 388-6407

4005 US Courthouse
300 Booth Street
Reno NV 89509
Phone: 702-784-5599,
    784-5550 or 784-5806

New Hampshire
275 Chestnut Street
722 Federal Building
Room 404
Manchester NH 03101
Phone: 603-666-7626 or
    666-7775

New Jersey
15 North 7th Street
PO Box 2067
Camden NJ 08102
Phone: 609-757-5424

50 Walnut Street
3rd Floor
Newark NJ 07102
Phone: 201-645-3930

US Courthouse, 2nd Floor
402 East State Street
Trenton NJ 08608
Phone: 609-989-2128

New Mexico
PO Box 546
Albuquerque NM 87103
Phone: 505-248-6500

New York
445 Breading
US Courthouse
Albany NY 12201
Phone: 518-431-0188

75 Clinton Street
Brooklyn NY 11201
Phone: 718-330-2188

250 U.S. Courthouse
300 Perl St., Ste. 250
Buffalo NY 14202
Phone: 716-551-4130

601 Veterans Highway
Hauppauge NY 11788
Phone: 516-361-8601

One Bowling Green
New York NY 10004
Phone: 212-668-2870 or
    212-791-2247

176 Church Street
Poughkeepsie NY 12601
Phone: 914-452-4200

100 State Street
1220 US Courthouse
Rochester NY 14614
Phone: 716-263-3148

10 Broad Street
230 US Courthouse
Utica NY 13501
Phone: 315-793-8101

1635 Privado Road
Westbury NY 11590
Phone: 516-832-8801

300 Quarropas, St
White Plains NY 10601
Phone: 914-682-6617

North Carolina
401 West Trade Street
209 Federal Building
Charlotte NC 28202
Phone: 704-350-7500

PO Box 26100
Greensboro NC 27402
Phone: 910-333-5647

PO Drawer 2807
Wilson, NC 27894-2807
Phone: 252-237-0248 x143

North Dakota
PO Box 1110
655 1st Avenue
Fargo ND 58102
Phone: 701-297-7140

Ohio
Federal Building
201 Cleveland Avenue SW
Canton OH 44702
Phone: 330-489-4426

US Courthouse
Room 735
Cincinnati OH 45202
Phone: 513-684-2572

3001 Society Center
127 Public Square
Cleveland OH 44114
Phone: 215-522-4373

124 US Courthouse
170 North High Street
Columbus OH 43215
Phone: 614-469-2087

120 West 3rd Street
Dayton OH 45402
Phone: 937-225-7274

411 US Courthouse
1716 Spielbusch Avenue
Toledo OH 43624
Phone: 419-259-6440

PO Box 147
337 US Courthouse
125 Market Street
Youngstown OH 44501
Phone: 330-746-7027

Oklahoma
Post Office-Courthouse
215 D A McGee Avenue
Oklahoma City OK 73102
Phone: 405-609-5700

PO Box 1347
US Courthouse
4th and Grand
Okmulgee OK 74447
Phone: 918-758-0127

Federal Building
224 South Boulder
Tulsa OK 74103
Phone: 918-581-7181

Oregon
PO Box 1335
404 Federal Building
151 W. 7th. Ave., Ste. 300
Eugene OR 97440
Phone: 503-465-6448

1001 SW 5th Avenue
#700
Portland OR 97204
Phone: 503-326-2231

Pennsylvania
PO Box 1755
717 State Street
Erie PA 16501
Phone: 814-453-7580

PO Box 908
Federal Building
3rd & Walnut Streets
Harrisburg PA 17108
Phone: 717-901-2800

900 Market Street
Philadelphia PA 19107
Phone: 215-408-2800

400 Washington, St., Rm. 300
Reading PA 19601
Phone: 610-320-5255

U.S. Bankruptcy Court
5414 USX Tower
600 Grant St.
Pittsburgh PA 15219
Phone: 412-355-3210

217 Federal Building
197 South Main Street
Wilkes-Barre PA 18701
Phone: 717-826-6450

Rhode Island
380 Westminster Mall
Federal Center
Providence RI 02903
Phone: 401-528-4477

South Carolina
PO Box 1448
1100 Laurel Street
Columbia SC 29202
Phone: 803-765-5436

South Dakota
PO Box 5060
US Courthouse
400 South Phillips Avenue
Sioux Falls SD 57117
Phone: 605-330-4541

203 Federal Building
225 South Pierre Street
Pierre SD 57501
Phone: 605-224-0560

Tennessee
31 East 11th Street
Chattanooga TN 37402
Phone: 865-545-4279

108 W Summer Street
Greenville TN 37743
Phone: 423-638-2264

1501 Tower Plaza
Knoxville TN 37929
Phone: 423-545-4279 or
    545-4284

200 Jefferson Avenue
Room 500
Memphis TN 38103
Phone: 901-328-3500

207 Customs House
701 Broadway
Nashville TN 37203
Phone: 615-736-7590

Texas
U.S. Bankruptcy Court
903 San Jacinto Blvd. #322
Austin TX 78701
Phone: 512-916-5238

300 Willow Street, Suite 100
Beaumont TX 77701
Phone: 409-839-2617

615 Leopard Street
113 Wilson Place N
Corpus Christi TX 78476
Phone: 512-888-3484

U.S. Bankruptcy Court
211 W. Ferguson St.
4th Floor
Tyler TX 75702
Phone: 903-590-1212

12-A-24 US Courthouse
1100 Commerce Street
Dallas TX 75242
Phone: 800-442-6850

8515 Lockheed
PO Box 971040
El Paso TX 79997
Phone: 915-779-7362

501 West 10th Street
Fort Worth TX 76102
Phone: 817-333-6000

US Courthouse
PO Box 61010
Houston TX 77008
Phone: 713-250-5115

102 Federal Building
1205 Texas Avenue
Lubbock TX 79401
Phone: 800-796-8262

PO Box 191
201 East 4th Street
Pecos TX 79772
Phone: 915-445-4228

PO Box 1439
615 East Houston Street
San Antonio TX 78295
Phone: 210-472-6722

660 North Central
    Expressway
Plano Texas 75074
Phone: 972-509-1240

U.S. Bankruptcy Court
600 Austin Ave.
St. Charels PL., Ste 28
Waco TX 76710
Phone: 254-754-1481

Utah
301 US Courthouse
350 Main Street
Salt Lake City UT 84101
Phone: 801-524-6687

Vermont
PO Box 6648
67 Merchants Row, 2nd Floor
Rutland VT 05702
Phone: 802-776-2000

Virginia
PO Box 19247
Alexandria VA 22320
Phone: 703-258-1200

PO Box 1407
116 North Main Street
Harrisonburg VA 22801
Phone: 530-434-8327

PO Box 6400
1100 Main St
Lynchburg VA 24505
Phone: 804-845-0317

PO Box 1938
US Courthouse
600 Granby Street
Norfolk VA 23510
Phone: 757-222-7500

US Courthouse Annex
  Building
Suite 301
1100 Elm Street
Richmond VA 23219
Phone: 804-916-2400

PO Box 2390
210 Church Avenue SW
Roanoke VA 24010
Phone: 540-857-2391

Washington
PO Box 2164
Spokane WA 99210
Phone: 509-353-2404

315 Park Place Building
1200 6th Avenue
Seattle WA 98101
Phone: 206-553-2751

U.S. Bankruptcy Court
1717 Pacific Ave.
Tacoma WA 98402
Phone: 206-593-6313

West Virginia
300 Virginia St. E.
Charleston WV 25301
Phone: 304-347-3000

PO Box 70
12th & Chapline Street
Wheeling WV 26003
Phone: 304-233-1655

Wisconsin
PO Box 5009
500 South Barstow Street
Eau Claire WI 54701
Phone: 715-839-2980

PO Box 548
120 North Henry
Madison WI 53701
Phone: 608-264-5178

216 Federal Building
517 East Wisconsin Avenue
Room 171
Milwaukee WI 53202
Phone: 414-297-3291,
   297-1583, or 297-4087

Wyoming
PO Box 1107
Cheyenne WY 82003
Phone: 307-772-2191

Room 101
111 South Wolcott St.
Casper WY 26003
Phone: 307-261-5444

Glossary of Bankruptcy Legal Terms

Annuity: An insurance contract that pays the insured person during his or her life, rather than paying a beneficiary after the insured person's death. An annuity is a type of retirement plan.

Asset: Anything of value. May be real estate or personal property. Personal property can be tangible or intangible property.

Attachment: The seizure or repossession of property by a governmental agent. Generally, attachment is carried out by a county sheriff or the Internal Revenue Service.

Automatic stay: An court order from the bankruptcy court that goes into effect automatically upon filing for bankruptcy. It orders creditors to stop taking any further action to collect on any debts owed by the debtor filing for bankruptcy including lawsuits, garnishments, foreclosures, and collections.

Bankruptcy Code: The U.S. Bankruptcy Code is the set of United States laws relating to bankruptcy. The laws are contained in Title 11, Sections 101-1330 of the United States Code.

Bankruptcy Court Rules: In addition to the Bankruptcy Code, there are three further sets of rules that govern the procedures in bankruptcy courts: the Federal Rules of Bankruptcy Procedure, the Federal Rules of Civil Procedure, and Local Bankruptcy Court Rules. Local bankruptcy court rules may not conflict with any of the federal rules.

Bankruptcy Courts: The United States is divided into various bankruptcy court districts. All bankruptcy court districts are referenced by the name of the state (for example, Federal Bankruptcy Court, Idaho District). Many districts are also referenced geographically, if there is more than one district within the state (i.e., Southern District of Illinois).

Bankruptcy estate: All property, whether real estate or personal property, that is owned by a debtor who files for bankruptcy. Control over the bankruptcy estate is given to the court by filing for bankruptcy.

Bankruptcy petition: A formal request of the court for the protection of the federal bankruptcy laws.

Bankruptcy petition preparer: A private non-lawyer paralegal who can assist persons in preparing the legal papers necessary for bankruptcy. He or she cannot, however, provide any legal advice. Preparers are now authorized and regulated by the Bankruptcy Code.

Bankruptcy trustee: A person who is appointed by the bankruptcy court to handle the bankruptcy estate of a debtor. The trustee will examine the papers, handle the creditors' meeting, collect and sell any non-exempt property, and pay off the creditors.

Chapter 7: The chapter of the Bankruptcy Code that provides for "liquidation" (the sale of the debtor's non-exempt property and distribution of the proceeds to the creditors).

Chapter 11: The chapter of the Bankruptcy Code that provides for reorganization (usually of a corporation or partnership).

Chapter 12: The chapter of the Bankruptcy Code that provides for an adjustment of the debts of a family farmer.

Chapter 13: The chapter of the Bankruptcy Code that provides for an adjustment of the debts of an individual with a regular income.

Claim: A creditor's assertion of a right to payment from a debtor.

Codebtor: A person who is jointly liable on a particular debt, either because of cosigning on the debt, acting as a guarantor on the debt, or by virtue of being a spouse or partner of the debtor.

Collateral: Property used to guarantee payment for a secured debt.

Cosignor: A person who has also signed a loan or contract with another and who is jointly liable on the loan or contract.

Common-law property: Property in those states that follow common-law property rules. In general, the ownership of common-law property is determined by the name on the title document for the property. This is true for married couples also, with the exception of gifts or inheritances that are received jointly and thus held jointly. See also *community property*.

Community debts: Those debts incurred during marriage in those states that follow community-property rules. See also *community property*.

Community property: Property held by a husband and wife in those states that follow community-property law rules (Alaska, Arizona, California, Idaho, Louisiana, Nevada, New Mexico, Texas, Washington, and Wisconsin). Generally, all property that either spouse receives during their marriage is owned jointly by both spouses and is referred to as community property. See also *common-law property*.

Contingent debt: A known debt with an uncertain value that has yet to be resolved by a court.

Creditor: A creditor is a person or entity (corporation, partnership, etc.) who is owed a debt of some type. Creditors may be secured creditors who hold the title or a lien or some form of collateral for the debt. Creditors may also be unsecured creditors who have no security for the debt.

Creditors' meeting: This meeting is held in all Chapter 7 bankruptcies approximately one month after filing. It is attended by the bankruptcy trustee and the debtor(s). It may also be attended by any of the creditors. At this meeting, the bankruptcy papers will be examined, priority claims determined, and the property that is exempt will be resolved.

Debtor: A debtor is a person (or entity) who owes a debt of some kind. The persons or entities who file for bankruptcy are referred to as "debtors" in the court papers.

Debts: A debt is an obligation of some type that is owed to another person or entity. A debt may be secured if collateral of some type has been pledged or if a lien exists against some type of property. A debt may also be unsecured if there is no collateral securing the debt. Debts may also be further classified as "contingent", "liquidated," "unliquidated." See also *contingent debt, liquidated debt,* or *unliquidated debt*.

Disability benefits: Payments made to a person under a disability insurance plan because of injury, disability, or sickness.

Discharge: The total elimination of all dischargeable debts. This is the final result of a Chapter 7 bankruptcy. A discharge also prohibits creditors from communicating in any way with the debtor regarding the discharged debts.

Dischargeable debts: Those debts that may, by bankruptcy law, be discharged (eliminated) by a bankruptcy action. See also *non-dischargeable debts*.

Disputed debts: Those debts that a debtor claims are in error, either in part or in whole.

Equity: The value of a debtor's interest in property that remains after all liens or creditor's interests (such as a mortgage) are deducted.

ERISA benefits: Payments made to a person under a pension or retirement plan that qualifies under the Federal Employees Retirement Income Security Act. IRAs, KEOGHs, and many other pensions are ERISA plans. Ask your retirement plan administrator.

Execution: The process of seizing and selling property under a court order or judgment for a money judgment against a person or entity.

Executory contract: A contract that is not fully completed, which has some obligation or action yet to be fulfilled.

Exempt property: Property that may not be seized, repossessed by a private creditor, or executed against by a government agent because of debts that the owner has incurred. Property may be exempt based on either state or federal law.

Expenditure: Money that is, or will be, spent by a debtor.
Family farm bankruptcy: A Chapter 12 bankruptcy. Similar to a Chapter 13 bankruptcy, but which is available only to those debtors who fit the description of a "family farmer."
Fee simple: Referst to full ownership.
Fraternal society benefits: Group life or other insurance benefits that are maintained and paid to members by fraternal societies, such as the Elks, Masons, Moose, etc.
Fraudulent transfer: A transfer of property by a debtor with the intent to defraud creditors.
Group Insurance: A single insurance policy under which a group of persons is covered. Often, employee insurance plans are based on group insurance policies.
Guarantor: A person who has agreed to guarantee payment on a debt should the original debtor fail to keep up on the required payments.
Health aids: Items or material that a person uses to maintain his or her own health, such as a wheelchair.
Health benefits: Payments made to a person under a health insurance policy.
Homestead declaration: A document that is placed on county property records that asserts your homestead exemption. Filing such a declaration is a requirement in certain states in order to take advantage of your homestead exemption. Check your state's listing in Appendix B.
Homestead exemption: A state or federal exemption that protects a personal residence from being seized to pay for the owner's debts. Is often limited to only a certain dollar value.
Household goods: Non-disposable items that are used to maintain a household, such as dishes, utensils, pots and pans, lamps, radios, etc.
Income: Money that is, or will be, earned by a debtor.
Insider: Any relative of an individual debtor.
Insurance benefits: Payments made to a person under an insurance policy.
Intangible property: Property that has no actual existence, such as stocks, bonds, copyrights, trademarks, etc. These items may be represented by some type of document, but the property itself has no physical existence. See also *tangible property*.
Involuntary bankruptcy: A bankruptcy action that is instituted by creditors against a debtor who has defaulted on debt obligations.
Joint petition: A single bankruptcy petition filed by a husband and wife together.
Joint tenancy: Joint ownership of property in which the owners of the property hold equal undivided ownership interest in the property and in which each owner has the right of survivorship (the survivor will automatically inherit the other's interest on death).
Judgment: The final determination by a court of the matter before that court.
Judgment lien: A real estate lien that has been established by a court order or judgment. The lien is recorded on official records and generally must be satisfied before the property is sold.
Lessee: A tenant.
Lessor: A landlord.
Liability: A legal obligation or debt.
Lien: A legal claim against property for the payment of a debt.
Life insurance: A contract under which an insurance company agrees to pay a specified sum to a beneficiary upon the death of the insured person.
Liquidate: To sell a debtor's property and pay off any debts. To finally settle all debts.
Liquidated debt: A debt for which a court judgment has been issued.
Liquidation bankruptcy: A Chapter 7 bankruptcy. A bankruptcy in which all non-exempt property is sold to pay off all debts.
Lost future earnings: The amount of money awarded in a personal injury lawsuit to cover the amount of future income that the plaintiff is determined to have lost because of the injury.

Mailing list: A particular column and row arrangement of mailing addresses. It is required by many bankruptcy courts in order to make duplicate mailing labels for notification of creditors and other parties to a bankruptcy.

Matured life insurance benefits: Life insurance benefits that are currently payable to a beneficiary (because the insured person has already died).

Motor vehicle: Any vehicle that is powered by a mechanical engine.

Nature of lien: The type of lien: either a tax, judgment, child support, or mechanic's lien.

Necessities: Items that are necessary to sustain life. Generally, food, clothing, and medical care are considered necessities.

Non-dischargeable debts: Those debts that cannot be eliminated in a bankruptcy proceeding. Certain taxes, student loans, alimony, child support, and other debts are non-dischargeable. See also *dischargeable debts*.

Non-purchase money debt: A debt that is incurred other than to purchase the collateral for the debt, such as a home equity loan.

Pain and suffering payments: The amount of money awarded in a personal injury lawsuit to cover the amount of pain and suffering that the plaintiff is determined to have suffered because of the injury.

Pension benefits: Benefits that a person receives or will receive upon retirement. Generally received from some type of pension fund.

Personal injury causes of action: The right to file a suit and claim a right to compensation for personal injuries that may have occurred.

Personal Property: All property, either intangible or tangible, that is not real estate. See also *real estate*.

Possessory lien: A right to seize and sell property that attaches to the property by law, such as a moving company's right to sell property that it has moved and which has not been paid for.

Possessory non-purchase money debt: A debt that is incurred other than to purchase the collateral for the debt, and for which the creditor obtains possession of the collateral, such as a loan by a pawnshop for a pawned item.

Priority claims: Those claims for unsecured debts that, by law, are to be paid off in a bankruptcy before any other unsecured debts are paid. The most common priority claim is for the payment of taxes.

Proof of Claim by Mail: A written statement describing why a debtor owes a creditor money. There is an official form for this.

Proof of Service: An official statement under oath that a person has delivered to (served) another a specific legal document.

Purchase money debt: A debt that is incurred to purchase the property which is the collateral for the debt.

Reaffirmation of a debt: An agreement by a debtor to pay off a debt, regardless of bankruptcy. Must be approved by both the creditor and the bankruptcy court. A reaffirmed debt is not eliminated by bankruptcy, even if the debt was dischargeable. Generally done for the purpose of keeping collateral or mortgaged property that would otherwise be subject to repossession.

Real estate: All land and any items that are permanently attached to the land, such as buildings.

Redemption of property: In bankruptcy, a debtor may purchase personal property that is subject to a creditor's lien by payment of the market value of the property.

Reorganization bankruptcy: A Chapter 11 bankruptcy under which a business attempts to reorganize its affairs in order to satisfy its debt obligations.

Repossession: The taking, by a creditor of a defaulted-upon loan, of the collateral for the loan.

Retirement benefits: Those benefits that are paid to persons by reason of their retirement from a job or by virtue of their employment for a certain number of years.

Secured claim: Any mortgage, deed of trust, loan, lien, or other claim against a property, that is in writing and for which the property acts as collateral.

Secured debts: Debts for which the creditors have some form of security for their repayment, such as collateral or a lien.

Security interest: A creditor's right to possess property held as collateral, upon a debtor's default on a loan.

Setoff: The application by a creditor of other assets of a debtor to lessen the amount of debt, such as the application of a debtor's bank account balance to a pay off a defaulted loan.

Tangible property: Property that has existence, that may be touched. See also *intangible property*.

Tenancy by the entireties: A form of joint ownership of property by wives and husbands only (only in certain states). Similar to joint tenancy with a right of survivorship, but for married couples only.

Tools: Those items that are necessary to perform a certain type of work. For bankruptcy, any items that are used in a trade or business may generally qualify as a tool, including computers, motor vehicles, etc.

Unexpired lease: A lease that is still in force.

Unliquidated debt: A known, undisputed debt that has not been the subject of a court action.

Unsecured nonpriority debts: Those debts that have no collateral pledged and which are not priority debts by law.

Unsecured priority debts: See *priority claims*.

Voluntary bankruptcy: A bankruptcy that is voluntarily filed by the debtor in an effort to obtain relief from debts.

Wages: The amount of money paid on a regular basis for work.

Wrongful death benefits: The amount of money awarded in a wrongful death lawsuit to compensate the plaintiff for having to live without the deceased person.

Index

accounts payable, 36
accounts receivable, 31
administrative fees, 21, 23
alimony, 12, 14, 20, 31, 63, 76
alternatives, 15
annuity, 29, 194, 247
Application to Pay Filing Fee in Installments (Official Form 3), 18–19, 22–23, 44, 107–110, 113–114, 119, 189–191
    instructions, 107–108
    official form, 189–191
    sample form, 109–110
assets, 17–18, 20, 25–26, 34, 41, 115, 247
attachment, 87, 247
auto loans, 118
automatic stay, 11, 13, 19–20, 114–115, 247

bank accounts, 21, 27
bankruptcy
    action checklist, 22–23
    code, 11, 14, 247
    completion, 112–118
    court, 13, 16–25, 42, 59, 76, 87, 104, 111–112, 114–117, 119, 247
    court clerk, 22–24, 111–115, 119
    court rules, 22, 247
    court trustee, 11
    estate, 20, 247
    exemptions, 13, 193
    forms, 12–13, 16–19, 21–25, 41–117, 119–191
        filling out, 16, 18, 41–42, 112
        filing, 16, 18–20, 22, 42, 107, 112–116
    judge, 14, 17–18, 117
    law, 107
    petition, 15, 247
    petition preparer, 24, 85, 90, 108, 247
    questionnaire, 25–41, 116
    schedule checklist, 23–24
    schedules, 18, 41–42
    trustee, 14, 16–17, 20–22, 87, 114–118, 247
benefits, 194
bonds, 31
business, 14–15, 30, 76, 89

cash, 21, 27, 116
changes, 87
Chapter 7
    bankruptcy, 11–12, 14–15, 17–24, 41, 48, 247
    checklists, 22–24
    Individual Debtor's Statement of Intention (Official Form 8), 19, 24, 59, 104–106, 113–116, 119, 187
        instructions, 104–105
        official form, 187
        sample form, 106
Chapter 11 bankruptcy, 14–15, 247
Chapter 12 bankruptcy, 15, 247
Chapter 13 bankruptcy, 14, 48, 247
checklists
    Action for Obtaining a Chapter 7 Bankruptcy, 22–23
    Schedules, Statements, and Fees for a Chapter 7 Bankruptcy, 23–24
child support, 12, 14, 20, 63
claim, 49, 63–64, 68, 104, 118, 247
codebtors, 18, 20, 74, 247
collateral, 12–14, 18, 20, 59–60, 63, 68, 104, 116, 118, 247
collection, 20
common-law property, 59, 68, 247–248
community debts, 22, 59, 68, 248
community property, 22, 51, 59, 68, 248
condominium fees, 12
consumer loans, 118
contingent debts, 18, 248
Continuation Sheet, 41, 48, 59, 81–82, 113, 157
    instructions, 81
    official form, 157
    sample form, 82
    Schedule E, 63
contracts, 13, 18, 68, 72
corporation, 15, 89
cosigners, 13, 15, 18, 74, 247
court hearing, 116–117
court order, 13, 19
court-ordered fines, 12

credit cards, 37, 68, 118
credit rebuilding, 118
credit record, 116–118
creditors, 11–15, 17–21, 23, 25, 42, 59, 68, 87, 104, 111, 113–117, 194, 248
creditors' meeting, 20, 22, 24, 112–113, 115–117, 248
criminal prosecution, 20
criminal restitution, 12, 14

debtor, 11–12, 24, 248
debts, 11–18, 20–22, 24–25, 31–32, 35–38, 41–43, 59, 63, 68, 74, 104, 113, 116–118, 248
Declaration Concerning Debtor's Schedules, 85–86, 161
    instructions, 85
    official form, 161
    sample form, 86
disability proceeds, 194, 248
discharge, 11–12, 14, 16, 20–22, 68, 112–113, 116–118, 248
dischargeable debts, 13–14, 21–22, 43, 112, 117, 248
discrimination, 117
dismissal, 21, 41, 85, 115
disputed debts, 18, 248
divorce settlement, 12, 118
double filing, 21

emergency filing, 19, 113
equity, 15, 248
ERISA, 52, 56, 248
eviction, 20
execution, 87, 248
executory contracts, 72, 248
exempt property, 11, 14, 18–19, 43, 56, 104, 112, 116, 193, 248
exemption laws, 18, 56
exemptions, 12–13, 18, 20, 193–194
expenditure, 41, 79, 248
expenses, 13, 18, 21, 25, 39–41, 79

farming, 15, 76, 248
Federal
    Bankruptcy Code, 11, 14, 21
    bankruptcy courts, 112, 240–246
    bankruptcy exemptions, 12–13, 18–19, 56, 193–194
    non-bankruptcy exemptions, 56, 193, 238–239

fee simple, 48
filing fee, 12, 22–23, 44, 107, 112–114
final discharge, 21–22, 117
financial
    affairs, 18, 22, 25, 41, 87, 116
    summary, 40
    transactions, 13, 18, 87
foreclosure, 19–20, 87
fraternal society benefits, 248
fraud, 12–13, 15, 17–18, 25, 41, 85, 116, 248

garnish, 19, 87
governmental benefits, 194
guarantors, 18, 74, 248

health aids, 19, 249
homestead declaration, 249
homestead exemptions, 194, 249
house, 14–15, 48, 194

income, 13, 18, 25, 38–39, 41, 76, 248
income taxes, 12, 16
inheritance, 118
insider, 87, 249
installments, 22–23, 44, 107
insurance, 29, 51, 194, 249
    benefits, 19
    proceeds, 118
intangible property, 193, 249
Internal Revenue Service, 20
investments, 76
involuntary bankruptcy, 249
IRAs, 29, 194

joint
    bankruptcy petition, 20
    filing, 18, 21–22, 25, 59, 68, 74, 79, 87, 113, 115, 194, 249
    tenancy, 51, 59, 68, 249
judgment, 59, 249

KEOGHs, 29, 194

landlords, 20, 28, 72, 114, 249
lawsuits, 20, 87
leases, 13, 18, 68
lessee, 72, 249
lessor, 72, 249
liability, 59, 68, 249
lien, 13, 16, 18, 59, 104, 249
lien avoidance, 104

liquidated debts, 18, 249
liquidation, 11
liquidation bankruptcy, 12, 249
loans, 25, 35, 59, 68, 118
local bankruptcy court, 112, 119
local court rules, 22, 24, 42, 113

Mailing List of Creditors' Names and
 Addresses, 19, 22, 24, 42, 111, 113, 115, 249
 instructions, 111
married couples, 21–22, 79
mechanic's lien, 59–60
mistake, 117–118
mortgage, 14, 18, 25, 35, 59, 118
mutual funds, 30–31

nature of lien, 59–60, 249
non-dischargeable debts, 12–13, 16, 68,
 116–117, 249
non-exempt property, 11, 14, 17, 21–22, 112,
 115–117
non-purchase money debt, 60, 249
non-wage income, 39

Official Form 1 (see *Voluntary Petition*)
Official Form 3 (see *Application to Pay Filing
 Fee in Installments*)
Official Form 6 (see *Summary of Schedules*)
Official Form 7 (see *Statement of Financial
 Affairs*)
Official Form 8 (see *Chapter 7 Individual
 Debtor's Statement of Intention*)
Official Form 21 (see *Statement of Social
 Security Number[s]*)

paperwork, 18, 22, 25
partnership, 15, 89, 194
pensions, 19, 29, 56, 76, 194, 250
perjury, 180
personal bankruptcy, 11
personal property, 11, 13, 17–18, 28–29, 32–34,
 48, 51, 193–194, 250
petition, 15
possessory lien, 60, 250
possessory non-purchase money debt, 60, 250
priority claim, 63–64, 250
profit-sharing, 29
Proof of Claim, 250
Proof of Service by Mail, 115
property settlements, 12, 31
purchase money debt, 60, 250

reaffirmation, 16, 104, 116, 250
real estate, 11–13, 17–19, 26–27, 48, 51, 76,
 193–194, 250
rebuilding credit, 118, 254
redemption, 16, 104
rent, 36
reorganization, 14, 250
repossession, 20, 87, 250
residence, 19, 26, 194
retirement plans, 194, 250
return of property, 87

Schedule A: Real Property, 18, 23, 48–50, 125,
 193
 instructions, 48–49
 official form, 125
 sample form, 50
Schedule B: Personal Property, 18, 23, 41, 48,
 51–56, 113, 127–131, 193
 instructions, 51–52
 official form, 127–131
 sample form, 53–55
Schedule C: Property Claimed as Exempt,
 18–19, 23, 56–58, 133, 193
 instructions, 56–57
 official form, 133
 sample form, 58
schedule checklist, 23–24
Schedule D: Creditors Holding Secured Claims,
 18, 23–24, 41, 59–62, 72, 74, 81, 104, 113,
 115, 135–137
 instructions, 59–60
 official form, 135–137
 sample form, 61–62
Schedule E: Creditors Holding Unsecured
 Priority Claims, 18, 23, 41, 63–67, 72, 74,
 81, 113, 139–143
 instructions, 63–64
 official form, 139–143
 sample form, 65–67
Schedule F: Creditors Holding Unsecured
 Nonpriority Claims, 18, 23, 41, 68–72, 74,
 81, 113, 145–147
 instructions, 68–69
 official form, 145–147
 sample form, 70–71
Schedule G: Executory Contracts and Unexpired
 Leases, 18, 23, 48, 72–73, 149
 instructions, 72
 official form, 149
 sample form, 73

Schedule H: Codebtors, 18, 23, 74–76, 151
   instructions, 74
   official form, 151
   sample form, 76
Schedule I: Current Income of Individual Debtor(s), 18, 23, 76–78, 153
   instructions, 76–77
   official form, 153
   sample form, 78
Schedule J: Current Expenditures of Individual Debtor(s), 18, 23, 79–80, 155
   instructions, 79
   official form, 155
   sample form, 80
schedules for Official Form 6, 23, 48–81
secured claim, 49
secured debts, 13–14, 18, 59, 68, 104, 115, 250
secured property, 11, 104, 116
security deposit, 28
security interest, 11, 250
setoff, 69, 88, 250
settlements, 31, 118
Social Security, 76
sole proprietorship, 14, 89
spouse, 18, 20–22, 25, 59, 68, 74, 79, 89, 113, 115, 194
state bankruptcy exemptions, 12–13, 18–19, 56, 193–238
statement
   checklist, 23–24
   Disclosing Compensation Paid or to Be Paid to an Attorney for the Debtor, 24
   of Financial Affairs (Official Form 7), 18, 24, 87–101, 113, 163–183
     instructions, 87–90
     official form, 163–183
     sample form, 91–101
   of Social Security Number(s) [Official Form 21], 24, 102–103, 185
     instructions, 102
     official form, 185
     sample form, 103
stocks, 30
student loans, 12, 14, 16, 68

summary of
   assets, 34
   debts, 38
   monthly income, 39
   Schedules (Official Form 6), 18, 81, 83–84, 113, 159
     instructions, 83
     official form, 159
     sample form, 84
surrender of property, 22, 104, 112, 116

tangible property, 193, 250
tax refunds, 32
tax returns, 87
taxes, 12, 14, 16, 20, 25, 37, 59, 63, 76
tenancy by the entireties, 51, 59, 68, 250
tenant, 72
trustee surcharge, 23

unemployment payments, 194
unexpired leases, 72, 250
unliquidated debts, 18
unsecured
   nonpriority claims, 68
   nonpriority debts, 13, 18
   priority claims, 63
   priority debts, 13, 18, 63, 68, 250
U.S. Bankruptcy Code, 42, 247 (See also *Federal Bankruptcy Code*)
U.S. Bankruptcy Court, 42, 114, 247
utilities, 20, 28, 68

veterans' benefits, 194
voluntary bankruptcy, 250
Voluntary Petition (Official Form 1), 18–20, 23–24, 42–47, 113–114, 121–123
   -instructions, 43–44, 46
   -official form, 121, 123
   -sample form, 45, 47

wages, 19, 38–39, 63, 76, 194, 250
waiver of filing fee, 44
welfare payments, 194
workers' compensation, 19, 194

Index   255

★ Nova Publishing Company ★
Small Business and Consumer Legal Books and Software

Law Made Simple Series
Basic Wills Simplified
    ISBN 0-935755-90-X   Book only $22.95
    ISBN 0-935755-89-6   Book w/Forms-on-CD $28.95
Divorce Agreements Simplified
    ISBN 0-935755-87-X   Book only $24.95
    ISBN 0-935755-86-1   Book w/Forms-on-CD $29.95
Living Trusts Simplified
    ISBN 0-935755-53-5   Book only $22.95
    ISBN 0-935755-51-9   Book w/Forms-on-CD $28.95
Living Wills Simplified
    ISBN 0-935755-52-7   Book only $22.95
    ISBN 0-935755-50-0   Book w/Forms-on-CD $28.95
Personal Bankruptcy Simplified (3rd Edition)
    ISBN 0-892949-01-6   Book only $22.95
    ISBN 0-892949-02-4   Book w/Forms-on-CD $28.95
Personal Legal Forms Simplified (3rd Edition)
    ISBN 0-935755-97-7   Book w/Forms-on-CD $28.95

Small Business Made Simple Series
C-Corporations: Small Business Start-up Kit
    ISBN 0-935755-78-0   Book w/Forms-on-CD $24.95
The Complete Book of Small Business Management Forms
    ISBN 0-935755-56-X   Book w/Forms-on-CD $24.95
Limited Liability Company: Small Business Start-up Kit (2nd Edition)
    ISBN 1-892949-04-0   Book w/Forms-on-CD $29.95
Partnerships: Small Business Start-up Kit
    ISBN 0-935755-75-6   Book w/Forms-on-CD $24.95
S-Corporation: Small Business Start-up Kit (2nd Edition)
    ISBN 1-892949-05-9   Book w/Forms-on-CD $29.95
Small Business Accounting Simplified (3rd Edition)
    ISBN 0-935755-91-8   Book only $22.95
Small Business Bookkeeping Systems Simplified
    ISBN 0-935755-74-8   Book only $14.95
Small Business Legal Forms Simplified (4th Edition)
    ISBN 0-935755-98-5   Book w/Forms-on-CD $29.95
Small Business Payroll Systems Simplified)
    ISBN 0-935755-55-1   Book only $14.95
Sole Proprietorship: Small Business Start-up Kit
    ISBN 0-935755-79-9   Book w/Forms-on-CD $24.95

Legal Self-Help Series
Divorce Yourself: The National No-Fault Divorce Kit (5th Edition)
    ISBN 0-935755-93-4   Book only $24.95
    ISBN 0-935755-94-2   Book w/Forms-on-CD $34.95
Incorporate Now!: The National Corporation Kit (4th Edition)
    ISBN 0-892949-00-8   Book w/Forms-on-CD $29.95
Prepare Your Own Will: The National Will Kit (5th Edition)
    ISBN 0-935755-72-1   Book only $17.95
    ISBN 0-935755-73-X   Book w/Forms-on-CD $27.95

National Legal Kits
Simplified Bankruptcy Kit
    ISBN 0-935755-83-7   Book only $17.95
Simplified Divorce Kit
    ISBN 0-935755-81-0   Book only $19.95
Simplified Will Kit
    ISBN 0-935755-96-9   Book only $16.95

★ Ordering Information ★

Distributed by:
National Book Network
4501 Forbes Blvd. Suite 200
Lanham MD 20706

Shipping: $4.50 for first & $.75 for each additional
Phone orders with Visa/MC: (800) 462-6420
Fax orders with Visa/MC: (800) 338-4550
Internet: www.novapublishing.com